HUMBLE SERVANT, SPIRITUAL GIANT

THE STORY OF HAROLD B. LEE

BLAINE M. YORGASON

The Living Scriptures®

Ogden, Utah

Published by The Living Scriptures®
Ogden, Utah

This book is a work of both fiction and non-fiction. Chapter beginning
narrative (printed in colored ink), which contains references to actual
historical characters, places, and incidents, is the product of the author's
creativity or is represented fictitiously. The majority of this book's content
(printed in black ink) is historical non-fiction based on the author's
research, containing endnotes and bibliography. The views expressed
herein are the responsibility of the author and do not necessarily
represent the position of Living Scriptures, Inc.

First Printing, 2001
Printed in the United States of America
10   9   8   7   6   5   4   3   2   1

ISBN 1-56473-176-6

In Appreciation:

For Jim and Carolyn Ockey,
dear friends,
whose timely assistance
helped make this book possible

*F*OREWORD

For persons looking for an easy and inspiring read, this biography of President Harold B. Lee can surely be recommended.

Through the writing genius of Blaine M. Yorgason the best of all the previously published stories about President Lee's life have been orchestrated in a masterful merger which rapidly unfolds the story of the life and service of this remarkable prophet-leader.

Harold B. Lee, Prophet and Seer, the biography of Harold B. Lee which I wrote, was comprehensive (519 pages) and yet so much still had to be left out. My second book, *He Changed My Life*, was written expressly as another witness (namely, what other people thought of the labors of Harold B. Lee), containing first-person testimonies and many faith-promoting stories which truly belonged in the original biography had there been room to contain them.

Now comes Brother Yorgason with his keen editorship and creative flair, free to choose from all previous books: my own *Harold B. Lee, Prophet and Seer*; Elder Francis M. Gibbons' *Man of Vision, Prophet of God*; Leonard J. Arrington's *The Presidents of the Church*; and others. These earlier texts give a decided advantage to Brother Yorgason, who has carefully chosen from among them for an accurate sampling of the total story. They are beautifully manipulated to hit most of the highlights in a delightful, unique digest.

The Harold B. Lee extended family is most grateful that through this book, *Humble Servant, Spiritual Giant: The Story of Harold B. Lee*, and companion Living Scriptures *Modern Prophets* video, *Harold B. Lee*, the story of his life can obtain a new telling. Hopefully, a new generation of readers can learn about and come to admire and love this amazing prophet of God—the eleventh president of The Church of Jesus Christ of Latter-day Saints.

Through the courtesy of Living Scriptures, producers of the video biography of President Lee, members of President Lee's progeny were invited to be in the costumed cast for many scenes enacting defining incidents in his life. Through not only learning the story in detail, but portraying it before the camera, these grandchildren and great-grandchildren now have an indelible memory to bless their lives forever. It has not only been a fun experience for the children, but one which has borne abundant learning experiences.

We are thankful also for the renewing of the family covenant these adventures have brought to us. Many spiritual experiences have come into our lives and the nearness of our family patriarch and his angelic court have already produced miracles, and many more will come, we are sure, from behind the veil.

We are so grateful that the work of this mighty prophet of God goes on, and we so testify.

L. Brent Goates
author and President Harold B. Lee's son-in-law
July 2001

One Foot in the Eternal World

Elder Harold B. Lee was exhausted! No, his wife, Joan, thought as the muted roar of the airliner's jet engines filled the cabin, he was more than exhausted. There was something terribly wrong with him, and with each passing moment she was growing more worried. His color was ashen, the skin around his mouth was a bluish white, his breathing was rapid and shallow, and— Well, she was no doctor, but it didn't take a doctor to tell that her husband—one of the Lord's beloved apostles—was in serious trouble.

Glancing over at her sister, Edna Cazier, who had accompanied her as a guest companion for those times when it would be impossible for her to be with her husband, Joan saw that she had fallen asleep. Poor dear! Yet it was no wonder she was exhausted, for who could ever grow used to such a grueling schedule as Harold and the other General Authorities were able—no, required—to keep.

For a moment Joan's mind wandered back, considering her seemingly miraculous marriage to Elder Lee following his beloved wife, Fern's, death in 1962. Joan had never married, and so it had come as a great surprise to find herself in love with and married not only to a wonderful man, but to a member of the Council of the Twelve Apostles. Moreover, she thought, to an apostle who because of his relative youth would almost certainly become

President of the Lord's Church. This was almost beyond her comprehension, and so she thought little of it, focusing instead on helping her new husband do the work he was presently called to accomplish.

And that, she thought with a sigh, was the difficulty. In spite of his relative youth, in spite of his intense inner drive, in spite even of his absolute certainty about being always on the Lord's errand, Harold was not a well man. For years he had suffered with migraine headaches and serious stomach troubles, experiencing pain and misery that would have completely disabled lesser men. Yet somehow he had pushed through such physical tortures as if they were mere inconveniences, never complaining, and hardly ever allowing anyone to even suspect how much he was suffering. Instead he had traveled the world under the direction of the First Presidency, experiencing privation of every sort, yet almost daily preaching, blessing, interviewing, and in every way giving himself to the people that he served.

Even now, after nearly four years at his side, Joan remained astounded by this incredible manifestation of Harold's faith. Yet still—

The previous year, 1966, Harold had undergone a complete physical examination. From it he had learned that his blood level was only fifty-six percent of normal—an extremely dangerous condition caused, the doctors felt, by bleeding ulcers. A series of blood transfusions had eliminated his pallid color and given him renewed energy, though he had remained weak and somewhat wobbly on his feet. Other tests, to determine the cause of his persistent headaches, had found nothing.

Then, the month before this one—March 1967—Joan had again observed Harold to be deathly pale. More tests had indicated the same problem as the previous year, and so, prior to their scheduled tour of the Florida Mission, she had admitted him to LDS Hospital for three days of additional transfusions and iron shots, hoping to build his strength before they departed for the east coast.

Joan smiled as she thought of Florida Mission President Glen L. Rudd and his excitement at having Harold be the one to tour his mission. President Rudd had been a friend and associate of the Lee family for many years, working in the Welfare Program with Harold and even naming his son Glen Lee in Harold's honor. In fact President Rudd had told her, during one of their long drives together, of a terrible, usually fatal illness that had overcome his son Lee shortly after his graduation from high school and of a marvelous blessing given by Harold that had begun Lee's lengthy but complete recovery. There was no doubt President Rudd loved her husband—not just because of his son's healing, he had assured her that day, but because Harold was a great man! Yet, he had declared, he suspected that few persons realized what a tremendous individual Harold really was.

Joan felt the same, for Harold's innate goodness never ceased to amaze her—that, and his complete humility and lack of ego!

So, in spite of his debilitating illness, Harold and she had begun the mission tour with President and Sister Rudd—which had lasted for eight intense days! There had been buildings to dedicate; five in all. There had been decisions to make on Church expansion and growth and on buildings yet to be built. There had been two hundred twenty-one missionaries to interview and encourage. There had been blessings to be given to the sick wherever they had gone, as well as other types of blessings. There had been special interviews with local members of the Church. Every single day had required traveling either by car or plane. Every day they had arisen early and retired late, and every moment of those unbelievably long days had seemed to involve another question that had to be answered, another problem that needed solving.

Almost never had Harold been given a personal moment in which to simply relax or see the lovely sights that graced the

Florida Mission. Instead his concern had ever been for her comfort and happiness, Edna's comfort and happiness, and the comfort and happiness of President and Sister Rudd. It was amazing how he seemed content to always look outward, never inward—ever focused on accomplishing the Lord's work.

And so for eight rugged days Harold had labored, enduring three or four long air rides (already she couldn't remember with certainty) and logging over 2,300 miles by automobile as he had carried out his assignment. And then, instead of taking a final weekend to rest and relax under the warm Florida sun, he—along with she and Edna—had flown to New York for meetings which had begun almost immediately and which had culminated two terribly long days later in the division of the New Jersey Stake. And even that, Joan thought with a sigh, had been possible only because Harold had received a priesthood blessing from W. Jay Eldredge, president of the Eastern States Mission, and two of his young missionaries. Harold had developed a terrible weakness throughout his body early Sunday morning, March 27. In fact he had been so weak and faint that he had been forced to lie down just to clear his head. Thank heaven, she thought, that she had felt inspired to call and ask for President Eldredge's help. Only through his blessing had the Lord imparted to Harold the strength to continue.

By that night, however, Harold had been so exhausted, both physically and mentally, that he had not been able to prepare for the business meetings he had scheduled for the next morning. Serving on the boards of directors of both Equitable Life Insurance Company and the Union Pacific Railroad, Harold was required to meet with them at least once each month. This time, Joan had felt certain he could not do it.

Still, as he retired for the night Harold had been insistent, and it had not been her place to tell him what to do—

To no one's surprise, upon awakening Monday morning, even after a full ten hours of sleep, Harold had felt no better. In fact, the weakness of Sunday morning was returning. More, the Spirit had rested upon him at the moment of waking, giving him the certain knowledge that he must skip his meetings and leave immediately for Salt Lake City and home.

"What is it?" Joan had asked after Harold's surprise announcement.

"I feel that I am again losing blood," Harold had replied weakly. "I must reach Dr. Orme as quickly as possible. Would you mind scheduling reservations for us, my dear?"

Joan had done so, though she had been unable to reach Dr. James F. Orme, Harold's physician in Salt Lake City. But at least they were now on their way home, seated in the comparative comfort of the forward cabin. In the section behind them sat some members of the Church they had encountered at the airport and who, of course, had recognized Harold. And even ill as he had been, he had been so gracious with them—

"Who was that?" Harold suddenly asked as he opened his eyes and raised his head to look around.

"What is it, dear?"

"Someone just laid his hand on my head. Was anyone standing here? One of the members of the Church we met earlier, perhaps?"

"I'm sorry, darling," Joan responded, perplexed, "but there has been no one."

"But, I'm certain I felt—"

Slowly Harold relaxed and drifted off, not sleeping deeply but at least dozing. Her heart sick with worry, Joan kept constant vigil.

"There it is again," Harold stated a little while later, his eyes once again wide as he glanced around the cabin. "Someone has just laid their hands upon my head, exactly as if they were giving me a blessing." Pausing as understanding formed, Harold looked at his wife. "Yes, that is what has happened! Someone, twice now, has given me a blessing, though I have no idea who it was, or for what reason—"

Illustration by Robert T. Barrett

It was eleven o'clock Monday night before Joan and her husband arrived at their home on Penrose Drive in Salt Lake City, and there had hardly been a moment since Harold's experiences in the plane that she had not been pondering them, praying that his life might be preserved according to the blessings of whomever it might have been.

"Dear," she said a few moments later, almost before Harold had had time to sit down, "Dr. Orme wishes to speak with you."

"You have called him already?" Harold questioned weakly. "Thank you!" Taking the phone from her, he held it to his ear. "Yes, Dr. Orme, we are very sorry to be troubling you at such a late hour."

"You are no trouble, Elder Lee," Dr. Orme responded. "You never are. Now, how are you? Tell me exactly how you feel!"

"Well, I am very tired, but I think I will be all right—at least through the night."

"Are you certain, Elder Lee? After all, it would be no trouble—"

"No, I feel quite confident I can last until the morning."

"Very well. But if anything should change—if you sense any passage of blood—have Sister Lee call me and then get you to the hospital immediately!"

Harold thanked him and hung up the telephone, sat back down to try and calm his spinning head, and it was only a few moments later when he began massive hemorrhaging. Prepared and knowing exactly what to do, Joan quickly called Dr. Orme and then rushed Harold to emergency, feeling thankful all the way for the unknown but divinely sent messenger who had, by the laying on of hands from the other side of the veil, preserved her dear husband's life until they could arrive home and be near qualified medical help. 1

Such a man, who throughout his mortal life seemed to walk with one foot in the eternal worlds, was Harold Bingham Lee. Yet such marvelous experiences as the one described in the vignette above made him neither pompous nor presumptuous. Instead they merely humbled him and filled him with an ever-increasing desire to share the tender mercies and miraculous workings of the Lord with his beloved Saints. Some years later, as President of the Church, Harold spoke in general conference concerning the above incident. At that time he said:

> On the way across the country, we were sitting in the forward section of the airplane. Some of our Church members were in the next section. As we approached a certain point en route, someone laid his hand upon my head. I looked up; I could see no one. That happened again before we arrived home, again with the same experience. Who it was, by what means or what medium, I may never know, except I knew that I was receiving a blessing that I came a few hours later to know I needed most desperately.
>
> As soon as we arrived home, my wife very anxiously called the doctor. It was now about eleven o'clock at night. He called me to come to the telephone, and he asked me how I was. I said, "Well, I am very tired; I think I will be all right." But shortly thereafter, there came massive hemorrhages, which had they occurred while we were in flight, I wouldn't be here today talking about it.
>
> I know that there are powers divine that reach out when all other help is not available.... Yes, I know that there are such powers. 2

And so he did know. Following a three-and-a-half-hour surgical procedure a few days after his return from New York, during which over half of his stomach was removed because of a perforated ulcer, a sobered Elder Lee recorded in his journal: " 'One can only suppose that the Almighty has it in his hand to give or to take and he alone keeps the timetable. To the thoroughness and the skill of the doctors I owe much, but I'm not unmindful of the spiritual power which has been in evidence in the events leading up to the operation as well as circumstances resulting therefrom. When I was released to come home I found I weighed but 150 pounds, a loss of 15 pounds.'"[3]

Who was this man who, during his years as a General Authority and as President of The Church of Jesus Christ of Latter-day Saints, was willing to pay such a price for his service and demonstrated such a remarkable spiritual transparency. Who was this man who "opened to view the office of prophet, seer, and revelator as it had never been exposed since the days of the Prophet Joseph Smith?"[4]

> At his birth on March 28, 1899, [Harold B. Lee] received as an earthly inheritance superior qualities of intelligence, devotion; and spirituality through ancestors of worth and good character, although none of his direct forebears achieved high reputation outside the small circles of family and village. There was a great uncle, Joseph W. McMurrin, his grandmother's brother, who had risen to become one of the General Authorities of The Church of Jesus Christ of Latter-day Saints, serving for thirty-five years as a member of the First Council of the Seventy. But, with this exception, the ancestry of Harold B. Lee is devoid of anyone who gained prominence of a kind which remotely resembled that which he attained. This lack, however, bears no relationship to the innate qualities they possessed and which were transmitted to him as a legacy by lineal descent.[5]

Throughout his life, which was wonderfully productive and far reaching, Harold developed these qualities to the very best of his ability. Thus, most with whom he came in contact, wanted to be near him. He "had an amazing faculty for making people feel important. He had a remarkable memory for names and faces, recalling incidents with clarity even after twenty or thirty years had passed.

He challenged many to be better than they were by telling them they already were what he knew they could become. His 'as if' approach was effective, yet it was not a contrived style, but merely an indigenous human relations magic which he possessed." 6

Of the power of his mind, Elder Neal A. Maxwell has written:

He was at home in the world of ideas. For instance, his brief experience in politics and government permitted him to distill from that short period what other men would have taken years to learn. Being secure spiritually and intellectually, he could be eclectic in gathering in ideas, concepts, and truths that would be helpful to the work of the kingdom. Though he had not had the opportunity for extensive education in the secular sense, he could cope with and even use ideas that his remarkable spiritual education encouraged him to reach out for. 7

"Being a very sensitive man," writes his son-in-law, L. Brent Goates, "[Harold B. Lee] had a genius to identify with people and their problems" Despite the fact that "it was wearying just to keep pace with their unintended demands," he "moved instinctively to the rescue of someone in danger. It was not done in a sense of duty; his natural reflex was to simply care for other people....

"He never compromised his ideals of a spiritual kingdom and a personal relationship with Deity, despite encounters along his Church career with an environment that featured the sophisticated learning of men. As a result he was consistently a worker of miracles and brought heaven closer to thousands.

"Spirituality thus became his greatest leadership tool. He took direction from the heavens. He knew how to talk with God and how to obtain answers to his prayers for the Saints." 8

The hearts of all good people yearn to be near such a man, to watch him, listen to him, learn from him, and to simply feel and bask in the radiance of his spirit. To that end, what follows is his story.

SCHOOLED IN SPIRITUAL MATTERS

It was while he was lying on his stomach fishing pollywogs out of the large puddle that Harold began thinking of what his father had said. The two had left their home in Clifton early that morning, young Harold being allowed to accompany his father because he had so willingly helped his mother the day before. Fortified with a hearty breakfast, and knowing that the morning chores around the home place were satisfactorily completed, Sam Lee had harnessed the team to the wagon, nodded approvingly as Harold scrambled up onto the bench, and then climbed up beside him.

"Daylight's burning," Harold's father had said simply and with a double cluck of his tongue and a snap of the reins, had set the team in motion, and he and his second son were on their way to the forty-acre farm on the flat below Dayton.

It was a beautiful summer morning in southern Idaho, and as the wagon and horses churned up the fine dust along what was called the Stringtown Road, young Harold was conscious of everything around him. Red-winged blackbirds warbled in the rushes that occasionally lined the road; a hungry hawk circled silently overhead. Several new colts frolicked around their mothers in a nearby pasture; in other pastures wobbly legged calves and long-tailed lambs were doing the same; and the fields that had been planted to winter wheat the fall before, or to alfalfa, were now lush with new green growth. Summer had finally come to the upper end of the Cache Valley, and all creatures seemed filled with the joy of it.

When they passed the Henderson place, the family's three dogs attacked the creaking wagon with yapping gusto, though the canines were smart enough to stay clear of the plodding team's massive hooves. Thank goodness, Harold had thought, that there had been no sign of the mean Henderson boy! And at the Humphries farm Sam halted the team for a moment to visit with Able Humphries who, though almost completely crippled with arthritis, was still considered one of the best and wisest farmers in the country.

And meanwhile Harold's father had kept up a running conversation with his young son, pointing out things of local interest, asking questions, and gently inserting thoughts and ideas into the boy's mind. Sam Lee did not believe in wasting time—to a farmer of the early 1900s every moment was precious—and so the hour in the wagon became an hour of schooling for young Harold. And this day, as the wagon had rumbled along beneath them, Sam had decided to sermonize upon the life and spiritual experiences of the boy prophet, Joseph Smith.

"Now remember, Harold," Sam Lee had instructed, "he was only fourteen when he headed into the woods to pray—not a whole lot older than you."

"Did he go far to the woods?"

Sam shook his head. "Not very—not much more than a quarter of a mile, or so I'm told. Joseph said he just wanted to be alone, and the woods were a good place for it. You see, he had never in his life prayed aloud, and he was feeling somewhat self-conscious even considering it."

"We pray aloud all the time," Harold declared as he gazed at the fir-covered mountains across the valley to the east—the only real woods he was aware of. And they were certainly a lot more than a quarter of a mile away. "The Smiths must not have had family prayer. Don't you think so, Pa?"

Sam chuckled. "I'd never thought of that, Harold, but I suppose you are right—at least not the way we do it. I guess the point is that Joseph was willing to make the effort, untrained and self-conscious or not. That is called exercising faith. Can you remember what happened next?"

"You mean about seeing God and Jesus?"

"Well, before that happened, Joseph said he was set upon by an unseen power that seemed determined to destroy him—a force of darkness that had terrible strength. Who might that have been?"

"The devil!"

"Good for you. And why do you suppose the devil would want to destroy young Joseph Smith?"

Harold grinned with his own memory of the well-rehearsed story. "Because he knew Joseph was going to be called as a prophet of God, and he didn't want that to happen!"

"Why not?"

"Because the devil is God's enemy, and he didn't want Joseph to start up the Lord's true Church or do anything else that God might ask him to do."

"Does Satan feel the same about us, Harold?"

Soberly, the boy nodded.

"You're right, son. He'll work to stop us from doing what we should at every opportunity! And each time he gains a small victory he is one step closer to destroying us, just as he was trying to destroy young Joseph Smith. But just as you gained a small victory over Satan yesterday when you helped your mother without arguing or fussing, Joseph gained a victory when he refused to stop praying. The devil was forced to give up and leave, and immediately thereafter Joseph looked up and saw the pillar of light coming down out of heaven—the light which surrounded the two personages."

"Heavenly Father and Jesus," young Harold breathed, trying to imagine in his mind what the Prophet had seen on that long-ago morning. "What did they look like, Pa? Did Joseph ever say?"

"Not much, except that they were glorious and beautiful beyond description. Later he said they looked exactly like each other—sort of like Sherman and Ollie Williams."

"Brother Williams' beard is a lot more gray than Ollie's," Harold grinned.

"Yes, but other than that, Ollie looks amazingly like his father. Can you tell me what happened next? With Joseph Smith, I mean?"

Harold nodded. "They talked to him."

"That's right. The boy Joseph heard the voices of the Father and the Son. Literally, he heard the voices of eternity. More than that, Harold, he listened to them and learned from them."

"Pa, have other people ever heard their voices?"

"Many. Adam, Moses, Nephi—and Heber C. Kimball among others in our day. Remember when we read about Enos in the Book of Mormon and how he heard the voice of the Lord in his mind when he went to hunt beasts in the forest?"

"Forests and woods seem like good places for hearing the Lord," Harold mused.

"That's because they're quiet, son. Fields, forests, mountains, deserts, church, the temple—it seems we're most likely to hear the Lord's voice when we are in the midst of silence and perhaps even solitude. That's a good lesson for all of us to learn."

"Have you ever heard the Lord's voice, Pa?"

For a long moment Sam Lee looked away. "I have," he finally replied, his voice husky with emotion. "Just like Enos, I have heard it in my mind, clear and unmistakable. You see, Harold, the veil between this and the eternal world is very thin, and whatever distance in miles may separate us seems to mean nothing. The Lord and his holy angels speak all the time, through the power of the Holy Ghost, but we only hear when we have prepared ourselves to do so."

"By going where it is silent and we can be alone?"

Sam Lee smiled at his son. "Yes, and by preparing our hearts so we will listen and obey. Obedience is vitally important, Harold. If we are to hear that still, small voice from the eternities, we must be endeavoring to be obedient to the commandments of God, and we must obey whatever we are told to do once we are spoken to."

"Angels like Gabriel can speak to us, too?"

"Of course they can. But remember, son, angels are more than just Gabriel and Raphael. Joseph Smith said their ranks included people who love us, perhaps even our own family members who have gone before. For instance, Grandfather or Grandmother Lee might be ministering as angels to us, or any of my brothers or sisters who died when they were babies. They are all part of the heavenly Church—the general assembly and Church of the Firstborn. The Book of Mormon says such beings speak the words of Christ by the power of the Holy Ghost, so if they speak it would be the same as hearing the voice of the Lord. And since we know that Heavenly Father and Jesus Christ cannot lie, when we hear a voice from the eternities, it must be telling us the truth. It would be silly not to obey the truth, wouldn't you say?"

Soberly, Harold had nodded. Now, as he lay by the puddle marveling that some of the pollywogs had legs while others didn't, meaning that they were that much closer to turning into frogs, he found himself rehearsing his father's words. Angels always spoke the truth, so it would be silly not to obey them. The question was, would he ever have the chance to hear the voice of an angel? Or maybe even the Lord's voice, as had his father, Joseph Smith, and others?

Perhaps, Harold thought as he rose to his feet and looked around, when he was a lot older. But now he was just a little kid, it was sunny and getting hot, and there was a mighty lot of exploring to do before his father pulled out his mother's packed lunch and called a temporary halt to the fence mending.

To the east of the Lee property, just across the barbed wire fence, some old abandoned outbuildings had collapsed under the weight of winter's snows. Now they were lying in a moldering heap. As Harold glanced at the jumbled pile of weathered timbers and boards, something caught his eye, perhaps some movement that might mean a den of ground squirrels. Whatever he had seen, the place certainly deserved closer inspection, and he was just the fellow to do it.

Wiping his muddy hands on his overalls, Harold started off through the tall grass, his eyes never leaving the intriguing wreckage on the other side of the fence. Why had he never noticed the place before, he wondered? And what great mystery lay in or under that heap of lumber, just waiting for him to discover it?

Coming at length to the rusty fence, Harold placed his hands on the top and second strands, being careful to avoid the steel barbs. Then, spreading the wires apart as he had seen his father do a hundred and more times, he bent over, lifted his leg, and was just putting it through his self-created aperture when it happened.

"Harold," someone commanded very distinctly from immediately behind him, "don't go near that lumber over there!"

Startled, the boy pulled his leg back, stood erect, and looked around. He expected to see that his father had drawn close and was warning him. But no, his father was still at the far end of the forty-acre spread, still working on the fence line there. So, who—

Abruptly nervous, for he had heard that voice as distinctly as anything he had ever heard in his life, Harold was still looking around for the source of it when his father's words concerning God, angels, and voices from the eternity came slamming into his mind, and he knew! Instantly, he turned and fled, for though the danger in the moldering lumber might be unknown to him, he had been warned away from it by a voice from the eternities! Like his father and the Prophet Joseph Smith, Harold had now heard the voice of the Lord, and he knew it could not lie.

"So," Harold's older brother, Perry, questioned that night after hearing Harold's fervently told experience at the dinner table, "what was over there in that old pile of wood that was so dangerous? What were you being warned against? Rattlesnakes, maybe?"

"I don't know," Harold replied softly as he wondered anew at the words of the heavenly voice. "I never went over to see!" 1

Born on March 28, 1899, a blustery day in Clifton, Idaho, tiny Harold Bingham Lee was the second child and son of Samuel Marion Lee Jr. and Louisa Emeline Bingham. Samuel Marion Lee Jr. had been born in Panaca, Nevada, where Harold's grandparents, Samuel Marion Lee Sr. and Margaret McMurrin, had been called, along with Samuel's parents and brother, to settle.

> From the time of their marriage in 1863 until 1875, [Harold's grandparents] were childless. It was not that they did not want children or had not tried to have them. Indeed, during that period, Margaret had conceived eleven times, but her babies were either stillborn or lived for only a few hours. After ten failures, Margaret, who during most of her married life was very frail, almost despaired of having a child who would survive. But while on a trip to Salt Lake to visit her family, she received a remarkable blessing from Patriarch Able Lamb who promised her, "you shall have a son and he shall be a mighty man in Israel and his name shall be the name of his father." 2

No doubt Harold's grandmother was excited to have her next child. One wonders how she dealt with the grief—as well as what would most certainly have been confusion—when her eleventh baby was once again stillborn. Yet she pressed on in faith, and in due time that great faith was rewarded. Her twelfth and last baby, a son, survived, "although the circumstances made it doubtful he would do so. The child, who was born prematurely on November 22, 1875, weighed only

Both photos courtesy of the Lee Family Collection

Harold B. Lee's grandparents   N.D.
Samuel Marion Lee, Sr. and Margaret McMurrin

three-and-a-half pounds. Margaret, exhausted by the ordeal, lived only eight days afterward, then passed away. She was twenty-nine. Her miracle child was named Samuel Marion Lee, Jr., as the patriarch had decreed. He would become the father of the prophet, Harold B. Lee....

"[But] there was serious doubt whether Margaret's son would grow to manhood. He was so weak and tiny, and after only eight days of life, he was also motherless. It was providential that at Margaret's death her sister, Mary, was nursing her own baby. She took Samuel into her home and, for six months, nursed him in tandem with her own child. However, by the spring of 1876, Mary was exhausted from the physical demands of nursing and caring for two babies. Out of family consultations came the decision to take Samuel to Salt Lake City to be cared for by [Grandfather Joseph and] Grandmother Margaret Leaing McMurrin. By then the baby was strong enough to endure the two-week trip to Salt Lake by horse and buggy." 3

Though Samuel Sr. no doubt intended that his namesake and only child would live with his mother-in-law in Salt Lake City just a short time, circumstances demanded otherwise. Until two months short of his eighteenth birthday, Samuel "was raised in the home of his grandparents.... His father, still living in Nevada, assisted in his support and came occasionally to Salt Lake City to see him. At the age of fourteen, Samuel M. Lee went [back] to Panaca, where he visited for a time with his father. There he saw his birthplace and the grave of his mother, and he personally thanked his Aunt Mary for the patient, loving care she had given to him. Without her valiant service this child of promise would not have lived to fulfill his special mission in mortality." 4

While in Panaca young Samuel learned much about his Lee ancestors—including their fortitude and courage. For instance, in the early days in Panaca the settlers had had quite a bit of trouble with the Indians—so much that Church authorities gave them permission to abandon the settlement. Yet:

> Jane Vail Johnson Lee [Harold's great-grandmother] ...said
> she was in Panaca to stay and refused to leave. One day two
> Indians came into her dugout home, and one of them spot-
> ted a rifle in the corner of the room. He demanded it, but
> Jane refused to give it to him. When he started for the gun,
> she struck him so hard with a piece of stove wood that it
> knocked him down. He staggered to his feet and drew his
> bow, attempting to aim an arrow at her. She used another
> piece of wood in defense, which smashed the Indian's bow
> and arrow. He and his companion fled for their lives. 5

On September 4, 1893, Samuel Jr.'s Grandmother McMurrin had
died in his arms. After her death, and because his father had passed
away three years earlier, grief-stricken seventeen-year-old Samuel Jr.
went to Clifton, Idaho, to live with his uncle and aunt, Riley and
Jeanette McMurrin Davis. There he learned during the next three
years how to farm, and there also he met and fell in love with Louisa
Emeline Bingham, who was four years his junior.

The second child of Perry Calvin and Rachel Elvira Bingham,
Louisa was born in Clifton on January 1, 1879. Louisa's older sister,
Sarah, died when she was three years old, leaving Louisa as the
eldest. Concerning his mother's youth, Harold wrote:

> When my mother was a young child she was obliged to
> shoulder the responsibility of caring for an invalid mother,
> as well as the younger children in the family, and to perform
> all the household duties in the home. In addition to doing
> the cooking, housework, and sewing, she often performed
> the outside chores as well. She was so small that she was
> required to stand on a box to enable her to reach far enough
> down into the tub to scrub the clothes on a washboard
> When she was sewing, her feet would hardly reach the

machine treadles.

Her father was away much of the time freighting into Montana, and it became my mother's responsibility to bathe, feed, and care for not only her younger brother and sister, but also her bedfast mother. They lived about a five-minute walk from school, and Mother would arise very early, fix breakfast, dress and care for her brother and sister, bathe and feed her mother, then dash off for school. When all the other children were enjoying their games at recess, Mother would run home to care for her mother and begin preparing lunch. At noon she would hurry home again to take care of the family responsibilities which came upon her early in her life....

At the age of fourteen, Mother was sustained as a Sunday School teacher in the Rushville School. 6

"Under this regimen, Louisa matured very fast. Indeed, it might be said that she never had the luxury of being a child." 7 But thus she was well prepared when handsome Sam Lee began paying attention to her.

In contrast to Louisa's intense frugality, strict work ethic, and outright enthusiasm for life and its labors, Sam Lee, who was rapidly developing his acumen as a farmer, was most often described as dignified and calm, a "quiet, gentle, compassionate, unassuming, thoughtful man ...[who,] if he had an obvious fault, it was perhaps his tendency to carry charity to the extreme. Once started, he seldom knew when to stop giving." 8 "Characteristic of his personality was the creation of his own 'patented' swear word. When he was wont to vent his anger or frustration, he would say, 'Oh, nickofishtoe.' That always seemed to take care of the situation, with a release that seemed harmless enough to all present." 9

Of those early days of acquaintance and courtship between Sam Lee and Louisa Bingham, Elder S. Dilworth Young wrote poetically:

Out on the farm
Louisa Bingham
Grew and blossomed
Into girlish womanhood.
Her blue eyes
Caught the color of the
Bright hills in spring,
And in the fall they
Danced with joy
At autumn's coloring.
At home she learned
To wash and cook and sew,
And winter
Saw her
Skating, sledding, and
Riding in the bobsleigh
Through the snow.

Then Samuel Lee, now
Working on his uncle's farm,
Watched her grow,
Saw with his heart
As well as with his eyes—
The slow unfolding
Of her girlish charm,
The bloom of girlhood
High upon her cheeks,
A budding woman,
Gentle, soft, and warm. 10

When she was asked, Louisa Bingham was ready to accept Samuel Lee Jr.'s proposal of marriage. Traveling to Logan, Utah, by horse and buggy on May 13, 1895, the couple was sealed in marriage in the Logan Temple by Elder Marriner W. Merrill, later of the Council of the Twelve. "They were young at the time of the marriage. Louisa was always somewhat sensitive about this point. She thought it might not be a proper example if her family discovered what a young, little bride she was at age sixteen. [Yet] they reared a fine family of six children in the little farming community of Clifton." 11

To them were sent Samuel Perry, who was born December 5, 1896; Harold Bingham, born on March 28, 1899; Clyde Bingham, who was born October 12, 1902; Waldo Bingham, who entered the world on November 24, 1905; Stella Bingham, their first daughter,

Harold B. Lee's parents
Louisa Bingham and Samuel Lee, Jr.

N.D.

Courtesy of the Lee Family Collection

who came on December 21, 1907; and finally Verda Bingham, who was born on July 1, 1910.

Cache Valley, where all the Lee children entered mortality, begins on the south near Logan and extends northward into Idaho beyond Preston, finally heading at Red Rock Pass, where, "geologists theorize, the walls of ancient Lake Bonneville were breached, allowing its waters to drain into the Snake River."12 Near this northern pass, on the western side of the valley, reposes the tiny farming village of Clifton—named because of a high rocky cliff that towers over the community to the west.

[Clifton] is one of several string towns [towns built as though along a long thin string of road] settled by Mormon colonists in the 1860s, including Oxford to the north and Dayton and Weston to the south, all of which are overshadowed by the mountains to the west. Several miles southeast of Clifton, in the center of the valley, is Franklin, Idaho, founded in 1855 by the Latter-day Saints. To the north of Franklin, on the east side of the valley, lies Whitney, the birthplace of Ezra Taft Benson, and Preston, the site of the Oneida Stake Academy. It was here that Harold Lee and "T" Benson, born only five months and several miles apart, would first become acquainted....

Because these communities had been founded of such recent date, they were very rudimentary at the time Samuel and Louisa set up housekeeping on a small farm in Clifton. They had no modern conveniences. There was no indoor plumbing, no electricity, and no central heating. At first, water was carried from a well or stream. Later when it was piped in, the water needed for laundering or personal hygiene was heated on the kitchen stove. Baths were taken in a washtub. Lighting was by kerosene or gas lamps. As electrification was introduced into the valley and as other

The old barn in Clifton, Idaho,
on the property where Harold B. Lee
was born and reared

CA. *1980*

Courtesy of the Lee Family Collection

modern conveniences were added, life became more comfortable. But it was never easy.

The high elevation of the Cache Valley greatly shortened the growing season, and late spring or early summer storms or freezes would sometimes blight the crops. There was ample fertile land available, but water was scarce. The farms were irrigated from the Twin Lake reservoir, which was fed by Mink Creek or from flowing wells that had been successfully dug. But there was seldom a surplus. Farming here was labor intensive, and before the Lee boys were old enough to do farm work, Louisa often pitched in to help with the lighter outside chores. She was an expert rider and had a pony named Maude that she rode often, either in helping Samuel or as a means of transportation. In addition to the crops needed to feed their cattle, the Lees had a truck garden and an orchard that provided vegetables and fruits for the table. Surpluses were bottled for use during the off-season. Chickens and a cow provided milk and eggs for their diet, and what meat they needed came from their own cattle and hogs. What little cash they had was derived chiefly from the sale of their cattle or surplus crops. A downturn in market prices could be as devastating as an unseasonable freeze.

While the Lees never went hungry, indeed they always had an ample diet, they, like other farmers in the area, lived frugally because of the lack of money to buy the things that could not be produced on the farm. This fostered a sense of ingenuity and resourcefulness to make do with what they had. So, notwithstanding a slender cash income, the Lee household presented an image of material abundance. 13

In such an atmosphere and under such conditions, Harold B. Lee entered the world and embarked upon his voyage through childhood and youth. To heaven's and his parents' credit, the Lee home provided the perfect atmosphere in which a future prophet of the Lord could make his start. As family patriarch and matriarch, it was Sam's and Louisa's delight to provide the sort of intellectual and spiritual leadership that imbued their children with a sense of purpose, as well as a firm conviction of the reality of the Lord Jesus Christ and their eternal relationship with him.

Church service, therefore, was paramount in the home. Besides serving for years as a Sunday School teacher, Louisa served as a counselor as well as president of the ward Young Woman's Mutual Improvement Association and also as counselor in the stake YWMIA. Simultaneously, she served in both the Primary and Relief Society organizations and was chosen to be on the sewing committee, having the responsibility of sewing temple clothing in which to bury the dead.

Samuel, meanwhile, shortly after his marriage was called as assistant to the superintendent of the Sunday School. Later he became the superintendent, in which position he served for five years. After being called into the ward bishopric as a counselor, he next became bishop of the Clifton Ward. In this position he served for nine years, not being released until after Harold had successfully completed his mission to the Western States.

> So, from the moment of Elder Lee's birth until the time he left the family home, his [parents were] heavily and continuously engaged in Church work. That influence carried into the home, where the principles and practices of [the gospel of Jesus Christ] were a dominant factor. Family prayers and scripture study were a regular part of the daily routine, and the children saw in their parents' conduct a demonstration of how religious principles are applied to daily living.
>
> In the Lee home there was a genuine concern for the

welfare of others. Bishop Lee was a devoted shepherd of his flock, attending to the temporal and spiritual needs of the widows and others in his ward who required special attention. Louisa, who was skilled in nursing and midwifery, was often called on to comfort the sick or to preside at the delivery of a baby. And, of course, she used her healing arts in aid of her own family, applying the well-known home remedies of the day, chief among which were the clammy mustard plaster for chest colds, a hot onion or camphor for the earache, and cloves for the toothache. Because of the prevalence of pulmonary ailments and children's diseases in these rural communities, and because of the scarcity of professionally trained doctors, there was a greater reliance at the time than at present on priesthood administrations to heal the sick. Accordingly, Harold and the other children in the Lee home became witnesses at an early age of their father exercising his priesthood authority to bless the sick or to bring comfort to those who were troubled or who mourned.

They also became aware, when very young, of special spiritual qualities that their mother possessed. Louisa was prayerful by nature and frequently offered special, secret prayers for the welfare of her family. 14

It was a good thing both parents were spiritually astute, for from an early age Harold and his family were forced to deal with the adversary's efforts to destroy him and therefore his future prophetic calling. In his personal life history, Harold wrote:

> In my young boyhood there were many occasions, as I recall the earlier years of my life, when my mother's instructive and intuitive understanding prompted her to know that help was needed. Once on a stormy night, she directed my father to go and search for me, only to find that my horse

had stumbled while crossing a stream of water and thrown me into a pool of half-frozen mud. My mother had known that help was needed....

Among my earliest recollections was an occasion when my instinctive meddling got me into some trouble. Mother was [canning] fruit, and as she finished there were sometimes juices left over which she allowed me to drink. On this occasion, I went to do the same thing, but after taking a few swallows I discovered that this was lye water she had put in to get rid of the burned fruit which was sticking to the inside of the pan. This time I remember my mother and Grandmother Bingham poured olive oil down my throat to save me from being fatally injured....

[Another] incident stands out vividly in my memory. There was a severe thunderstorm raging near the mountain where our home was located. Our family, consisting of my grandmother, my mother, and two or three of the younger children, were seated in the kitchen before an open door, watching the great display of nature's fireworks. A flash of chain lightning followed by an immediate loud clap of thunder indicated that the lightning had struck very close.

I was playing back and forth in the doorway when suddenly and without warning, my mother gave me a vigorous push that sent me sprawling backwards out of the doorway. At that instant, a bolt of lightning came down the chimney of the kitchen stove, [shot] out through the kitchen's open doorway, and split a huge gash from top to bottom in a large tree immediately in front of the house....

My mother could never explain her split-second decision. All I know is that my life was spared because of her impulsive, intuitive nature.

Years later, when I saw the deep scar on that large tree at the old family home, I could only say from a grateful

heart, "Thank the Lord for that precious gift possessed in abundant measure by my own mother and by many of the faithful mothers, through whom heaven can be very near in time of need."...

[One time] Mother was making soap and had a large tub of lye preparation stored on a high shelf to keep it out of the reach of the younger children. She wanted to take it down, and since I was the only one home she enlisted my help. We climbed up on a chair and began to steady it down. When it was exactly above my head, our hold slipped and the tub and its burning lye water dashed over my face, head, and arms. As quickly as she could act, Mother seized me so I wouldn't run and kicked off the lid from a jar of beet pickles she had just made, and with her right hand cupped, dipped out the reddened, pickle vinegar from the beets over my burning face, neck and arms to stop the eating of the lye and save me from being badly scarred. What could have been a tragedy was averted because of her inspired action....

On another occasion, Father was away on the header and Perry and I had just finished doing the morning chores. I had just finished pouring the milk through the separator, which was a machine which separated the milk from the cream. While waiting for the separator to stop, I foolishly and absentmindedly was tapping my fingers on the outside wheel as it turned around. Not paying attention to what I was doing, I unwittingly put my fingers into the cogs and suffered a severe injury that tore the flesh from the first joint of the third finger of my right hand. Mother was sitting at the table under a bowery just outside and I ran out and put my finger, with the bone protruding, in front of her. She turned ill at the sight. Miraculously, Bishop Erastus E. Farmer appeared on the scene at the moment needed and squeezed the mashed flesh around the bone so it would heal. Mother bound up the wounded finger and the flesh began to grow. While my finger in adult life was somewhat disfigured, it never prevented me from playing the piano....

I had accompanied Father to the "flat" below Dayton, where we owned a forty-acre farm. Just over the fence to the east of the property, some old sheds and barns had blown down, and I set out on a tour of exploration. I had just parted the wires to crawl through when I heard a voice as distinctly as a person could speak, command: "Harold, don't go near that lumber over there!" I looked around quickly, wondering where the voice had come from and frightened at the unusual experience, and then ran as fast as possible away from some unknown danger. I have wondered what the danger could have been and have imagined everything from rattlesnakes to rusty nails.

During my early childhood, my grandmother lived in the old home and Mother used to send meals down with my older brother, Perry, and myself. It was a dark, stormy night when we went down this time, and I stood on the porch cleaning my feet, holding onto the sill, but my foot slipped and I fell backwards; my left hand fell on a broken bottle and cut a gash four or five inches long. I bear the scar of that accident. The treatment Mother gave me was to burn a sock and sift the ashes from the sock down into the open wound. Somehow it worked and avoided the possibility of blood poisoning. This injury kept me from attending school most of the year.... 15

No wonder Harold exclaimed in later years, " 'Through my childhood there seemed to be a guiding hand over me.' " 16

"While Samuel and Louisa Lee lacked opportunities for higher education, they were studious, enjoyed books, and cultivated a sense of scholarship in their home. This attitude was enhanced when, during the early years of their marriage, Samuel taught school during the off-season to supplement the income generated from the family farm. In such an environment, children were inclined toward intellectual and scholarly pursuits." 17 This was made evident when, one morning when he was five years of age, Harold accompanied his older brother, Perry, to school. Harold remembers:

> In 1904, I went with Perry to visit school. Chloe Howell, the teacher, set me at some work to keep me busy, and I surprised her by writing the ABCs and by writing my name. She persuaded Mother to permit me to start school, and although I was only five years of age and the school house was located over two miles from our home, Mother consented. 18

There was only one problem. When Harold was born, it seems that Louisa had her heart set on a girl. Harold was a beautiful enough baby to pass for one, and as he grew into childhood, his most striking features "were his large, searching brown eyes and an abundant growth of dark, wavy hair.... Louisa insisted on letting the baby's hair grow; and when it was sufficiently long, she began to fashion it into long ringlets in the style of Little Lord Fauntleroy [a very popular fictional character of the time]. In keeping with that image, Louisa spent long hours making clothes for Harold worthy of his hair: white shirts with ruffles in front, starched cuffs, and a white middy that was draped over the shoulder of a handsome coat, all set off with a large, flamboyant black tie." 19

The neighborhood ladies thought him a beautiful picture, but it didn't take Harold long to realize that their view was severely limited. In fact, the image he presented was not in the least in harmony with what one should expect from a little boy from an

Samuel Perry, Clyde and
"Little Lord Fauntleroy" Harold B. Lee

CA. *1903*

Courtesy of the Lee Family Collection

extremely rural Idaho farm village at the turn of the century. Perry continues:

> We arrived at the small school every day dressed in knee pants with white starched cuffs folded back over the coat sleeves and white, sailor-collars draped down over the shoulders. And those ringlets were carefully combed and painstakingly curled, dangling down [Harold's back] for all the world to see, and pull—and scoff....
>
> Suffice to record that those curls caused more skinned knuckles and black eyes than either politics or religion. Finally, he had had enough. I remember now how our mother wept when he purloined a pair of scissors and literally "sawed" off one of the frontal danglers, spoiling the whole effect, which made it necessary to delete the remainder—a welcomed relief. He was at last a boy—a fat, chubby one and a pet of all the teachers. 20

On June 9, 1907, a Sunday, Harold was baptized in Bybee's Pond at the old lime kiln near Clifton. He was baptized by Lester Bybee and confirmed a member of the Church the same day by Bishop E. G. Farmer. Two years later, at age ten, he was ordained a deacon in the Clifton Ward. "This seemed to set a pattern that was repeated often throughout his life, a pattern that saw Harold B. Lee reach milestones at a younger age than his peers. He [started school at age five,] was ordained a deacon at age ten, was a school principal in his teens, became both a stake president and a Salt Lake City commissioner in his early thirties, was the managing director of the Church Welfare Department in his mid-thirties, and was ordained a member of the Twelve in his early forties. His precocity and maturity always belied his chronological age. His confident demeanor and bearing made Harold B. Lee seem older than he actually was. There was a certain dignity there, a certain sense about him, which conveyed the impression that he had always

35

been an adult. It was an inherent quality whose roots seemed to extend back beyond the moment of his earthly birth. It was a spiritual quality that implied a pre-earth life where his character and personality had been molded and honed." 21

Yet to all outward appearances, Harold was as common and ordinary as Ezra Taft "T" Benson or any of the other farm boys of southern Idaho. He made his way the two miles to and from school each day through whatever conditions the weather and the dirt road dictated and by whatever means of transportation happened to be available. At home he did his share of indoor chores such as churning the cream into butter; doing up the dirty dishes; dusting and sweeping; and helping his mother bake bread, make soap, wash and hang out the laundry, and put up preserves and other foodstuffs. Outdoors he took his turn with the morning and evening chores, feeding, watering, and otherwise caring for the livestock and poultry; milking the cows; gathering the eggs; and so on. Then there was the actual work of farming—plowing the fields, harrowing, drilling, irrigating, harvesting, and then plowing the fields again so the whole process could be repeated the next season. And never—not one day in the entire year—were any of them absolutely certain that their work would pay off with good crops. Yet the Lees were fortunate, for in their family were one, two, three, and then four growing sons, all of whom could help Samuel and Louisa shoulder the burdens of rural life.

On the other hand, life in the Lee home was not always work without relief. Occasionally there were family outings, picnics, and two memorable trips. One was to Pocatello and then via the railroad to the huge city of Boise to visit with Louisa's parents. Grandfather Bingham was deputy warden at the prison, and while the Lees were visiting, a prisoner escaped, was captured by guards with dogs, and was placed in solitary confinement as a punishment. Harold never forgot the incident, nor his feelings at seeing so many prisoners in their black-and-white striped prison uniforms.

Harold B. and Samuel Perry Lee   CA. *1905–6*

The second trip, which both Harold and Perry took with their father, was south on the train to Salt Lake City to attend general conference. Harold remembered:

> My father had grown up in Salt Lake City....
>
> Naturally, [he] was anxious for his boys to see some of the scenes he had remembered as a boy...so it was decided that we would go down to attend general conference. He took his two oldest boys; I was second oldest. Of course, the pending conference, as such, was not our most immediate interest. We wanted to see the sights of the big city....
>
> I still recall...that Mother fixed food for us. I remember we had fried chicken, and all we needed, too....
>
> My earliest recollection [of general conference]—I was just a young lad—was sitting in the south gallery of the Salt Lake Tabernacle and looking down at the pulpit and seeing President Joseph F. Smith sitting there. I was impressed at seeing for the first time the President of the Church....
>
> That was my first visit to Salt Lake City. 22

Simply being at home with the family was also remembered with fondness. According to Harold's sisters Verda and Stella, their mother's "motto was 'You can always do a little bit better,' her example [preaching] the most potent sermon of all. Her home was shining and she was the most immaculate housekeeper. [Their father Samuel] once said: 'Mother, I do believe that you make dirt just because you enjoy cleaning it up so much!' And her personal grooming was just as neat and tidy as her home."23

According to Harold, two things about life in his mother's home stood out in his memory. The first was her skill as a seamstress. Always considered well dressed as children, few outsiders knew that practically all their outer clothing had been made over by their mother from secondhand clothes. Harold continues:

[Mother's] other outstanding skill was in caring for the

sick. She always began with castor oil, and so successful was she that never was a doctor in our home excepting when the babies came. I recall the many weary days and nights when four of us were down in bed at the same time with scarlet fever. Father was away much of the time, and for several days, my brother Clyde, particularly, was at death's door. I remember also Mother's bitterly successful fight to save his life when he suffered with diphtheria. She swabbed his throat constantly for several days and nights to prevent its closing. 24

The girls continued: "Our home reflected a great love of beauty and fine taste. [Mother] was gifted in the art of flower arranging and her beautiful handiwork lent the stamp of her personality in our home." 25

There was also much kindness in the Lee home. Again according to Harold's sisters:

The simple joys created by a loving mother of hot, home-made tomato soup after sacrament meeting on Sundays; the "lumpy-dick," of which Harold was so fond [a thick "pudding" of flour, milk and cream served with butter and sugar]; a very special evening when mother had made new flannel nightgowns for us as little girls; and the nights when we couldn't sleep, because the delicious aroma of baking bread cast its tantalizing aroma through the house to our nostrils in the bedroom—all will never be forgotten. It was on such occasions that, late at night, Father would open our bedroom door quietly, pick up his little girls in his arms, and carry us into the bright light of the kitchen and sit us on the table. Then Mother would place a plate of delectable slices of hot bread and honey on the table, along with a glass of cold milk for each of us. That was a treat for princesses, and we were treated that way. We did have the sweetest childhood. 26

Courtesy of the Lee Family Collection. N.D.

To those sentiments about his dear mother, Louisa, Harold would later utter a frequent and heartfelt, "Amen!"

TEACHER BY DAY,
MUSICIAN BY NIGHT

"Mother?"

"Yes, Harold?" Concerned by the terrible weakness in her seventeen-year-old son's voice, Louisa Lee nevertheless rejoiced that he was at least talking. Only the night before he had been on the edge of unconsciousness, and the gasping and wheezing that had come from deep in his lungs was far too close to the death rattle she had heard so many times in others.

"What...what caused you to...to think of onions?"

Waiting for the young man's spasm of coughing to subside, Louisa glanced at the damp, reeking flour sack she had only moments before removed from his chest.

"I didn't think of them," she replied simply. Reaching forward, she wiped her son's brow. "I was listening to your breathing during the night, pleading with the Lord to spare your life, when the thought of placing crushed onions on your chest came into my mind. In that instant I knew the Lord was telling me how to save your life. All I had to do was obey."

"So, the Lord told you...to cut up a bunch of onions and...crush them inside a flour sack?"

Louisa chuckled. "Of course not, Harold. His Spirit whispered only the basics—that crushed onions on your chest would save your life. It was left up to me how to do it. I emptied a dozen or more large onions out of the sack on the porch into my apron, carried them to the sideboard in the kitchen, cut and diced them as rapidly as possible, and it was while doing that, meanwhile wiping the flow of tears from my eyes with whatever was handy, that the flour sack came to mind. It was what I'd grasped when I was blinded by the onion-caused tears."

"Well, th...thank you for saving my life."

"I didn't save it, darling. I told you, the Lord took care of that. All I did was obey his instructions."

"I don't know what...what healing properties God put into onions," Harold gasped as he tried to smile, "but I'm thankful he told you about it."

"So am I." Again Louisa smiled, but quickly she grew serious. The sun had not yet crested the mountains to the east, yet out in the corral the family cow was already complaining about her overly full udder; several hens were cackling over the early success of their egg-laying efforts; a meadowlark was trilling from a nearby fence post; and the large-hoofed Percheron work horses were whinnying up a storm as they waited for the bags of bran and shorts her husband gave them each morning. It was going to be a good day both indoors and out, she thought—a fine day, for now she knew without doubt that her son was going to live. Still, there was something he needed to be told, something difficult to say even for one as plainspoken as herself. For most of the night the Spirit had been whispering it to her, preparing her mind for it, and now she had it to do. Steeling herself, she began.

"Harold, you brought this pneumonia upon yourself, you know."

"Mother—"

"I don't want you arguing with me, or trying to tease me out of what I have to say. Be still, Harold, and listen!"

"Yes, ma'am," Harold nodded, though he was fairly certain he knew exactly what was coming.

"The fact of the matter is, Harold, you aren't getting anywhere near enough rest."

"I know that, Mother."

"Yes, you do, and that's the worst part of it. To be ignorant of a fact is forgivable, but to be knowledgeable and then do nothing can only be grievous in the eyes of the Lord."

She was right about that, Louisa knew. Willfully being foolish was a sin. Of course Harold was still very young, only eighteen, and so he hadn't had time to develop a vast store of wisdom. Yet before leaving home he had always been so responsible—

"Think about it, Harold. As principal of the Oxford School your day begins by six in the morning at least—"

"More usually five. You just don't see me until six."

"That only makes it worse. You eat your breakfast as you're flying out the door, you often skip the lunches I make because you're playing basketball with the schoolboys—"

"And the fellows from the community."

"Of course, and them. After school you spend an hour or so practicing with the girls chorus you organized—"

"The girls need an extracurricular activity as much as do the fellows, Mother."

"Yes, yes, I'm certain they do. But the point is, you have no time during the day for any sort of rest. After girls chorus you meet with the fellows of the orchestra and practice with them until practically bedtime. At least that's when you arrive here at home. And that doesn't count the two or three nights a week when you travel with the orchestra to play for dances. Even when the dances end at midnight, Harold, you don't get back to the school until four or five in the morning. And if you happen to play in Pocatello, or all the way down to Logan or Brigham City, or if the dances are scheduled to last all night long—"

"I know, Mother." Harold was staring at the ceiling. "Then I don't get any sleep at all."

"Harold, no one can entirely miss two or three nights of sleep a week, week in and week out, and not have it catch up with him. You are simply pushing yourself too hard, and you came very near to losing your life because of it."

"It doesn't seem to bother the other fellows."

"Not one of them is doing any real work in the daytime, either." Louisa was obviously upset, and it showed in her voice. "Besides, they have Sundays to lay around and rest, whereas now that you are president of the elders quorum, you have no time even then. Mercy sakes alive, Harold! Don't you ever know when to quit?"

"Do you?" Harold asked as he smiled playfully up at his mother.

"We are not discussing me, Harold, and you know it!"

With a sigh Harold turned his gaze back toward the ceiling. "If I didn't play with the orchestra, Mother, I couldn't afford to give you and Father all my teaching salary. And I know how badly you need it."

For a moment Louisa smoothed the bedding around her, thinking of how to reply. "Yes," she finally responded, "that money is a great blessing to us, and we are more thankful for it than you know. But both your father and I would a thousand times rather have nothing than to end up losing you before your time."

"You won't lose me—"

"We very nearly did last night, and you know it!" Louisa took a deep breath to steady herself. "But Harold, there's something else, something more serious even than loss of sleep, that both your father and I have been anguishing over for some time. Both of the Frew boys, and maybe even the rest of the orchestra, have been seen drinking and smoking cigars. Last week we heard that one of them was even fall-down drunk and had to be carried out of the dance hall!"

"And you think I'm drinking?" Harold asked angrily.

"Oh, Harold, of course we don't! We know you better than that, and we trust you completely."

"Then, why—"

"We worry that others don't know you so well. Oh, my darling son, what might happen if one of your precious young singers heard that you were drinking—and she didn't know you as well as we do? Or one of the young men you are working so hard to educate? Or what about one of the members of your quorum, one who also doesn't know you well enough? Do you suppose any of them would listen to you after hearing such a report? Or respect you enough to learn from you?"

"I…hadn't thought of it quite like that."

"Harold, I believe such a situation is what our Savior was referring to when he admonished us to avoid even the appearance of evil. It isn't necessarily that such an appearance damages us, as that it can so easily damage the good we might otherwise be able to do."

"But appearance *can* damage us as well," Harold's father said from the doorway, his presence surprising both his wife and his son.

"Father," Louisa said as she spun around, referring to her husband by the same title her children used, "I thought you were doing the chores."

Samuel Lee smiled. "It's all right, Mother. I wanted to see how Harold was doing this morning. When I heard what was being discussed, I decided to keep my mouth shut, stand still, and listen."

"Good morning, Father." Harold's voice was already gaining strength—at least a little.

"Morning, Harold. I'm delighted to see you're feeling some better. You gave us a real fright, you know."

"So I've heard."

Stepping into the room, Samuel sat in the chair next to his son's bed. "The way the stock's carrying on out back, I don't have much time. So, what say we talk about appearances?"

"I think I'd like to hear what you have to say."

Sam Lee smiled. "Good. Makes it easier that way. As with what your mother told you, my thought also has to do with the company you keep—but in a slightly different way."

"Okay," Harold responded hesitantly.

"Let me see if I can explain. I'm thinking of your God-given gifts, and of your eternal mission—that which you were fore-ordained by the Lord God Jehovah to accomplish for him during your mortal life. Do you remember how you were promised by Bishop Farmer when he confirmed you after your baptism that in addition to the Holy Ghost, you would have the ministering of angels to help you magnify your gifts and give you the power to accomplish your life's work?"

Harold smiled weakly. "You've never let me forget it."

"Nor will I. And that brings me to my point. If you spend your days in teaching, educating, loving, serving, and otherwise doing the Lord's work, and so enjoying the help of God's holy angels and the Holy Ghost, and then spend your evenings as well as two or three nights a week laboring in the presence of the prince of darkness and his angels of misery, which power will have the greatest influence upon you?"

"I...I don't know. I suppose whichever one I try most sincerely to obey."

"Perhaps in an ultimate sense, that is so. But in the short run, Harold, do you see how you might be conflicted? Torn apart inside? Day in and day out you are intentionally inviting both forces into your personal temple, and whereas Satan and his evil followers make no promise about not trying to be where the Spirit of the Lord is, the Lord is very clear that he cannot allow his Spirit to remain where evil exists. In such a situation, particularly when it is intentional, Satan will always outstay the Holy Ghost. In other words, son, for a time the battle within you will rage hot and heavy, but there is no doubt who the short-term victor will be. And given enough short-term victories, old Scratch will win the final battle, too."

"But...why?"

"Because of your agency, Harold, your choices. No matter your
spiritual gifts or your foreordained promises, you cannot obtain
the blessings and glories of heaven so long as you choose to keep on
walking with one foot in Babylon. As surely as the sun came up this
morning, you will be dooming yourself to failure! The Lord's spirit
will be forced to withdraw from you, and in that instant Satan will
have gained power in your life. That, dear son, is why your mother
and I worry."

Harold's head was spinning, for each of his parents had introduced a thought he had never before considered. And both, he
knew instinctively, were right! The thing was, now he had to figure
out what to do about it. And considering the commitments he had
made to the fellows in the orchestra, that was going to be a major
challenge—

As a small child Harold Bingham Lee showed an aptitude for music,
and his parents did all in their power to encourage the development
of his talent. He started with piano and then organ, being instructed
by one Sarah Gerard, a rather stern technician who was inclined to
rap his knuckles when he played wrong notes. Soon he was serving
as accompanist in the Clifton Primary and Sunday School, enjoying
himself so much that whenever there was a rest from the labors of
the farm he could be found at the piano, adding to his skill while
providing pleasure and delight to all who might be near to listen.
"This skill followed him into the mission field where he was
frequently called on to provide the music for various gatherings. It
even followed him into the Quorum of the Twelve, where, for many
years, he served as the organist at the weekly meetings of the
First Presidency and the Quorum of the Twelve held in the upper
room of the Salt Lake Temple. Indeed, he was still performing that
function in the spring of 1970, but soon thereafter relinquished it to
Elder Spencer W. Kimball, who continued as the official organist of

the Brethren until after he became the president of the Church."1

But Harold's musical talents went beyond the piano and the organ. According to his elder brother, Perry:

> Our father surprised us one day as we were convalescing from a bout with scarlet fever by bringing into our sickroom two shining instruments—a baritone horn for Harold and a cornet for me. That cured the fever in jig time, but I'm afraid the raucous sounds that came from those shiny horns in the learning process gave our parents many a headache.2

It wasn't long before Harold was playing brass instruments well enough to be invited into membership in the Clifton Silver Concert Band. Neither would that be the end of his career as a professional musician.

At age twelve Harold successfully completed the last of the eight grades of study offered at Clifton's school. "The next scholastic step for the graduates of Clifton's grammar school was the Oneida Stake Academy at Preston, Idaho, across the valley and south of Clifton. The academy was organized in 1888 under the direction of the Oneida Stake Presidency. Its first home was in Franklin, Idaho. It remained there until 1898 when it moved to Preston where a new two-story, cut-stone building had been erected for its use. Nine years later, a second building was added. In Harold's junior year, a well-equipped gymnasium was constructed. These buildings, with the nearby playing fields, comprised the campus of the academy. Here the new student from Clifton would spend four years, except during the summer months when he would return home to help on the farm. Here he would begin to reveal the qualities of leadership that would characterize all his adult years.

"In his beginnings at the Oneida Academy, it is doubtful that young Harold Lee, soon to be called Hal by his friends, felt like much of a leader. He was the youngest student in his class and, therefore, the youngest in the entire school. Moreover, except for one other poor, benighted freshman, he was the only boy in the academy who still wore knee pants. While Louisa had yielded on the issue of Little Lord Fauntleroy outfits for her son, she had remained adamant that he wear knee pants. Had it not been for the protective guidance of Perry, who had preceded him at the academy, Harold's first days there could have been very rough, indeed. It is inferred that with urgent counsel from Perry, knee pants quite soon disappeared from the freshman's wardrobe."3

Of his own experiences at the academy, Harold wrote:

> Perry and I were fitted up in a room and started our house-keeping in the home of Robert Daines, located across the street from the Oneida Stake Academy....
>
> Living in the same house were a total of thirteen boys, and one could easily guess the impromptu parties staged. Underneath our room were the quarters of the principal of the school, J. Robert Robinson. On various occasions, he appeared and soundly scolded us for the "ceiling-cracking" performance we sometimes staged....
>
> When I entered school I was anxious to continue my music training. The high school band offered the best opportunity. My first instruments were an alto [sax] and the French horn. Later in my school, when I had attained a bit more ability, I was invited to join the Preston Military Band, and the second year I took up the baritone [sax]. Under the tutelage of Professor Charles J. Engar, I played through the summer and winter with the Preston Band. For these four years we concertized on all patriotic and civic occasions and were paid a fee for our services....
>
> In my second year at high school I became acquainted with Ethel Cole of Fairview, Idaho, and during our high school years and until I went on my mission in 1920, she

and I kept up a rather constant, intimate friendship either by correspondence or by occasional visits. I remember her as my first "sweetheart" and the only girl with whom I kept steady company prior to my mission. I always admired her as a genuine friend....

My favorite sport was basketball, and at the time I attended high school it was the major athletic sport. In my junior year I was elected athletic reporter for the Oneida, the school paper; and in my senior year, I was elected the student manager of athletics, which was the "plum" of all school offices because it carried the privilege of accompanying all athletic teams on their trips to handle the business affairs while en route, all expenses being paid by the school. Art Rynearson was the coach, and we were fortunate in having a team that competed on even terms with college teams like the UAC. Our team played games that took us from Rexburg, Idaho, on the north to Ogden, Utah, on the south. It was often my responsibility, also, to "scout" rival teams.

Besides managing the team, I gained considerable skill as a player. I was a member of the senior team that won the class championship. Following my graduation I continued to play and enjoyed some reputation as a basketball player. 4

It was during Harold's senior year that an incident occurred that was to cement forever in his mind the spiritual prowess of his mother, as well as the humility she insisted that he and his siblings must always display. After all, she told them repeatedly, it was by God's power that they were enabled to display gifts and skills, not their own. Therefore they had nothing of which to boast. Harold's account of this incident begins:

In my senior year at high school, 1915–16, I was extremely busy with a number of school activities outside of my school work. One of my debating teammates was Sparrel Huff. The

Both photos courtesy of the Lea Family Collection

Above: Oneida Stake Academy's basketball team   CA. *1915–16*
Below: Debating partners Sparrel Huff and Harold B. Lee

Oneida Academy was in a league with the Fielding Academy of Paris, Idaho, and the subject to be debated was "Resolved That the Monroe Doctrine Should Be Abolished." We defended the negative side and Louis Ballif and Irel Lowe the affirmative. Prior to the finals with the Paris teams, we staged debates all over the adjoining counties.

Never in the history of our school had a team [beaten] Fielding Academy at Paris, but we succeeded in turning the tables in a thrilling two-to-one decision over a Paris team, composed of Nellie Parker and George Bateman. They gave us a banquet following the debate, and the next day we returned to Preston as conquering "heroes," where our home team was victorious and our student body gave us a real reception in a special assembly. 5

Quite appropriately pleased with his success, Harold telephoned home to tell his mother of the triumph. To his surprise she responded, "'Never mind, son. I know all about it. I will tell you when you get home at the end of the week." Harold continues: "When I came home she took me aside and said, 'When I knew it was just time for this performance to start, I went out among the willows by the creekside, and there, all by myself, I remembered you and prayed God you would not fail.'" 6

Abruptly, Harold knew several things. First, that his mother had faith sufficient to open the heavens and call down blessings upon her son. Second, that it had been by God's power rather than his own that he had succeeded. And third, that his mother's love for him had been the motivator that had brought the power of God into play. Harold concluded his account by stating: "I have come to know that that kind of love is necessary for every son and daughter who seeks to achieve in this world." 7

There was little resemblance between the young boy in knee pants who enrolled in the Oneida Academy in the fall of 1912 and the handsome, accomplished, and self-assured young man who graduated in the spring of 1916. Hal Lee had left his mark on the academy. There may have been other students who excelled him in one activity or the other, but it is doubtful there was anyone whose overall performance outshone his. He was not a one-dimensional student, pouring all his energies into one aspect of the school's curriculum. He sampled them all, and he was remarkably adept in everything he sampled. Yet, with all his prominence in athletics, music, debate, and the school's social and administrative affairs, Harold was still one of the boys, enjoying the high jinks so often associated with teenagers. He was very much part of the "ceiling cracking" episodes at the Daines boardinghouse that evoked Mr. Robinson's little sermonettes. And he was very much involved in the brawl that erupted between the senior and junior classmen during the founders' day celebration in 1916. Moved, perhaps, by feelings of nostalgia as their careers at Oneida wound down, the seniors fixed their class flag to the academy's flagpole. Then, in turn, each of them climbed the pole to kiss the flag as a symbol of class unity and loyalty. After singing together and giving the class yell, they retired, presumably in an expansive, mellow mood. That turned quickly to anger when they awakened the next morning to find that the juniors had removed their flag. These underclassmen discovered too late that what to them was a harmless prank was to the seniors a major affront to their honor. The brawl that ensued ended only with the intervention of the Preston police force. Since "T" Benson was a year behind Hal Lee at Oneida, we are left to wonder whether the two future prophets were arrayed against each other in the sound and fury of this meaningless brawl. If so, we can be assured that

Both photos courtesy of the Lee Family Collection

Above: Oneida Stake Academy class picture
Below: High-school-age Harold B. Lee

CA. 1915–16

in later years, it afforded them many a good chuckle when the incident was put in proper perspective. 8

After graduating from the Oneida Stake Academy in the spring of 1916, Harold departed almost immediately for Albion, Idaho, some thirty miles south of Burley. There he enrolled for the summer in the Albion State Normal School to receive preparatory training to become a teacher. He continues: "The laws of Idaho required a rigid test in fifteen subjects in order to qualify [as a teacher], and I spent a very strenuous summer in intensive study, losing twenty pounds in weight, but [I] gained my objective, passing the required examination with an average grade of 89 percent.

"Albion was a quaint little old-fashioned town.... Practically nothing was there but the school.... There were no amusements except at the school, and the old board sidewalks indicated the general backwardness of the inhabitants. Removed as it was from all attractions that might detract from school, I think I never absorbed so much knowledge as during the summers of 1916 and 1917 when I earned my second- and third-class certificates. The second year I played in the town band with Lee M. Lockhard, and played baseball on the team from the school." 9

By the end of his first summer, seventeen-year-old Harold was qualified to enter into the profession of teaching. There was an opening for a teacher in nearby Weston, and Harold signed a contract to teach there. He remembers:

I was employed to teach my first school during the winter of 1916–17, at the Silver Star School, about five miles south of Weston, Idaho. Here in a one-room school, I had some real experience. With about twenty to twenty-five pupils, I had most of the grades represented from the first to the eighth grade. My program consisted of twenty-eight classes each day. So conscientious was I that I would count the youngsters on the grounds, and if they were all there, I would ring

Above: The one-room Silver Star school in Weston, Idaho   CA. *1917–18*
Below: Harold B. Lee as principal at Oxford, Idaho

the bell, although it was many times not much after 8:30 A.M. Almost nightly I placed my school problems before the Lord, and although I never worried so much over a work, the Lord never deserted me and I learned some of the most valuable lessons of self-mastery of my life....

This one-room school was the community center where all dances were held. A banjo, violin, and a portable organ served as instruments in an orchestra. The dances would go until midnight, when a halt was called while the women prepared their coffee, cake, and sandwiches, and the men went outside to get their whiskey and beer which had been hauled from Utida, the state line, and kept for the occasion. Following this interlude the dance continued until daylight. 10

For just one year Harold taught at the Silver Star School. Returning to Albion for a second summer, he obtained his certificate for administration as well as teaching at a higher level. In the fall he contracted to become the principal of the school at Oxford, near his home in Clifton.

Harold turned over to his father most of the salary [$50/month] he earned during the year he taught at the Silver Star school. He also did that when he transferred to the school at Oxford [$90/month], continuing to do so during the three years he taught there. This was a godsend to Bishop Lee, who constantly struggled to obtain the means to maintain his family and to educate Harold's younger brothers and sisters. 11

At Oxford School, which was a two-story stone structure, the most impressive building in town, Harold was no longer the only teacher. Velma Sperry and Tressie Lincoln taught the younger grades, leaving him to focus on the older grades as well as his administrative responsibilities. Unfortunately, a few of the students were older than he, and some of the boys were bigger. He records:

> Oxford had the reputation of having a rough crowd of boys, and the threat had been reported to me that I wouldn't last long in the school as the principal. In solving the situation, my basketball experience stood me in good stead. Because of my good size, I taught these big boys, some of whom were older than I, to play basketball, and during the lunch hours, I dressed in basketball togs and played with and against them, but as fortune would have it, I maintained sufficient dignity to win their confidence as their principal, and also win the kind of friendship that has lasted even to this day....
>
> While I was there we organized the Oxford Athletic Club, composed of the town fellows. I played a forward position on the first team and we traveled into all the neighboring towns to play. This activity gave me some prestige in the town." 12

Along with his athletic activities with the boys, Harold recognized that the young ladies of his school also needed attention through some sort of extracurricular activity. This was accomplished when the eighteen-year-old principal "organized and trained a women's chorus.... The chorus was comprised of ten young ladies who sang at various school, church, and civic functions. Since there were few entertainments in Oxford and the surrounding rural communities, a chorus such as this was doubtless very much in demand. So grateful were the members of this group for Harold's efforts in bringing them together and training them, that when he left for the mission field [three years later] they gave him a gold ring as a remembrance of their association." 13

Because of his age and relative inexperience, this was a difficult time for Harold, fraught with hidden dangers. Since he was now

Oxford's young women's chorus organized, trained
and conducted by Principal Harold B. Lee   CA. *1918*

living at home, for Oxford was not too many miles from Clifton, he turned often to his mother for counsel and advice. In his personal history he wrote:

> I think I came to appreciate her first while teaching at Oxford, Idaho. Mother guessed the dangers that beset an eighteen-year-old school principal, susceptible to temptation and always in danger of a fatal step in such a responsible job. Never did she go to bed at night until I had come home. While I ate the hot lunch she always had for me, she questioned me about the day's work. She had a keen intuition and on some occasions compelled Dad to hitch up a team and go to meet me. This companionship has always continued, and in my manhood I value greatly Mother's wisdom. Mother was always blunt and outspoken and had a way of correcting that sometimes antagonized, but was always effective. [14]

During this period Harold received his first significant priesthood calling—as president of his elders quorum. This quorum included members from the Clifton, Oxford, and Dayton wards, and his visits with the quorum members, combined with his callings to provide piano and organ accompaniment at most Clifton ward meetings, left him little time on Sundays for anything but church work.

Nevertheless, he also found time to join a dance orchestra that had been "organized by Dick and Chap Frew, whose parents purchased a ranch at Oxford while he was the school principal.... In organizing what they called the Frew Orchestra, the brothers conducted auditions for musicians who could play the cornet, piano, and trombone. They found their cornet and piano player in Marion Howell and Reese Davis. The only trombonist who auditioned lacked the necessary skill. Learning of Harold's musical background, the Frews invited him to try out. Although he had never before played the trombone, his experience with other wind instruments, which he played in the bands at Clifton, Preston, and Albion, enabled Harold to play the trombone readily.... After practicing together for a time to become acquainted with each other's styles and skills and to synchronize their instruments into a whole, and after developing a wide repertoire of catchy dance tunes, the Frew Orchestra went public. It did not take long for the group to catch on." 15

This period, immediately before and after World War I, saw the emergence of a whole new concept of ballroom dancing. It was a time that also saw the emergence of the so-called liberated woman, the flapper, with her bobbed hair, her short skirts, and her saucy attitudes. This spawned a set of new dance steps, among which were the Charleston and the Black Bottom, which gave energetic expression to the mood of the times. It was during this period that various temperance societies, with widespread public support, were able to shepherd through Congress the wartime Prohibition Act, passed in November 1918, and to obtain ratification of the Prohibition Amendment to the United States Constitution in January 1919. This in turn gave rise to the prevalent use of "the flask" by non-abstainers in which to carry their forbidden liquor about with them.

This, then, was the character of the era during which the Frew Orchestra and its members, including the trombonist Harold B. Lee, acquired a wide reputation in an area that extended from Logan, Utah, on the south to Pocatello, Idaho, on the north. Once its reputation had been established, it was not uncommon for the orchestra to play for dances two and three nights a week. This became a rich source of extra income for Harold and the other members of the orchestra, and made it possible for him to turn over to his father the entire amount of his school salary. But this also became a source of concern for Harold's parents. They disliked the idea that their son was repeatedly thrown into an environment that fostered attitudes and practices contrary to the standards of the Church. Their concerns were intensified by the knowledge that some members of the Frew Orchestra were known to drink and to engage in other conduct unbecoming a Latter-day Saint. While they had confidence in the integrity of their son, still they knew he was not immune to temptation. Harold later expressed the feeling that during this period, his parents "held their breath" out of fear that he might succumb to the enticements that surrounded him. And, they were concerned about his health. When the orchestra had a midweek engagement, Harold would have little sleep during a period of thirty-six hours. If, for instance, the musicians were scheduled to play on a Wednesday night, after working at school all day Harold would leave Oxford as soon as he could break away in the late afternoon. There would then be a long ride over a rough, unsurfaced road to the town where the dance was to be held. Usually these lasted well into the early-morning hours. After packing instruments and riding home, it would be nearing the time when Thursday's workday would begin. With the duties facing him at school that day, he could not hope to get any sleep until Thursday night, except for a short nap he might steal during the day. If this were a week, as often happened, when the orchestra also had commitments on Friday and Saturday nights, the musicians could look forward to little rest over the weekend, except on Sunday...[though] Harold's Sunday commitments left little room for leisure on that day. With such a heavy schedule, it is small wonder that Harold contracted a serious case of pneumonia during this period. His mother, ever solicitous over his well-being, carefully nursed him back to health. 16

Louisa's inspired cure, reminiscent of those she had used during the travails of Harold's childhood, is worthy of note. One can imagine the worried mother as she "bent over her seventeen-year-old son once more to feel his feverish head and listen to his tight, labored breathing. It was after midnight, and Harold's chest disease had not seemed to respond to [her] mustard plasters. Anxiety clutched at her heart and she knew she must do something quickly, or her son would die in a few hours.

"She hurried to the back porch and opened a large sack of onions, filled her apron, and went into the kitchen. After slicing a large panful of onions she dumped them into an empty flour sack and covered her son's chest with that wet, juicy sack. Then she prayed and waited for a miracle.

"By morning his breathing was improved, and he was over the crisis. When the family praised Harold's mother for saving his life, she merely said: 'Oh, but I didn't save his life. The Lord did. He just expects us to do everything we can do to help.'" 17

No wonder Harold later exclaimed: "'I thank God today for my parentage…. I have been blessed with a splendid father and a grand and lovely mother.'" 18

One other incident at Oxford School was worthy of note in Harold's history. He recorded: "I was principal of this school… during the severe influenza epidemic of 1918, our school being quarantined for some months. We had just reopened the school when every family but two came down with the disease, and it became necessary for neighboring towns to assist in supplying food and nursing until their recovery."19 Worldwide, tens of millions of people died during this terrible epidemic, including many in Idaho. Considering his weakened condition and horrific schedule, it is surprising that

Harold himself did not succumb at least somewhat to the disease.

Thankfully he didn't, but managed to keep on working. Then, not very long after the quarantine was lifted, Harold's father recommended as his bishop that his son serve a full-time mission. Shortly thereafter, Harold was prepared and ready when the President of The Church of Jesus Christ of Latter-day Saints called him into full-time missionary service.

AN AURA OF
DIVINE LEADERSHIP

As darkness closed in around the long train, and the people aboard settled in for the journey from Sheridan, Wyoming, to Denver, Colorado, Elder Harold B. Lee closed his eyes. He was not tired and did not wish to sleep, but in the car were too many distractions for him to concentrate, and concentrate is what he wished most earnestly to do. Beside him his mission president, John M. Knight, was already sleeping soundly, though with the commotion of crying children and a knot of giggling and laughing young people just two seats ahead, Harold wondered how the man had accomplished it.

President Knight was a remarkable man, no doubt about it. The grandson of Vinson Knight, who had been bishop of the Nauvoo Lower Ward and thus Joseph Smith's bishop before becoming Presiding Bishop of the Church, grandson John M. Knight was also serving as counselor in the Ensign Stake in Salt Lake City, though while serving as mission president he reported to the stake only for stake conferences. In serving under him, Harold had discovered the president to be fearless in his missionary endeavors and always on the go, traveling from one end of the vast Western States Mission to the other as frequently as possible. Since there were no organized stakes or wards in the mission, it meant that President Knight presided over every single member, rather than just the missionaries.

Since his own call as president of the Denver Conference at the nine-month mark of his mission, Harold had carried the same responsibility for the members there. He had performed marriages, counseled couples who wished to divorce or get married, conducted funerals, and filled every other ecclesiastical assignment imaginable. These things he had been called to do. But the assignment to travel to Sheridan that he had just completed was no part of any call he had ever been given, at least until the past week, and Harold was still wondering about it.

He was wondering even more about the sister who had approached him the afternoon before, following his second major sermon of the day. Why was it always sisters, he found himself asking? And why did they always zero in on a thing that gave a fellow like him so much discomfort?

Behind him a man was explaining to the woman at his side the history of Sheridan as well as the Bighorn Mountain country of northern Wyoming, and for a moment Harold listened in, hoping to ease his mind. Sheridan, it seemed, had been named after General Phillip Henry Sheridan of Civil War fame and was the trading and cultural center for a wide area of farms and cattle ranches in the vicinity of the Bighorn Mountains. It was also the center of an area that for many centuries had been home to several significant tribes of American Indians. One indication of their civilization, built atop the Bighorn Mountains between Sheridan and the Bighorn Basin country to the west, was the huge stone Medicine Wheel, a vast circle of stones whose spokes pointed true north and other accurate directions. And speaking of Indians, the man continued, just seventy miles north of Sheridan, in 1876, General George A. Custer had made his famous last stand against a huge force of them at the battle of the Little Bighorn.

There were also a goodly number of Latter-day Saints living in the area, Harold now knew, fine people who had come to ply their farming and ranching skills in building up the country. Many of them had been at the train station to greet President Knight prior to the conference, and keen disappointment had shown on their faces when Harold instead of the mission president had stepped down into the cold November morning.

The president's decision to have Harold take over for him had been last minute, leaving the young elder with little time to do anything but pack and depart. Certainly he had not prepared any sermons, save for while traveling to Sheridan on the train. "Elder Lee," President Knight had stated, "I know Sheridan is nowhere near your assigned field of labor, but there is no one else I would rather trust. Why, you're a regular triple-threat man, so I have no concerns for you whatsoever." And so Harold, twenty-three and almost ready to be released from his mission, had gone to Wyoming to conduct and be visiting authority during the first two days of a three-day conference.

What the Saints in Sheridan hadn't known or expected when he had introduced himself to them, Harold thought with modest satisfaction, was that he was indeed what President Knight had claimed—a triple-threat man. He had not only preached the gospel, but had played the piano and conducted the music with equal competence. And between meetings on Sunday, as he had been doing for more than a year in the Denver Conference, he had interviewed members, mediated disputes, and done his best to put the Church in order. He must have been at least moderately successful in all three areas, too, he thought as the man's voice droned on behind him. When President Knight had arrived on Monday, some of the Saints had pleaded that Elder Lee be allowed to speak again. He had declined, of course, in favor of his mission president. But still, the requests had left him with a good feeling—except, of course, for that one elderly sister.

As the steel wheels clattered rhythmically along the seemingly endless rails beneath the train, finally lulling even the quasi-historian

Illustration by Robert T. Barrett

behind him to sleep, Harold continued to ponder the woman's words. What could they mean to him? How on earth was he supposed to interpret her experience, or deal with it once he had?

Even more disconcerting, at least to Harold, was that it had happened before—to Sister Harriet Jensen, one of the finer sister missionaries under his supervision. One night he and his companion, along with Sister Jensen and her companion, had gone by invitation to a Denver area Protestant Church, where Elder Lee had been invited to explain the doctrines of The Church of Jesus Christ of Latter-day Saints.

"Elder Lee," Sister Jensen had said once they had left the church, speaking quietly enough that only he could hear, "while you were speaking tonight, I saw a hallowed light encircle your head."

"Excuse me," Harold had asked, stunned. "You saw what?"

"A hallowed or divine light that surrounded your head. Actually it extended beyond that, but it was much brighter right around your head, and it was mingled with several beautiful colors. It made it appear as though your head was framed in a half-circle of heavenly light from the top of one shoulder to the top of the other."

Too surprised to respond, Harold had simply stared.

"Elder Lee," she said then, and though her voice was no louder, it suddenly carried an unmistakable ring of conviction, "I have the impression that you are going to someday be the President of the Church."

"Sister," he had immediately responded with just as much firmness, "I won't be worthy enough to be the President."

"Be that as it may," she had responded with a slight smile. "One day, after I have sustained you as the President in general conference, I will remind you of what I said tonight, and you will remember."

Now, as the train clattered southward into the night, Harold's mind felt all awhirl. He remembered, all right. But just as it had happened to Sister Jensen, so had it happened again the day before.

After the afternoon meeting an elderly sister had come to him, quietly, and had described the same sort of aura or light that Sister Jensen had seen back in Denver. Thank goodness, he thought wryly, she hadn't added what he thought of as Sister Jensen's terribly blasphemous prophecy.

Still, as even the giggling young people ahead of him finally settled themselves for sleep, Harold could not rest. The hallowed light was too astounding for him to imagine, much less understand. That was why he had to stop thinking about it. Such thoughts distracted him from missionary work. Only, and this was the real puzzler, how was he to go about getting these two sisters' sincerely expressed experiences out of his mind?

"Dear Father in Heaven," he breathed with deep concern and honest humility, "I don't have a lot of time left on my mission. Wilt thou please help me to focus only on thy work—" 1

Once Harold B. Lee's father had recommended him to the Office of the First Presidency as a missionary candidate, all Harold could do was wait. And while he waited he no doubt reflected, for the decision to serve must not have been easy. He was twenty-one years of age, had worked as a professional educator for four years, "was mature physically, well educated, emotionally stable, and possessed of a rare spiritual instinct. He was of marriageable age and had the training and the skills that would have enabled him to comfortably support a wife and children. If he had settled down at the time into domestic life, one could have predicted a rewarding future for him as a pillar of strength in his local community and church, while enjoying all the blessings of married love and family life. It was not an easy thing, therefore, for Harold Lee to turn away from that prospect toward two years of austere and demanding missionary service during which he not only would be unable to earn an income, but would be a financial burden on his already overburdened father. As for the parents, they knew that with the loss of their son's income, with the need to regularly send money to him in the mission field, and with the obligation to finance the education of the younger children, they would be financially strapped as never before. Yet, there was never a serious question that their second son would willingly accept a call to serve, and that they would support him fully." 2

The call to serve in the Western States Mission, in the form of a letter from Church President Heber J. Grant, arrived in September, 1920. Harold was to report to the Church Offices in Salt Lake City in early November to be set apart, after which he would board the train for Denver, Colorado, his mission headquarters. In preparation he did much of what is done by newly called missionaries today, including traveling to the nearest temple to be endowed "with power from on high." 3 Harold was endowed in the Logan Temple on November 6, 1920.

> What he saw and learned [in the temple] comprised what Harold B. Lee later referred to frequently as the training provided by the "University of the Lord." There he gained further insight into his relationship to Deity, learned about the marvels and purposes of the Creation, was taught the plan of salvation, was shown the exaltation he might obtain through obedience and diligence, and was put under solemn covenant to observe basic laws of morality and godliness. With all this, he became obligated to wear a new garment, night and day, bearing symbolic markings that were to remind him of his identity and of the covenants he had made. Judging from the intense interest he later showed in temples, and from the frequency with which he taught the significance of temple ordinances, especially to young people, it is reasonable to assume that the experience young Elder Harold B. Lee had in the Logan Temple that day had a profound influence on his

mission and on his later life. 4

Like all missionaries, Harold experienced pangs of homesickness and loneliness when it came time to bid his family farewell. In his journal he recorded: "I never realized how great a gap my family filled in my life until I bade them good-bye.

"The parting words of my father when I left for the mission field were, 'Harold, my boy, your father and mother are looking for big things from you.'

"No one was 'greener' and more unused to city life than I was, and as a result, I lost my bearings and got turned around in Salt Lake. At the hands of the Presiding Patriarch, Hyrum G. Smith, I received my second patriarchal blessing.

"After a one-hour meeting at the Church Office Building, I was set apart on November 9, 1920, by Brigham H. Roberts of the First Council of the Seventy. Elder Roberts promised me I would go and return in safety.

"In company with Elder Owen H. Martin, of Salt Lake, I left for my mission at 5:30 P.M. on November 10, 1920, over the Union Pacific Railroad. We arrived in Denver the next day, Armistice Day, at noon." 5

> Rumpled and much in need of a shave, a shower, and a change of clothing, they were met at the Denver depot by their mission president, John M. Knight, and members of the mission office staff. This man would play an important role in the development of Harold B. Lee, not only during his mission, but afterward. He was a seasoned leader, forty-nine years old, who was not only the mission president, but was also a counselor in the Ensign Stake Presidency in Salt Lake City. When the Ensign Stake was organized on April 1, 1904, as part of the breakup of the original Salt Lake Stake (a breakup that also saw the creation of the Pioneer and Liberty Stakes), John M. Knight was called as the second

President John M. Knight Courtesy of the Lee Family Collection   CA. *1920*

counselor to Stake President Richard W. Young, who was a son of Brigham Young. Under a practice that was followed often in years past, when John Knight was called to preside over the Western States Mission, he retained his position in the Ensign Stake Presidency, which he actively resumed when he was released as mission president. 6

Taken to the mission home, located next door to the LDS chapel on the corner of Seventh Avenue and Pearl Street, the missionaries witnessed a baptism then in progress, after which Harold did some Relief Society visiting in company with Elder Daniel Peterson and the sister missionaries. After a night's rest he was assigned to labor in Denver with Elder Willis J. Woodbury of Salt Lake City. These two lived with two other missionaries—Owen H. Martin and Harry Jensen, the conference president. Harold recalls: "We lived on the upper floor of a home at 1145 Ogden Street. The lower floor was occupied by a family by the name of Hickman—a mother and three daughters. We became somewhat acquainted with this family in our going and coming, and after the mother and younger daughter had left for California, a Mrs. Ogden came to live with Florence and Mabel Hickman, the two remaining daughters." 7

Harold began his mission that first day by tracting. The woman at his first stop slammed her door in his face, a fairly typical experience, yet he and his companion persisted, and after a day had held eight gospel conversations, given out literature to all but two, and had obtained a promise from a woman that she would attend church the following Sunday.

Meanwhile, as the two companions got better acquainted, each discovered that the other had musical ability. Harold recorded that Elder Woodbury "was a cello player, and when he discovered I could play the piano, he insisted on regular musical practices.

"We often carried his cello and some music with us when we

went tracting, and during the day we were invited in to sing and play, thereby opening the way for the preaching of the gospel. With this approach usually we succeeded in being invited into three homes a day, which was about a record for us. In every home we were complimented and invited back again. After playing and preaching, we made real friends at each visit." 8

Like nearly all new missionaries, Elder Lee experienced the jitters each time he approached a "first-time" assignment. Concerning his first experience in anointing a sick person, he declared that he "forgot the whole prayer and made a mess of things. While we were going home Elder Woodbury asked me if I would get sore at him if he told me something. Reassured, he said, 'For pete's sake, don't ever do it like that.' I will never forget that lesson." 9

Another nerve-jarring experience for most new missionaries is public speaking—especially at what are commonly called street meetings. Again from Harold's journal:

> We held our first street meeting last Saturday night, and they gave me the "honor" of being one of the speakers, along with Sister Dunn and Elder Bergeson. If you want a thrill you sure want to try street preaching. "Scared," did you say? I thought I would surely faint until I got started, then somehow I forgot myself and everyone else, I'm afraid. We are preaching on the corner of 19TH and Welton Streets in Denver, and succeeded in keeping a few people sticking around all the time. I think if I keep on finding out how little I know, by the time my mission is over I will be convinced I don't know anything. Like the old professor at school used to say: "It's all right to say you don't know if you don't say it too often." But with me, it's getting quite frequent. 10

And again:

Courtesy of the Lee Family Collection

Elder Harold B. Lee
with missionary companions

CA. *1920–22*

While tracting I sold a lady two small books and promised to bring back to her a Book of Mormon the next day. I was as tickled as a boy with new shoes, but when I went back the lady wouldn't even come to the door. I sure thought I had a convert there. 11

Despite such typical setbacks and discouragements, Harold brought to his mission a knowledge of how to work. More importantly, all his experiences, all his training, had taught him to work with goals in mind. Farming, teaching, his music, his athletics—all these demanded well-formed goals if any measure of success was to be achieved. The more he focused and concentrated his efforts, therefore, the faster those goals could be reached. It didn't take him long to realize that missionary work was little different. It required diligent work, and if success was to be achieved, that work needed to be focused through specific goals.

Very quickly he began to experience real success—under his direction and tutelage individuals began coming to Christ and joining the Church through the ordinance of baptism. He records:

The first converts I baptized were Mabel and Florence Hickman, at whose home we were rooming. Mabel was an active member of the First Christian Church, and when she and Florence joined the Church, their family and the Christian Church members accused them of everything from immorality to insanity. They proved their conversion to the gospel and became splendid aids in the Denver Branch. They were both expert stenographers. 12

Altogether, I baptized about forty-five converts into the Church. 13

Seven months into his mission, Harold wrote: "We have, all totaled in the conference, about fourteen baptisms for this month, and if ever I felt like working, it is now, when I am just beginning to appreciate the responsibility that rests upon me. I am praying that I will always be kept just a 'high private in the rear ranks' so that I can continue to do the work I am beginning to love." 15

Fortunately, such desires for obscurity were not to be. When he had been serving only six months, Harold was invited to meet with President Knight, who informed him that he had been selected to preside over the Denver Conference, the strongest, most productive conference in the mission. President Knight's words were, "'I am just giving you a chance to show what is in you.'" 15

> As the conference president, he supervised the proselyting of thirty-five missionaries who served in an area extending from Littleton, Colorado, south of Denver, to the Wyoming border on the north and thence east to the Nebraska border. The western boundary of the conference generally followed the eastern flank of the Rockies. He also presided over the Church units and the members within that area, which included branches in Littleton, Denver, Boulder, Greeley, and Fort Collins. Because Elder Lee's headquarters were in Denver, close to the mission office, he had frequent contact with President Knight. As this relationship developed, President Knight began to give Elder Lee assignments beyond his duties as conference president, which, in effect, made him an assistant to the president. 16

Harold records:

> It was here also that I became acquainted with Sister Mary Van, the Relief Society President. She was so helpful to the missionaries that we called her the mission mother.
>
> Here I had some delightful experiences with the above-named missionaries, along with Dr. David S. Murdock, who was a veterinary surgeon whom I had known in Preston,

Idaho, and some others. 17

Three months later, Harold wrote, "I know now I have gained what I'm sure Father would call 'big things'—the confidence of President Knight.

"Only nine short months today since I arrived in Denver; and when I think back on all the wonderful experiences that have been mine in that time, I feel as though it had been but a dream, but I thank the Lord continually. The crying necessities of today wake me up to the fact that I must be working always if God is to accomplish anything through me." 18

As conference president, Harold went to work with a new companion, Elder Vernal Bergeson. Determined to set an appropriate example for the missionaries now under his charge, Harold increased his and his companion's personal work output and then required the same of the other missionaries. "Street meetings were accelerated to two a week. Tracting was intensified, and with that came an increase in cottage meetings. The end result was a significant increase in baptisms. Elder Lee reported seventy-two baptisms through the first nine months of 1922, one more than during the entire previous year.

"Although Harold knew that missionary success could not be measured exclusively in terms of baptisms, yet this was a vital aspect of the work. 'I almost feel as a little kid today,' he wrote several months after becoming conference president, 'and I cannot help but be happy. If all those who have promised to be baptized appear, there will be twelve or fourteen new members of the church after our baptismal service today. Of course, many have experienced the satisfaction that comes when you are able to measure the effectiveness of your work by converts. Although success can't possibly be measured in that way, yet therein is the fascination of missionary work.' The essence of that fascination was to see the changes made in the lives of people through the teaching of the missionaries." 19

Harold's "chief orientation and skill was that of a teacher. Those who knew him well observed that he seldom, if ever, missed an opportunity to teach a lesson to his associates. He was always on duty, as it were, and therefore took advantage of the moment to drive home a lesson regardless of the time or place." 20 Two examples will illustrate. One day he was training two new missionaries in the art of tracting. " 'I sent them alone and when I got around the block I found them sitting under a tree utterly disgusted because they couldn't talk at the homes. After I preached 'Mormonism' to them for fifteen minutes to give them an idea what to say, they started out and had a very successful time, some of the conversations lasting half an hour.' " 21

A second example of Harold using teaching moments to improve his missionaries' performances occurred with two sister missionaries. Harold insisted that the elders and sisters under his supervision strictly follow the rules of the mission. When he learned of violations, he was prompt and direct in speaking out. On one occasion he learned that two sisters had gone to a fashion show in downtown Denver rather than to a choir practice. The next morning, according to one of the sisters, he asked, "Where were you two last night?" When they told him, he replied, "Don't let it happen again."

That was all, no preaching or lectures, just five simple words, spoken with calm authority. One of the sisters wrote of the incident: "As I looked at him, I wished the floor would swallow me up. His look said more than words and made me feel like I had committed a huge crime.... Later,...we came to appreciate and respect the high standards that he held for all of us." 22

Francis M. Gibbons, a member of both the First and Second Quorums of the Seventy, who knew Harold as a General Authority, indicated that there were a great number who felt as the sister missionaries had felt. "It is safe to say that his looks and demeanor always conveyed as much or more meaning than his words. There was some indefinable something in the man, which spoke out by means other than words. It lay in the spiritual realm beyond normal, human understanding."23

It was in such a context that Sister Harriet Jensen described an evening when she, with Harold and his companion, attended by invitation another church. Harold had been asked to explain his church's doctrines from the pulpit.

> "It was while Elder Lee was speaking that night," wrote Sister Jensen, "that I saw a hallowed light encircle his head. The light was much brighter around his head than was the surrounding light, and it was mingled with several beautiful colors. His head was framed in a half circle from the top of one shoulder to the other." Such was the impact of this extraordinary experience on her that after the meeting Sister Jensen went to the speaker and said: "Elder Lee, you are going to someday be the president of the church." His modest reply was, "Sister, I won't be worthy enough to be the president." Sister Jensen added, "But from that day on, I was convinced that he would become our Prophet."
>
> This was not the last time such an aura would be seen surrounding or hovering over Elder Lee. "Stewart Mason and his wife drove me in their car over to Boise," he recorded in his diary on March 23, 1942, "where I was to board the train for Salt Lake. Sister Mason told me she had witnessed an 'aura' as she called it, surrounding me as I spoke." In the same entry, Elder Lee noted, "Fern had previously seen the same thing in the First Ward." 24

As conference president, Harold "was constantly engaged in reorganizing the branches, advising the Saints on their personal lives — including marital counseling on pending divorces — administering to and blessing the Saints, solving the problems of the missionaries, and attempting, as much as time permitted, to continue to do active proselyting work. The demands on his time, energy, physical strength, and moral character were heavy and unrelenting. But such burdens were also the training for his amazing leadership skills as they developed and tested the young spiritual giant growing within him." [25]

The most singular aspect of this spiritual growth was the intense love that filled Harold's heart as he entered into the labors of his calling. Called by many the "mantle" of authority, in reality this mantle is nothing more nor less than a divine manifestation of charity, or the pure love of Christ, thus giving to one called to leadership service a certainty, through the love that miraculously fills his own heart, of the amazing and overpowering love that Christ himself has for those the leader has been called to serve. In speaking of his love for those he served, Harold recorded:

> With such a splendid bunch of missionaries, I'm sure the president expects a great deal to be accomplished. Many times have I prayed that God would make me worthy to be a leader among such fine people. [26]

And:

> When conference finally arrived I was as happy as a little child, so much so, in fact, that when my turn came to talk it was very nearly impossible. Through sheer joy I could hardly speak. Never before have I been able to appreciate real people who are doing their best to help in God's great work, and words fail me in expressing my love toward them. [27]

Despite such significant accomplishments, Harold was still a young man in his early twenties with a great deal to learn. And like most who seek diligently to serve the Lord, he was allowed to learn many of his lessons the hard way. One day following a street meeting he had participated in, he wrote: " 'I made a miserable mess of my part of the meeting, apparently because I was relying upon my strength and ability and not upon the Lord.'" 28 Another day, after visiting with the Denver Branch president, who was moving from the area, Harold wrote:

> When he left me, he told me he respected me and was glad for the opportunity of working with me, saying that I was a hard one to say that about, because of the peculiar qualities that were distinctly mine that kept people long in the dark as to superior abilities that I might possess. That one fact of my makeup has caused me more misgivings as to my ability to succeed than any other. I wish someone would give me a recipe of instruction so I might overcome. 29

Perhaps the one incident of Harold's mission that proved most instructional was the visit of Elder James E. Talmage of the Council of the Twelve. Harold was conducting a baptismal service at the time of Elder Talmage's arrival, and not being too familiar with Church protocol, "went forward with the service without consulting Elder Talmage.

> During the baptism, Elder Talmage stepped forward to the edge of the font and carefully watched what went on. When the confirmations started, the apostle again stepped forward, uninvited, and said, "Here, I will confirm this one." In performing the confirmation, he deliberately reversed the order and first said, "Receive ye the Holy Ghost," and then he confirmed the candidate a member of the Church. After the ceremony, when they were alone, Elder Talmage said, "Elder Lee, you did a splendid job, but..." and then proceeded to point out his error in not recognizing the presiding authority and in not checking with him before he proceeded. He also emphasized that there was no special way to confirm someone a member of the Church. 30

Deeply humbled and thoroughly apologetic, Harold was then able to enjoy the remainder of the apostle's visit. Elder Talmage proved to be both knowledgeable and eloquent. "His extemporaneous remarks, so precise and closely reasoned, sounded like a carefully crafted sermon he might have toiled over for hours, or days. Such was the reputation of the man for gospel scholarship, gained chiefly through his major works, *The Articles of Faith* and *Jesus the Christ*... [that Harold's] experience at the baptismal service made a profound impression upon him....

"It is obvious that [Harold] did not take offense at the counsel given to him by Elder Talmage. On the contrary, he seemed to appreciate it and to profit from it." 31

Following Harold's private interview with Elder Talmage, the apostle "made suggestions freely during the missionary meeting that followed, teaching the Elders how to meet all forms of opposition while proselyting. That night Elder Talmage spoke on 'Heaven's First Law—Obedience.' Sunday night he spoke on the subject, 'Will Many or Few Be Saved?' The Pearl and Seventh Avenue chapel was crowded to overflowing with the largest crowd of Latter-day Saints and their friends ever assembled to that point in Denver. Four hundred and fifty people assembled within the chapel walls. Many were compelled to sit on the floor, and about twenty-five persons were turned away because of lack of space to see and hear. That night Elder Lee played a piano accompaniment for a ladies' vocal duet, and, with President Knight, assisted Elder Talmage in blessing many people after the meeting." 32

As Harold's mission drew toward the end of its second year, and though he remained president of the Denver Conference, President Knight involved him more and more in the affairs of the entire mission. There is no doubt that the young missionary and his president had developed an unusual affinity for each other. There is also no doubt that the Spirit was impressing upon President Knight at least some understanding of Harold's unique and significant future and that he needed special training for it. At one point he told Harold he felt certain he would one day be a mission president, and on another occasion he actually introduced him to a woman as the future president of the Western States Mission. Though neither of these occurred quite as President Knight thought they would, at a later time Harold most certainly did preside over the Western States Mission—as well as every other mission in the Church.

Apparently it was Harold's true humility, and his willingness to be taught, that attracted the young missionary to his president. Harold's "early success as a teacher and school administrator had not given [him] an exaggerated idea about his ability or his importance. Therefore, notwithstanding his father's prediction of 'big things' for him, he had entered the mission field with a cooperative, submissive attitude, anxious to do the work in whatever capacity, even as a 'high private in the rear rank.' This attitude doubtless inspired a sense of confidence in President Knight and was a chief factor in Elder Lee's appointment as the president of the most prestigious conference in the mission after only nine months in the field. As that attitude persisted after his appointment, and Elder Lee's leadership abilities were more clearly revealed, the mission president continued to show preference to him and to give him special assignments." 33

For instance, Harold

was invited to accompany President Knight to Pueblo, Colorado, to inspect the damage caused by a devastating flood and to direct reclamation efforts among the Saints there....

On arriving in Pueblo, President Knight and his young companion faced a scene of terrible devastation. An unusually heavy snowpack on the upper reaches of the Arkansas River and a late, rapid thaw had sent torrents of water cascading through the Royal Gorge and other deep, narrow, rocky canyons to the plain below, inundating Pueblo and its surrounding farms. This overwhelming volume of water had been augmented by an unusually heavy runoff on Fountain Creek, which converges with the Arkansas River at Pueblo. So sudden and unexpectedly heavy was the flooding that the townspeople were caught unaware and an estimated fifteen hundred of them were drowned. Property damage was estimated at thirty thousand dollars, a large sum for that day. As he was the presiding priesthood authority in the area, President Knight took the lead in efforts to comfort and to care for those who had lost loved ones or whose homes had been destroyed and to reclaim, as far as possible, their damaged properties. [Harold] witnessed at firsthand how, in an emergency, the priesthood, the Relief Society, and the other resources of the Church could be marshalled to alleviate suffering and to provide a glimmer of hope to those caught up in adversity. It is likely that some of the lessons Elder Lee learned at Pueblo were useful years later when he struggled to find solutions to a different kind of emergency that faced the members of the Pioneer Stake. 34

A short time later President Knight took Harold on a tour of the conferences located in the eastern part of the mission. This tour provided Harold with an extraordinary opportunity to travel with, room with, pray with, and share the pulpit with a man who was well seasoned in Church administration and doctrine. Acting under the spirit of inspiration, while on the tour President Knight took Harold across the boundary of the mission [the Mississippi River] to visit Nauvoo and Carthage, Illinois.

As Elder Lee walked these streets [of Nauvoo] with his mission president, reflecting on the events that had transpired there long ago, he could not have failed to remember that his great-grandfather, Francis Lee, and his family had lived in Nauvoo during its heyday and had been forcibly driven from it across the river to Montrose, Iowa, on the Mississippi's west bank and from thence had struggled forward to the valleys of the mountains. Here were some of Harold B. Lee's earliest Mormon roots, which extended in an unbroken line to Winter Quarters, to Tooele, to Panaca, to Salt Lake City, and finally to Clifton.

If Elder Lee was exhilarated by his visit to Nauvoo, he was probably depressed by his visit to nearby Carthage. Here he and President Knight inspected the dreary, forbidding jail where Joseph and Hyrum were slaughtered by a mob with painted faces. As the pair stood in the upper room where the murders had occurred, what earthly wisdom could have foretold that the dark-haired, earnest young man who stood there with his mission president would one day stand as number eleven in a line of modern-day prophets that began with the enigmatic Joseph Smith who was martyred there. That Harold B. Lee's visit to Nauvoo and Carthage had a profound effect on him is evidenced by the frequency with which he referred to it [in later years] and by the detailed description he made of it. 35

In November 1922, shortly after his return from the eastern tour, President Knight gave Harold another unusual assignment. Calling him into his office, President Knight asked Harold to take his place in conducting the first two days of a three-day conference in Sheridan, Wyoming. Harold was given just two hours to accept the assignment and make the train, and only the duration of the train ride to prepare. In a letter to his parents, Harold wrote:

> I told the president he was giving me a bigger bite than I could chew, but if the best I could do was all right, that I

would go. He said there was no one else he would rather trust and the Church would pay my expenses. I did the best I could—preached, played the piano, conducted the singing, and helped settle the difficulties in the branch. When President Knight arrived on Monday, Elder Scadlock insisted that I talk again, but I graciously declined and played the part of wisdom. While there, the president took me into his confidence more than he has ever done before and took me with him wherever he went. I wish I could tell you more details (letters are unable to convey the thoughts intended) regarding the value of this trip to me, coming, as it has, at the close of my mission when many thoughts have crowded themselves upon me to make me more appreciative and humble in the responsibility that is mine—to determine whether or not I can make good among strangers, etc. 36

With all these "extracurricular" activities, it is a wonder that Harold found any time for his work in the Denver Conference. Yet he wrote: "When I tell you we are having to hold eighteen cottage meetings this week, besides street meetings and Mutual and choir practice, and only fifteen missionaries here in Denver, you can know that we have but little spare time…the pace is fast and furious…. But don't think I'm getting too straight-backed to admit of foolishness at times, because my indulgence in that on occasions has kept me alive. Times are so strenuous that we don't have time to get sick or die. This week, too, I have been fighting off a bad cold, but have been unable to slacken up because of the work demanded of me. A number of the missionaries have likewise had colds, but with twenty-four cottage meetings to hold, we haven't had much time to lose." 37

Meanwhile, conditions at home were worrying Harold more and more. When reports came that his father was aging dramatically because of the stress of being bishop, Harold felt that his mission was adding to the problem, which, as he put it, "makes my heart ache." [38] Then he vowed that, despite the uncertainty of his future, he would never knowingly allow his parents to be in such a position again.

In early December, 1922, President Knight again called Harold into his office. After expressing that he had hoped to keep Harold in the mission until the next spring, he told him that with circumstances at home being what they were, he recommended releasing him immediately. Feeling "up in the air" over the announcement, Harold began a mad dash to tie up all the loose ends of his labors and finish his mission appropriately. These loose ends included a thorough housecleaning of the meetinghouse, including washing and oiling all the woodwork and chairs. He wrote, "'I crawled up and down the floors on my knees until my knees were calloused and my back ached.'" [39]

Two days later, during what would be Harold's final conference, he found himself overcome with emotion. "When my turn came to speak, after all the others had talked, I found I was up against a hard proposition. I was finally able to control myself after a time, and then say what I wanted. The president likewise experienced the same difficulty when he attempted to speak." [40]

During the Sunday meetings of this conference, Harold sang in a male quartet, spoke, and played the accompaniments for all the music sung by the congregation. In one of those meetings President Knight announced Harold's release. Of that announcement, Harold wrote:

> When the president announced that I was released, he said that it would bankrupt the English language to tell how much he thought of me and said that I had been on the firing line from the time I had arrived in Denver. Elder Andrew Hood was chosen in my place. He is sixty-two

years old....

There followed a busy week of leave-taking, last-minute converts to baptize, babies of close friends to bless, and many good-byes. 41

On Thursday morning, December 14, 1922, Harold boarded the train and departed for Salt Lake City. Traveling with him was his mission president, who was returning to attend the Ensign Stake quarterly conference. Harold was bid good-bye by a throng of missionaries and others, including Mabel Hickman, his first convert. For many reasons his heart yearned to stay, but none more than because of the depth of love he felt for the missionaries, Saints, and the people of Denver.

On Sunday, December 17, Harold attended the quarterly conference at the Ensign Stake in Salt Lake City. To his surprise he was asked by the stake presidency to speak for ten minutes. Afterward, as they came forward and complimented him on his remarks, Harold discovered that many of the General Authorities lived in the stake and had been in the congregation.

The next day President Knight took Harold to the Church Office Building and introduced him to a number of the Brethren, including President Charles W. Penrose of the First Presidency. After being formally released and receiving a recommend to perform ordinances in the Salt Lake Temple from President Penrose, Harold set out to visit some of his former missionary friends, as well as friends and family of others. His main goal, however, was to locate and visit with one particular missionary sister.

One of the more unusual aspects of Harold's mission had begun three days into it and continued somewhat steadily thereafter. On that date, November 14, 1920, he had met a sister missionary from Utah whose name was Fern L. Tanner. She was four years older than Harold, had been on her mission just two weeks, and was the junior companion of F. Elinor Johnson, an older sister who had been placed "in charge" of the sister missionaries in the mission. These sisters lived in an apartment across the street from the chapel and mission home and offices, and because Elders Lee and Wolley were there in the line of duty, Harold and the sisters had become well acquainted. Although there had been no romantic involvement between Harold and either of the sisters, there seemed to be a strong affinity between them. Of this acquaintance, Harold had written, "'Among the three of us there was formed a 'trinity' that 'sat in judgment' on most of the affairs of the mission.'" 42

Some time before Harold was appointed president of the Denver Conference, Sister Tanner had been transferred to Pueblo, Colorado, which was in another district, where she had spent most of the rest of her mission. "During that interval, she and Elder Lee retained their platonic relationship through occasional correspondence. She was transferred back to Denver near the end of [her] mission, where she served for a short while under...[Harold's] direction...

"When Sister Tanner was transferred back to Denver, Elder Lee's success as conference president was just beginning to crest. By that time the initiatives of organization, delegation, training, and discipline he had put in place were beginning to bear significant fruit. There was an optimistic attitude among the missionaries, which, in no small part, could be traced to the inspired, energetic leadership of their conference president." 43 There is little doubt that Sister Tanner noticed this prior to her departure for home and appreciated it.

Following her release the correspondence between Harold and Fern Tanner had increased dramatically. "So, despite the brevity of their personal contacts before then, by the time Harold arrived in Salt Lake City...he and Fern were well acquainted with each other at the intellectual and spiritual level." 44 Thus Harold was determined to once again make personal contact with the woman who would become his first wife and the mother of his children.

Of the evening when they finally got together, Harold wrote:

My first thought upon arriving in Salt Lake was to find Fern
L. Tanner, with whom I had corresponded practically dur-
ing our entire mission, she having returned from the
Western States Mission in July 1922.

Fern met me with her brother, Bud, and his wife, Ethel,
that night at the Kenyon Hotel, and I went to her home,
where I first met Daddy and Mother Tanner.

We talked far into the night, I think more as missionary
friends than as sweethearts. There was much to ask and
much to tell. Both of us had experienced joys and
disappointments, but through it all we had gained a deep
testimony of the gospel of Jesus Christ, the real value of
which we then but little realized. 45

In a rather interesting twist of fate, earlier that afternoon Harold
had visited a girl named Freda Joan Jensen, the girlfriend of one of
his favorite missionary companions, Elder David S. Murdock, the
veterinary surgeon who had practiced in Preston, Idaho prior to
his mission. 46 Though he went in an attempt to cement the young
woman's relationship with Elder Murdock, that marriage never
materialized. As a matter of fact, Freda Joan Jensen ended up
marrying no one until many years later when, following the death
of Fern Tanner Lee, she was asked to become Elder Lee's second
wife. Thus, on the same day at the honorable conclusion of his mission, Harold first met and/or visited "as a civilian" with both his
future wives.

After a week of such adventures in Salt Lake City, Harold
arrived home to his waiting family in Clifton just a few days before
Christmas, 1922.

Meanwhile, President John M. Knight had written and
submitted to Church headquarters a simple yet graphic report on
the missionary services of Harold B. Lee from November 11, 1920,

Both photos courtesy of the Lee Family Collection

Fern Tanner and Harold B. Lee

CA. *1923*

to December 18, 1922. The brief character sketch fit him well.

Qualifications—As a speaker, "Very Good." As a presiding officer, "Very Good." Has he a good knowledge of the Gospel? "Very Good." Has he been energetic? "Very." Is he discreet and does he carry a good influence? "Yes." Remarks: "Elder Lee presided over the Denver Conference with marked distinction from August 8, 1921, to December 18, 1922. An exceptional missionary." 47

A Mature Calling
for a Young Man

"That's it, Maurine. Sit right there beside Daddy, and be sure to fold your arms like a big girl." Fern Tanner Lee smiled as her eldest daughter quickly obeyed. Then she reached over and took Maurine's younger sister from the arms of her husband. "Thank you, dear," she whispered. "I'll see if I can keep baby Helen quiet through at least the opening prayer."

Harold B. Lee nodded at his wife and smiled tenderly. He didn't know why she was feeling so anxious about this last session of quarterly conference, but he was very happy to let Helen's presence soothe and comfort her. Of course he absolutely adored his two daughters and loved to hold them, but with his name being presented for a new stake calling, he should probably appear to be paying at least a modicum of attention. Sweet little Helen made that difficult if not outright impossible—

Maybe that was why Fern was feeling so unsettled, he suddenly thought. Maybe something about his new calling was troubling her. But that made no sense either. After all, stake superintendent of the Sunday School was not a calling he would have difficulty handling. If anything, the calling he was being released from— stake superintendent of religion classes—took a whale of a lot more time and required constant preparation on his part to teach the classes. In this new calling he wouldn't be doing any actual classroom teaching, so the pressures would ease significantly. Of course, not teaching was giving him somewhat of a letdown, for he loved to teach, and he was very much going to miss the classroom. Still, he accepted wholeheartedly President Hammond's inspiration, and he had been trained since childhood to never turn down a calling—

Quickly the Assembly Hall on Temple Square filled with members of the Pioneer Stake—so named because the stake encompassed Pioneer Square, site of the pioneers' first encampment after they had entered the Valley. The stake, on the west side of the Salt Lake Valley, now included ten wards and a Mexican branch and had a population of something over ten thousand people. Presiding over the stake was President D. E. Hammond, a professional Scouter who was absolutely wonderful with the young people of the stake. Harold, who as a former educator cherished similar feelings for the youth, admired and sustained the stake president and looked forward to even the limited association with the man his new calling would give him.

October 1928 stake quarterly conference. Harold smiled, remembering when he had been called by his mission president, John M. Knight, to speak to the Ensign Stake conference the day after he had returned from his mission. How things had changed in the six years since then! Instead of a newly returned missionary wondering what was to become of himself, he was now a blessed and happy husband, as well as the proud father of two sweet little girls. He owned a home. He held a responsible position as a salesman with a company called Foundation Press, headquartered in Denver. He made a pretty decent salary, plus bonuses on his sales. And, he was privileged to travel in his job over a good part of the western United States at company expense, often with his family for company. Those journeys were always enjoyable, and he loved the adventure of them.

Try as he might, Harold could think of nothing significant that he lacked. Truly he was a blessed man. Why, even his parents and family were now nearby, having moved from Clifton at his and his brother Perry's encouragement some three years before. Thus he and Fern were close to both sets of parents as well as their brothers and sisters, and their two little girls were being spoiled terribly by all of them. In the midst of a typically difficult world, it might easily be said that he and Fern were living the idyllic life.

So why, he wondered again, would Fern be feeling such a sense of anxiety—

As the last session of conference opened with a hymn, Harold briefly lost himself in the music, rejoicing as the sacred strains lifted his soul to soaring heights But following the prayer he saw the anxious look back on his wife's face, and as the stake clerk stood to read the names of the stake officers for sustaining vote, Harold steeled himself for what he was beginning to expect would be a negative reaction to his new calling.

Was that what Fern was being warned against? Was the Holy Ghost letting her know that such a trial was coming for herself and her husband? Of course he didn't know, but if it were to happen, how would he react? It had never happened to him before; in fact, he had never seen anyone receive a negative vote. But if he received some, and because of any number of reasons it was surely possible, then he needed to remain calm—

"Harold," Fern whispered as she reached across the still silent four-year-old Maurine, her concern obvious on her face, "I love you."

Squeezing her proffered hand, Harold nodded. Then, to reassure her that all would be well, he winked. Fern smiled in response, and Harold, still gripping his wife's hand, once again focused on the stake clerk. However, he was not really listening as the man prepared to read the names of the current stake presidency. Instead he was now worrying about what could happen in a few minutes when his own name was read.

"As president of the Pioneer Stake of Zion," the man was intoning, "Datus E. Hammond."

Harold smiled a little. What a great man! There would certainly be no difficulty in his being sustained! It would be the same with his counselors, Presidents J. A. Hancock and Charles S. Hyde. They were all three great and wonderful men—

"As first counselor, Charles S. Hyde."

Startled, Harold looked up at the clerk. President Hyde had been second counselor, not first. That meant there was going to be a change in the stake presidency—

"And as second counselor, Harold B. Lee."

For Harold, it was as if, at least for a moment, time stopped. Had it been he whose name the clerk had read? It couldn't have been, but—

Fern was squeezing his hand, hard! She was also looking at him, her eyes wide with wonder. But surely they could be no wider than his own. He was being sustained as second counselor in the stake presidency? Him? Harold B. Lee? But, he was supposed to be sustained as superintendent of the stake Sunday School! He was supposed—

"All who can sustain these three brethren as the stake presidency of the Pioneer Stake of Zion, please signify by raising your right hands."

Feeling almost numb, Harold felt his right hand lift automatically into the air. Out of the corner of his eye he saw both tiny hands of his daughter Maurine go up, and he almost smiled until he realized that he could also see Fern's right arm raised to the square. Of course she would sustain him, but this still could not be happening—

"Any opposed, please signify by the same sign."

Harold's hand was back down, but he did not dare look to see how many hands would be raised in opposition to the calling of a young twenty-nine-year-old into a stake presidency. Why, such an action was unheard of; service in such a position required maturity, seasoning, vast experience—

"President Hammond," the clerk's voice finally sounded a bit more animated, "it appears that the voting has been unanimous in the affirmative." From behind the clerk President Hammond nodded and made a quiet comment, and quickly the clerk nodded in return.

"President Lee? I assume you are here in the congregation. While I am reading the names of the stake clerks and other stake officers, President Hammond has requested that you make your way to the stand and take your place at his side."

After receiving and then giving back another hand squeeze from his beloved Fern, Harold rose shakily to his feet and made his way awkwardly to the aisle. Then he started forward toward the Assembly Hall stand, completely unaware that never again in his life would he enjoy the peaceful anonymity of sitting with his wife in the midst of a congregation of the Saints. 1

Harold arrived in Clifton on December 23, 1922, excited to see his family after more than two years' absence on his mission, but thoroughly ambivalent about his future. He knew he needed to go to work—somewhere; and he felt fairly certain his future did not lie in Clifton. Though where in the world he was supposed to go in order to establish himself, he had no idea. Of course, his interests and his training were in education, but it was the middle of the school year, so a teaching contract for the balance of the year was not available. Then, too, if he hoped to teach at the high school level, which would provide him a better salary, ever-increasing accreditation standards would require that he obtain more education—which took money that he didn't have. So, at least for the moment, the returned missionary's entire future appeared to be stymied.

To make matters worse, his father's financial condition was far worse than Harold had been led to believe or was able to imagine. "In order to maintain his son in the mission field, Bishop Lee had incurred heavy indebtedness, which, in view of the depressed farm conditions of the day, he had no prospect of repaying. 'I thank the Lord that my parents didn't tell me all their difficulties,' [Harold] wrote on learning of the financial peril they faced. Had he known earlier, it is likely he would not have remained in the mission field. Yet, the discouraging financial prospects facing the family were temporarily submerged in the festivities of the season." 2 He wrote: "Although people have no money in their pockets, they have bushels of love in their hearts and I believe there has never been a time when there was more of the real Christmas spirit." 3

After the joyful reunion and Christmas celebration with his family was over, however, Harold descended almost immediately into the typical "post-mission blues," a letdown or sense of depression many missionaries experience because the growth and progression engendered by a mission seems to have been stopped dead in its tracks. "For two years he had been strung taut with the responsibilities of his calling, which had kept him fully occupied during most of his waking hours. During most of his mission, his calling as the conference president had stretched his capacities to the limit and had given him a status and prestige he had never known before. Now at home he had reverted to the obscure role as one of the six children of Bishop Samuel Lee and his wife Louisa, without employment and without any immediate prospects of obtaining any. It was a most stressful time for one as able and creative as he." 4

Another issue troubling Harold was the less-heightened level of spirituality he was discovering among a good many of the Church members in the area. Yes, "he enjoyed visiting with his family and friends, sharing his missionary experiences and his convictions about the Church. While this was enjoyable and aroused fond memories, [however,] it had its down side. The fact is Harold was disappointed at the lowered level of spirituality and commitment he found among the members at home compared to those in the mission field.... So, while recalling incidents in the mission field evoked pleasant memories of the past, it caused feelings of regret that those days were gone." 5

Steeling himself to put his best foot forward, Harold did his best to immerse himself in his family's activities, including church. Besides taking part in the chores both indoors and out, he worked diligently to spend time with each of his siblings: Clyde, who was twenty; Waldo, seventeen; Stella, fifteen; and Verda, who was twelve. He also helped his older brother, Perry, organize and stage a minstrel show. At church he enthusiastically accepted a calling from his bishop/father

> to teach a class in theology in his home ward. It was absorbing to prepare his lesson, delving into the scriptures, which he loved. He enjoyed the challenging interplay between teacher and students in the classroom. Here Harold was in his proper element. He was a natural teacher, born to the task, as it were. His intelligence, his spirituality, his eloquence, and his genuine love for people combined in a classroom setting to provide ideal conditions for sharing knowledge and for kindling testimony and resolves to improve. 6

In addition to his teaching, Harold was called by the stake president to once again serve as elders quorum president in the Clifton, Oxford, and Dayton wards. Apparently the activity level was such that it took combining three quorums to get an extremely modest turnout. In January 1923 he was set apart during the Oneida Stake Quarterly Conference at Preston, and he launched immediately into his work.

Still, his family continued calling out to him for his companionship. It seemed especially important that he spend time with Clyde, who at twenty needed his positive influence. Clyde had become the foremost basketball player in the area, and after Harold had been home about three weeks, Clyde cajoled him into joining with him and the other local athletes in a pickup game. Little did Harold imagine how much the Lord's hand was in what was about to transpire.

Weakened by two years of physical inactivity and a hernia developed during his mission, Harold seems to have forgotten how intensely physical basketball was played.

> During the game, which was marked by rough physical contact, he was knocked to the floor where he lay, writhing, until he was carried off with a severely wrenched back. This injury further aggravated a hernia that had developed in the mission field. When his condition worsened a few weeks later, surgery became necessary. He travelled to Utah for this purpose, where in February 1923 the operation was performed in a Salt Lake City hospital. Afterward, he gladly accepted the invitation of Fern's parents to stay at their house while he convalesced. 7

Since their one-evening visit in December, Harold and Fern had corresponded even more frequently than before, but now with Harold convalescing in her home, Fern experienced a dramatic change in their relationship. Within a week or so both she and Harold were speaking of their future wedding, and though there was never an exact moment when both of them knew they were to become man and wife, it seemed to both of them that it was the right and only thing to do, and always had been.

A month after his surgery, Harold received a letter from his mother telling him that his father had been released as bishop and hinting at some unnamed problems at home. A short time later he returned to Clifton with Perry, who filled him in on some of the details. In a family gathering after his arrival they expressed their worries that Harold might be feeling that his mission had placed too much of a burden on them, thus weakening his faith in the gospel and the blessings of the Lord. Harold wrote:

> It gave me a joy I am unable to express to see their pride and satisfaction in my missionary service. I could cry when I think that in the midst of all their trouble and grief they have placed uppermost the spiritual values, and in their great stress, have found peace and rest through the gospel.
>
> Father and Mother have gone through a veritable hell and appear to have aged years since I last saw them. Even in the short time I have been gone to Salt Lake, Father's hair is more gray than ever and I'm sure that only love and hard work will ever make back to them what they have lost....
>
> We have decided unanimously that I should go to work to get ahead financially, so I will return to Salt Lake and find employment as soon as possible. I'm going to do the right, as the Lord directs. [8]

Back in Salt Lake City, Harold enrolled in summer school at the University of Utah to improve his teaching certification and then obtained part-time work at the Paris department store to earn funding for his schooling. On such meager wages he survived, but just barely. He was also too busy to see Fern except on Sundays, when they planned their wedding for the coming fall.

In August he secured a one-year contract to both teach and serve as principal at the Whittier School in the Granite School District for $135 a month. With an income thus assured, wedding plans were finalized and pressed forward.

> On November 14, 1923, I was married to Fern L. Tanner in the Salt Lake Temple, with Elder George F. Richards of

Courtesy of the Lee Family Collection

Harold B. and Fern Lee in their
earliest photo as husband and wife

CA. *early 1920s*

the Council of the Twelve officiating. Never doubting our ability to get ahead together, we put our full trust in each other and moved into our first home at 1538 West 800 South, owned by Daddy Tanner, and obligated ourselves for $800 of furniture and a used Ford automobile for $300, on my salary of $135 per month. 9

Fern was "bright, talented, and beautiful...[and] a scripturalist of unusual ability." 10 Harold, speaking of her years later, added the following:

It has been my joy to see perpetuated in Fern many of the fine traits of her mother. Like her mother, Fern is quiet and unassuming and yet vigorous in her denunciation of unfairness and calumny, generous to a fault, sensitive, impressionable, a splendid mother, and an ideal homemaker. Mother Tanner endured the hardships of pioneer life without a murmur, but was not content until their farm house in Granger was the finest in that community. A close parallel is to be found in Fern. No matter how often public duty takes me away from home, there is always an assurance of her loyal support. We began married life on a borrowed $300. Due to her high standards, our present home has all the conveniences possible, and while small and not the most convenient, it has breathed the influence of a charming wife and a loving mother. These sterling qualities were apparent on the first night of our marriage when she reminded me of our family prayers. 11

Despite such efforts at righteousness, the young couple struggled in many ways, learning and drawing closer to each other through each adversity. Harold continues:

The first year of our married life was a glorious honeymoon in which we made preparations for our first baby. Despite the fact that we carefully followed the instructions of Dr. A. C. Callister, Fern came near losing her life from a serious hemorrhage when our baby [Maurine] was born.

Maurine was born September 1, 1924. Within fifteen months our second baby came. Fern had been in constant labor pain for sixty hours before Helen was born on November 25, 1925. With her birth we saw the beginning of a sweet companionship of close sisters that developed with each year of their lives. They were both born in the Latter-day Saints Hospital in Salt Lake City....

During the first years of our married life I struggled to complete my education at the University of Utah by extension study and summer school work while I taught school. I was forced to seek new employment each summer to support my little family until school would begin in the fall. One summer I sold meats and produce for Swift and Company, the next I dispensed gas and oil and checked out equipment at the Salt Lake City Street Department under Commissioner T. T. Burton from 3:00 P.M. to 11:00 P.M. The next two summers I was a watchman and train checker at the Union Pacific north yards under the special agent's department. Some of my choicest friends during these years were Superintendent D. W. Parratt, of the Granite Schools, Commissioner T. T. Burton, and Edward H. Eardley.

Fern was never content that I should remain in the school teaching profession. [To help makes ends meet] I sold Nash automobiles...and later worked for the grocery department of ZCMI, and for the Bennett Gas and Oil Company. Finally, in 1928, I was invited by L. A. Ray to become a salesman for the Foundation Press, Inc. I was guaranteed a salary of $50 per week, and an over-writing on all sales of the salesmen whom I had trained. I resigned in

Helen (left) and Maurine Lee (right) were reared in a home of culture and modest refinement

CA. *1933–34*

the fall of 1928 from the Granite schools. My new work took me into Wyoming, Colorado, Washington, Oregon, and Idaho, and on many of these trips I was accompanied by Fern and our two girls. 12

Harold's and Fern's first home was located in the Poplar Grove Ward of the Pioneer Stake. "It was here they planted their marital roots, deep and firm, roots that grew into an extraordinary life career in the coming years. One wonders what life would have been like for the Lees had they lived in some other part of Salt Lake City or in some other city. So many critical things occurred to them along the path that led to the presidency of the Church, which had their roots in the Pioneer Stake, as to suggest that establishing their home there was based on some divine purpose." 13

For instance, "On January 1, 1922, Paul C. Child was called as the new bishop of the Poplar Grove Ward. Some time after Bishop Child was installed, he and his counselors began to pray fervently that the Lord would bring into their ward persons who would provide good leadership for its members. In not too long a time after this, both Harold B. Lee and [his brother] S. Perry Lee and their wives moved there." 14

His spirit in tune with the Lord's whisperings concerning the potential of the younger of the Lee brothers, Bishop Child quickly called Harold as the M-Men instructor. "At the time, there was an able but dispirited group of young men in the ward whose activities had no sense of direction due to a lack of leadership. In only one year, this same group, who had previously enjoyed the reputation of being the doormats in stake competition, led out in basketball, debating, male quartet, and public speaking.... While the technical skills Elder Lee taught were vital to their success, it is undoubtedly true that new attitudes of self-confidence he instilled in his M-Men were equally if not more important. This quality was evident in every position of leadership Harold B. Lee occupied. It was certainly true during his second year in Poplar Grove Ward when he served as the superintendent of the Sunday School. His previous experience as a teacher and principal in Idaho and his everyday employment as a teacher and principal at Whittier enabled him to instill a sense of professionalism and commitment in the Sunday School faculty." 15

Of course, no stake president worth his salt would fail to note the increased activity due to the efforts of a certain extraordinary young man in the Poplar Grove Ward, and President Datus E. Hammond was certainly worth his salt. Of what followed, Harold writes:

> After two years in ward work in the Sunday School, I was drafted in 1926 as the superintendent of religion classes in the Pioneer Stake by President D. E. Hammond. This was a pioneer experience with almost a complete rejuvenation and reorganization necessary.
>
> In 1927 I was chosen as a member of the Pioneer Stake high council, along with Joseph Jenkins. I was ordained a high priest and set apart as a high councilor by Elder Richard R. Lyman of the Council of the Twelve.
>
> Upon the release of T. T. Burton in 1928, I was released as superintendent of religion classes and made stake superintendent of Sunday Schools. My counselors were Edwin Bronson and E. Albert Rosenvall.
>
> Before I had [even] been set apart to this position, and while attending the October Pioneer Stake quarterly conference, I was startled to hear my name announced as the selection of President D. E. Hammond for the position of second counselor in the stake presidency. Charles S. Hyde was advanced to first counselor and J. A. Hancock was released. 16

Meanwhile, shortly after his marriage Harold had written his parents, suggesting that they also move to Salt Lake City where there were greater opportunities for work. They did so, ultimately ending up in a home located at 213 F Street, where they remained for the remainder of their lives. After some initial struggles during the Great Depression of the early 1930s, Samuel Lee gained permanent employment as a night watchman for the ZCMI department store, eventually becoming the night supervisor. He was respectfully called Bishop Lee by those who worked under him, including those who were not members of the Church, and he quietly exerted a positive influence over all of them.

Unlike his parents, who seemed to enjoy staying put, Harold and Fern did a certain amount of moving. According to Harold:

> When Maurine was born we were forced to move into a larger home at 1534 West 8TH South Street. In 1928, Fern's father and mother gave up their home at 1310 Indiana Avenue, because of their old age, to live with their daughter, Emily, in Granger, Utah. We purchased the old home for $2,700 at $25 per month at 7 percent interest.
>
> Fern's father, Stewart T. Tanner, died July 23, 1931, and her mother, Janet Coats Tanner, died July 6, 1932.
>
> From the time our two babies were born their Grandpa and Grandma Tanner seemed to take a great interest in their care and never less than once or twice a day did they plan to see the girls. Grandpa Tanner always called Maurine his "pal." They were a lovable father and mother, wise and just, making no distinction between their own children and their sons- and daughters-in-law. 17

"What was it like to grow up in the Lee family in the 1920s? Helen Lee Goates says that her earliest memories relate to the nightly ritual in which the family of four (Father Harold, Mother Fern, Maurine, and Helen) knelt in family prayer. They lived in a little home Brother Lee had bought from his father-in-law, on Eighth

South in Salt Lake City. A sleeping porch had been added to the back of the house and was equipped with space heaters designed to keep out the frost. Maurine and Helen, just fifteen months apart in age, slept on the porch, which was very cold in winter. So they had their prayers in the living room, and their father would take one of them in each arm and carry them out to the sleeping room and tuck them in. When they were a little older and were too big for him to carry in that way, the gentle father would put one of his daughters on his back and carry the other in his arms—and out they'd go to bed each night. As he tucked them in, according to Helen, he always had some endearing words to say to them. 'Daddy knew how important it was in the lives of his little girls to feel that he loved them. We were with Mother a great deal, of course, but this little nightly ritual demonstrated that he loved us, was concerned for his little girls.'" 18

For just over a year Harold served as second counselor to President Hammond, meanwhile continuing his employment with the Foundation Press. He wrote:

> In 1930, I was called to Denver by E. H. Ferris, president of the Foundation Press, and notified that I was to continue in the promotion of Master Library sales, and L. A. Ray was to spend his time with the "Pageant of the Nation," a collection of pictures. This move caused friction between myself and Mr. Ray, and consequently, in September 1930, I was designated to continue alone as the Intermountain manager, with offices in the McIntyre Building in Salt Lake City. 19

By great effort, Harold's business was prospering, and he felt fairly certain that, if left to himself, he could continue to produce a good living. Nevertheless, after just a year as second counselor in the stake presidency, the next major change in Harold's life occurred, and he was no longer left to himself. He wrote:

On the Friday preceding the quarterly conference, I was called to the office of President Rudger Clawson, where I was told by President Clawson and Elder George Albert Smith that I had been chosen by the First Presidency and the Twelve as the new president of Pioneer Stake. I told them I would much prefer working as a counselor to Brother Hyde, and was bluntly told by George Albert Smith that I had been invited to meet with them, not to tell them what should be done, but to find out if I was willing to do what the Lord wanted me to do. There followed a discussion on the selection of my counselors. Again I was told when I asked if they had any suggestions on that, "We have suggestions, but we are not going to tell you—that is your responsibility. If you are guided by the Spirit of the Lord, you will choose those whom we have in mind."...

I retired that night, or rather early morning, to a fitful sleep, about three o'clock in the morning, after earnest prayer for guidance. During the few hours I tried to sleep it would seem that I had chosen two counselors and was trying to hold council meetings with them. Disagreements, obstacles, and misunderstandings would arise, and I would awake with a start to realize that my first choices were wrong. This process was repeated with ten or twelve of my brethren until, when morning came, I was certain the Lord had guided me to choose Charles S. Hyde and Paul C. Child as my counselors. When I announced to the Brethren my decision the next morning, they smiled their approval. The men whom they had desired had been selected.

On the Saturday night following our conference priesthood convention, I went for a long ride with Brother Hyde, who was many years my senior in age and experience, and informed him of the proposed change and of my desire for him to be my first counselor. It was like a thunderbolt to him, and he deferred his answer until he could think it over and talk with President Clawson the next day. Paul C. Child had been my bishop in the Poplar Grove Ward for seven years, and he was not aware of his selection until his name was placed before the conference. 20

Harold B. Lee was thirty-one years old, at that time the youngest stake president in the Church, and he had been called over Charles S. Hyde, the scion of one of the oldest and most distinguished families in the stake. What a jolt that must have given the members of the Pioneer Stake that day! It is a mark of both Brother Hyde's and Bishop Child's spiritual maturity that they not only sustained the action of the Brethren, but willingly and faithfully served as counselors to the young leader.

Now, just as had been the case when he had been called to preside over the Denver Conference after only nine months as a missionary, it would be up to Harold to prove whether or not he himself was "big enough" for this new calling.

COMPASSIONATE AND VISIONARY LEADER

"Maurine told you that?" Harold B. Lee's eyes were sparking he was so upset, though he was doing his best to control his infamous temper. "That she'd be home soon?"

Helen, Harold's youngest daughter, fidgeted nervously. It was not often that her father was upset with her. In fact it was extremely rare—in part, at least, because she so zealously endeavored to please him and make him proud. And such zeal was necessary, Helen knew, for even with her best efforts she would never be quite as good her father thought she already was. For instance, she played the violin and Maurine the piano—or at least they were learning to play. Yet when they practiced together and their father was at home, he would tell them that together they made the most beautiful music this side of heaven! In reality, of course, they were squeaking and squawking and playing all sorts of wrong notes. Yet his sweet praise, always uttered most sincerely, convinced the two girls that he really did believe they were better than they were. And so they practiced constantly just to fulfill his beliefs.

He did the same thing regarding their awkward, adolescent appearances, calling them his beautiful, charming daughters when both of them knew they were anything but. Helen, for instance, had her hair cut short, was "pudgy" and overweight, wore corrective shoes, and stared out at the world through ugly horn-rimmed glasses. Yet, she found herself reasoning, if her father thought she was beautiful, then she must try very hard to be what he expected, for she couldn't bear to disappoint him. Constantly, therefore, she practiced the kind of natural beauty and grace exhibited by her mother, and every night she asked God to help her become as lovely and beautiful as her daddy thought she already was.

But that was her approach, Helen knew, and not necessarily the approach of her older sister. Maurine was always stretching things, reaching to tickle and maybe even probe the limits of her relationship with their parents. Yes, she wanted to please them—but not necessarily at the expense of something else she might happen to desire. Oh, she didn't do awful things, of course, but she didn't mind taking a stab at the family's rules now and then, just to see if they really were enforced. That was why their father called her "his little harness-fighter." Mar sometimes fought the bit!

And so it had been that night, when the two girls had been left by their parents at a party and dance following a weeknight missionary farewell. Having been told to be home at a certain hour, they were expected to come home together. Maurine knew that, too, for they had been taught to take care of each other and to never leave the other one alone. There was safety in that—for both of them. Yet as the hour of departure had arrived, Maurine had calmly said to Helen: "Why don't you just run on home, and I'll be along in a little while."

Stunned, Helen had done little more than stutter a protest.

Maurine was aloof. "Just go and tell Mother and Dad I'll come home soon; it'll be okay."

Despite her misgivings Helen had left the party alone, and now she stood all atremble as her father's eyes flashed his displeasure. "How much later does she intend to come?" he demanded to know.

"Well, I don't really know, Daddy. But she'll come soon, I think."

"Soon," Harold muttered as he turned away, "what is that supposed to mean? Who does she think she is, anyway? She knows she's not supposed to send Helen off alone like that! Why, anything might have happened! Anything!"

"But it didn't, dear," Helen's mother soothed from where she sat at her stitching. "Helen's just fine, you see, and I'm certain Mar will be along any moment."

"That isn't the point, Fern!" Harold responded, speaking quite sharply to his wife. "She broke the rules, you see, and she can't be allowed—"

"She only wanted to be alone for a few moments," Helen's mother interrupted, her voice calm and soothing. "Growing girls sometimes need a little space."

Helen was growing increasingly nervous, for she had never found herself in the midst of such a conversation. Moreover, she was growing more convinced by the second that she didn't want to be a part of it any longer—

"I think I'll drive over there and make sure she knows when to come home!" Harold was standing at the window.

"Well now, dear," Fern responded, her voice more calm and quiet than ever, "let's just wait a little bit longer and see if she will come home on her own."

Nodding his agreement in such a way that Helen could see it was only temporary, Harold busied himself in the kitchen. Taking a seat near the door, Helen silently began leafing through a magazine, her mind meanwhile on her older sister. "Oh, Maurine," she breathed as she anxiously flipped the pages, "if only you could see what your harness-testing does to Daddy—"

"Well," Harold abruptly declared a few minutes later as he strode into the room, "I'm going to go and get her! She must learn that when we tell her to be home at a certain time, she must be here!"

As her father reached for his hat, his face clearly showing how upset he was, Helen slowly lowered her magazine. This was something new they were encountering, a sign of dramatically changing times in their family, she sensed. And though she was not yet old enough to understand things fully, she still recognized and was amazed by how her parents were reacting.

Helen's mother, who had the ability to always meet issues quietly and with composure, slowly put down her stitching. "Now, dear," she said with a smile that never failed to disarm her husband, "don't go in an angry way and insist that she come home."

"And why shouldn't I?"

"Why, just think what that would do to Mar in front of her friends. Remember who you are, dear, and remember how much time you've spent over the years building her up, showing her and telling her how much you love and respect her."

His hat in his hand, Harold studied his wife. "But, I must do something, Fern; you know that!"

"Yes, dear, I know you must."

"Then what do you suggest?"

For a moment there was silence, the only sound the ticking of the mantel clock. Helen looked from one to the other of her parents, sensing that a communication she could not understand was somehow passing between them. That her father was concerned about his standing as a Church leader, she knew, for he had spoken to her and Mar on several occasions about the fact that his best sermons would never be better than his, or their, personal behavior. Yet there was more here that was at stake, something indefinable to Helen, something her mother was trying to get her father to see—

"If you feel you must go, Harold, then go on the pretense of accomplishing something else—like going to see someone about some unfinished business at the ward. Make some other reason for going, dear, but don't confront our precious Mar with the idea that she's been bad and that you have come for her."

For a few seconds more Harold stood silently, regarding his

wife. Then, with a sly wink that Helen knew could mean any number of things, all of them good, he put on his hat and went out through the door.

"Helen," her mother said as she returned to her stitching, "I don't want you to be afraid for Maurine."

"But...Daddy was so upset."

"Yes, he was. But one of the things I love the very most about your father is that he recognizes and accepts good counsel—mine included. Mark my words; Mar will come home smiling! Now, don't you think it's about time you got ready for bed?"

Nodding silently, Helen rose and headed for her room. Her mind was whirling with thoughts—of her father's frustration and anger, Maurine's rebellion and disobedience, her mother's quiet suggestions, her father's wink—well, for the life of her she didn't understand how a person could do something bad and then be defended in it, like her mother seemed to be doing. Yet her father had obviously been listening, and his wink had to mean that he had agreed. So, what did that mean about Mar's disobedience? Was she in trouble, or wasn't she? Did she and Helen have to follow the rules, or not? And if not, then what was her father going to do with poor, foolish Mar—

"Wasn't that a grand party!" Maurine enthused a half an hour later as she came bursting into the room, her face all smiling and aglow. It was obvious to Helen that she had undergone no severe chastisement or abrasive confrontation.

"Didn't...I mean, did Daddy find you?"

"Oh, yes," Maurine replied as she fussed for a moment with her hair, studying herself rather critically in the mirror. "He was over there for something or other, some Church business I suppose, and when he saw me he asked if I wanted a ride home. Of course I knew that would mean a stop at the root beer stand; Daddy can't resist stopping there—"

"He got you a treat?" Helen was stunned. "But I thought...

I mean, he didn't say anything—"

"He said I was radiant. Do you think I look radiant, Helen? Or beautiful? I think my nose is too short for my face, and I absolutely detest my hair!"

"But...Daddy didn't say anything—"

"Oh, yes!" Maurine turned around, her eyes wide with remembrance. "We got a malt for you, too, Helen! Chocolate. He said you'd be wanting one the same as me. It's in the kitchen."

"But...but he—"

"Oh," Maurine interrupted as she began unbuttoning her dress, "I almost forgot! I'm sorry I sent you off alone tonight, Helen. I don't know what got into me, but I certainly wasn't being very thoughtful."

"Or obedient," Helen added a little snidely as she slipped out of bed, with the kitchen as her destination.

Maurine's look sobered. "Yes, that, too. It's funny, but Daddy never said a word about it, either. Oh well, it won't happen again, I promise you that! From now on," and instantly Maurine twisted her mouth to look like one of the popular movie stars they both tried to imitate, "it's just the two of us, kid, together!" Abruptly she laughed. "But Helen, I wish you had been there to see Dougie, the silly boy—"

And feeling immensely relieved though she had no real idea why, Helen laughed with her sister and then slipped into the kitchen for her wonderful chocolate malt. 1

Once Harold became stake president there were some immediate issues to be resolved. A first order of business was to call three new bishops for wards that had been affected by the change in stake leadership. At the conclusion of the accounting proceedings required for changes in bishops, it was discovered that in one ward there was a serious shortage in the tithing and building funds. A complete audit was called for, and the new stake presidency launched a thorough investigation into the matter. It quickly became apparent that a high council court would be needed for a former bishop in that ward, who at the moment was serving as a member of the stake high council.

Because there were many intertwining personal relationships between this former bishop and the other members of the council, and because many in the council had close ties with the man's family, an atmosphere of extreme tension developed when the man appeared to stand accused before them. "What made it especially difficult for the thirty-one-year-old stake president was that he had never before presided over a high council court. He was, therefore, apprehensive about following the court procedures while subjected to the personal anguish of having to sit in judgment on a dear friend and co-worker. The trial was long and wearing.... After the detailed evidence developed by the audit was introduced showing a pattern of dishonesty and misappropriation, the accused was allowed to respond with evidence by way of mitigation or in justification for what he had done. Then followed the customary procedure when half of the high council spoke in favor of the accused and the other half spoke for the court. President Lee then retired with his counselors to prayerfully mull over the evidence and to discuss the complex ramifications of the trial and the consequences of any decision to be reached. At length, President Lee decided that the circumstances required that the accused be disfellowshipped from the Church, and being supported in that decision by his counselors, returned to announce it to the high council."[2]

Harold continues the account:

This was my first experience in conducting a high council trial. The trial involved the straining of friendships formed over a period of ten years. When the decision of the presidency was announced after the trial had gone on until four o'clock A.M., the high council refused to vote their approval, whereupon I merely announced that the decision of the presidency was not the decision of the council, and promptly dismissed the trial.

It is difficult to imagine how a young stake president might feel after being rebuffed by the entire high council. This was the first real test of his leadership, and its apparent failure did not bode well for the future—for himself or the Pioneer Stake. Yet, with wisdom far beyond his years, Harold did not argue, lecture, threaten, or anything else one might have been tempted to do. Instead, he simply dismissed the court and went home, leaving the rest of the brethren to ponder—for the next several days—over what had just transpired.

As it turned out, he had chosen the perfect course to bring unanimity back to the high council and stake presidency. Upon reflection the brethren apparently concluded that the evidence fully justified the decision of the new stake president and that they had been swayed by their emotional attachment to the accused. Harold continues:

> On the next Sunday morning, the council was reconvened to show why our decision should not be sustained, and we then received their unanimous vote. The suddenness of our decision had seemed to stun them until they could be given a chance to think the matter over more carefully. 3

"It is not difficult to appraise the impact and the significance of this decision upon the members of the Pioneer Stake. It assuredly conveyed the message that high position in the Church would not insulate one from the consequences of misconduct. And the way in which the young and inexperienced stake president had adroitly brought about unanimity in the court undoubtedly enhanced his leadership role in the stake. Here was a man of strong mind and purpose who showed qualities of leadership and judgment far beyond his years. These qualities, and the confidence they engendered in his followers, would be of vital importance in the years ahead as Harold B. Lee and his associates forged an instrument for the relief of their people and infused it with an extraordinary enthusiasm and sense of purpose." 4

> Following that stressful experience came many other excommunications for adultery, polygamy, and apostasy. Some of the most trying were the cases of those charged with immorality and adultery, one involving a nineteen-year-old girl, as well as one for alleged dishonesty against a member of the high council. 5

Not all, however, was grim effort for the new stake president. He was given another assignment which he found to be absolutely delightful. His history continues:

> In 1931 the Church decided to establish a seminary in connection with the newly constructed South High School in Salt Lake City, and I was asked to be associated with Merrill D. Clayson as a teacher. Two classes each day were held, at eight o'clock each morning and three-thirty after school. I worked with some splendid youngsters during two winters and a part of the third. Coming early in the morning I found it possible to teach the morning class before office hours, and this I did without much difficulty until the late fall of 1933 when the demands of my position...made necessary my resignation. This was the most enjoyable teaching I ever did. My associate, Merrill Clayson, was a master at directing the social activities, which ranged from bonfire parties to dancing and Sunday night programs. This association to me was life at its best, and I was loathe to leave a work where I saw such possibilities for doing good. 6

In 1929 the U.S. stock market had crashed, which began the tumul-
tuous economic upheavals of the next decade. The crash, in turn,
ushered in what came to be known as the Great Depression.
Although it shared the basic characteristics of other such crises,
the Great Depression was unprecedented in its length and in the
wholesale poverty and tragedy it inflicted on American society.
At the depth of the Depression (1932–33), there were 16 million
unemployed—about one third of the available labor force. The
gross national product declined from the 1929 figure of
$103,828,000,000 to $55,760,000,000 in 1933.

Many members of the Pioneer Stake were immediately hit by
the effects of the Depression, and prior to Harold's becoming stake
president, the former presidency had hardly had time to consider
how to alleviate the suffering of the people. All around them businesses were folding and people were losing their jobs, until by 1933
more than half the members of the Pioneer Stake were dependent on
assistance outside the family for their livelihood. Harold recorded:

> Some of the most notable businesses to fold in Salt Lake
> City were Walker Brothers store, Columbia Trust Company,
> Deseret Savings Bank, Western Building and Loan
> Company, Consolidated Music Company, Ashton Jenkins
> Real Estate, and many others. It was no uncommon sight to
> see dozens of vacant stores along Main Street with a For
> Rent sign in each window.
>
> My business with the Foundation Press, Inc., suffered
> along with others, but I was able, by exerting all my energy,
> to maintain my office and keep up some production....
>
> Many of the meetings of the Pioneer Stake presidency
> were devoted to a prayerful study of our stressful condi-
> tions and of plans to cooperate in relieving the economic
> distress of our Saints. 7

Christmas seasons were especially difficult for the unemployed.

Because he had been so busy focusing on what seemed to be larger problems, however, Harold hadn't given enough thought to the Christmas-type needs of the individual families in his stake. In a Christmas dinner talk to the Deseret Industries workers in 1973, he remembered:

> Our little girl went across the street with her Christmas doll to show the neighbor, and soon came back crying. She was crying because Donna Mae, the neighbor girl, didn't have any gifts for Christmas. Santa Claus had not come to her house.
>
> Then, too late, we remembered that the father of the family had been out of work. Although he was not a member of the Church, we tried to share our Christmas with the children. For me it was a very difficult Christmas. I did not enjoy the dinner that I sat down to that day, because I, as stake president, had not become acquainted with the people in my stake.
>
> The next Christmas we made preparations. We made a survey, and we found that we had more than a thousand people who needed help during those difficult times. So we made ready by gathering toys and taking them to the old storehouse. Then the fathers and mothers came and helped fix the toys, putting them together, dressing dolls, and sewing things.
>
> We had oranges and apples. There was roast beef and all the trimmings for Christmas dinner. The bishops arranged to have it delivered to all the needy families, and then called me to let me know that all had been visited. 8

One morning just before that second Christmas, while Harold as a city commissioner was out supervising the removal of a night's deposit of heavy snow from Salt Lake City's streets, he:

saw a little boy. He didn't have a warm coat, or gloves, or overshoes. It was bitter cold so I stopped and brought him into the car. The heater was going, and as he got warm I inquired if he was ready for Christmas.

"Mister, we aren't going to have any Christmas. Daddy died six months ago. Now there is only Mom and me and two younger children. We don't have much."

Probing deeper, I asked where he was going and he replied that there was a free movie uptown that morning and he wanted to go to that. That was all the Christmas he was going to have. I got his name and address and I told him that I would see to it that he did have a Christmas at his home. 9

"President Lee [then] told his family about the little boy who was to have no Christmas. They too were concerned. He called the bishop to be assured that the family had been provided for. He concluded, 'That year when I sat down to my Christmas dinner I felt that I could enjoy it, because, as far as I knew, every family in my stake was having a good Christmas.'" 10

To bring to pass such blessings as these on a stakewide basis, the new stake presidency came up with a system of determining needs and resources and then matching them together—which would become a model for the entire Church in the years ahead. "The needs were apparent from a survey that revealed about forty-eight hundred members of the stake needed help from outside the family in providing for their food, clothing, and shelter. The main resource available in the stake to fill these needs was idle manpower. The challenge, therefore, was to put the manpower to work to fill the needs. After long hours of study, fasting, and prayer, President Lee appointed a committee to take the leadership in meeting this challenge. The strategy, as outlined by President Lee, was to negotiate contracts with farmers in the area to harvest their crops in exchange for a percentage of the harvest. The produce obtained from these contracts was then to be gathered in a central place for distribution to needy members of the stake, with the surplus to be canned for future use. The implementation of the strategy involved these essential steps: obtain a facility for the warehousing and distribution of commodities, organize a staff to manage this facility, negotiate contracts with farmers to harvest their crops, and organize and supervise the harvesting crews. The first step was taken when the central committee obtained, without cost, a warehouse at 333 Pierpont Avenue, which was within the boundaries of the stake and which was owned by the Browning family of Ogden, Utah. Jesse M. Drury, bishop of the Fifth Ward, who was then unemployed, was appointed as the manager of the storehouse. Three other unemployed bishops in the stake, C. E. Davey, R. F. W. Nickel, and James Graham were appointed to contact farmers in the surrounding area to negotiate harvesting contracts. They and others were then involved in recruiting and supervising the volunteer harvesting crews drawn from the membership of the stake. In anticipation of the flood of produce that would be garnered at harvest time, the storehouse crew was fleshed out to include numerous people who received, merchandised, and distributed the produce and who canned the surplus for use in the off-season. The storehouse organization also came to include many sisters who were productively involved in mending or making clothing and bedding for the use of the needy in the stake. In time, the stake contracted with local industries to provide work parties to help in times of emergency or seasonal overload. As this vast self-help organization was perfected, there developed with it an extensive network of volunteers and patrons, many of whom were not members of the stake, who donated items of clothing or equipment necessary for the successful operation of the system. As the work projects got into full swing, a system of welfare entitlement was perfected. Those who performed direct services, whether in the fieldwork crews or at the storehouse, were given 'pay' slips that could be presented at the storehouse to obtain food or other commodities they needed. The needy in a ward who could not render services in the program could go to their bishop, who, with the aid of the ward Relief Society president, would determine worthiness and need and would then issue orders on the storehouse for designated items of food and clothing or other commodities. In exchange for this assistance, recipients were expected to render some kind of charitable service of which they were capable, thereby removing any stigma of a dole or a mere handout." 11

According to Harold's account:

Hundreds of tons of produce soon began to roll in—peaches, tomatoes, fruits, vegetables, and meats. Relief Society women were organized and two canning machines were purchased for their own use. After exhausting all surplus bottles in the area through a "drive," we purchased ten to twenty thousand cans from the American Can Company at 1½ cents each.

After supplying our families and stocking our storehouse, we were able to sell considerable surplus to outside people.

The storehouse was known as the Pioneer Stake bishop's storehouse and the bishops of our eleven wards were organized into an executive committee, with Bishop Joseph H. McPhie of the 25TH Ward as chairman. They were instructed to meet regularly and to manage and initiate the policies of the storehouse. The First Presidency, after hearing our plan, agreed to permit withdrawals from the tithes to supplement the food received from our own efforts. With these funds we purchased at wholesale prices butter, eggs, flour, sugar, coal, etc., to provide a wide variety of foodstuffs for our people. 12

An account of this interesting agreement between Harold's stake presidency and the Church's First Presidency was provided by President Paul C. Child, who said that the decision-making process was much more intense and significant than Harold's terse account would indicate.

No, President Lee just didn't take those funds. We had been authorized to use the tithing, but even this wasn't enough. After appealing to the Presiding Bishop for more money [and being turned down], President Lee asked for a meeting with the First Presidency. We went in and presented our problem to President Grant and his counselors.

President Grant, after listening carefully, turned to President Ivins, his first counselor, and said, "What do you think, Tone?"

President Ivins said, "I think these brethren had better take care of their people."

President Grant turned to President Clark, asking, "What do you think, Reub?"

President Clark said: "I agree with President Ivins. These brethren ought to take care of their people, and we ought to be grateful that we have the one stake presidency in the Church that strongly feels the way they do."

President Grant then banged his fist on the table to emphasize his support for the welfare program of Pioneer Stake, saying: "Brethren, take care of your people, and that is the instruction from the First Presidency of the Church. If you need additional money, more than your tithing and fast offering, you are to come directly to the Presidency of the Church from now on, and get the help you need." 13

As the program developed and implemented by the Pioneer Stake picked up steam, actually providing for the needs of the Saints without any sort of government assistance and without resorting to the dole, it began to attract attention. After John F. Fitzpatrick, non-Mormon owner of the [*Salt Lake*] *Tribune*, visited the storehouse, he was so impressed that he assigned a reporter to do a feature article on the plan. Very favorable in its view, the article attracted national interest. "'Several Eastern men came to visit our projects,'" Harold recorded, "'among whom was a Mr. Pearmain from Washington, who was connected with government relief; Mr. Mackey, a friend of President Clark's from New York; and a brother of the Reverend Webb, who years ago wrote "The Case Against the Mormons" ...Each was the same in saying without hesitation, "We dream of these accomplishments being possible in the east, but never hoped to have it worked out as practically as you have it here."'" 14

Near the end of October 1932, as truckloads of Pioneer Stake workers scattered daily across northern Utah to assist with the various harvests their leaders had contracted for, one of those vehicles was involved in a serious accident. On October 27 an editorial concerning the accident appeared in one of the local papers. Because of what it revealed about Pioneer Stake's welfare program, Harold clipped this editorial and included it with his history. Under the heading, "The Wreck at the Crossing," the editorial readily describes the specifics of what the Pioneer Stake was doing to help its people find economic relief. It reads:

> With the news that 13 men had been seriously injured, one perhaps fatally, when an interurban car struck a loaded truck in the northern part of this city, the sympathy of the people went out to the injured and their families. The men were among the 20,000 of this county who have no regular work and were being employed through the efforts of the Pioneer Stake organization, whose work in meeting this depression has been most commendable....

Meanwhile the injured men are being cared for, and President Harold B. Lee, of the Pioneer Stake, states that the accident has drawn the people more closely together than he would have believed possible. In the southwestern quarter of the city, where there is a very large proportion of unemployment, the stake authorities have been sending out some 75 to 100 men a day, alternating them in work that they have secured from farmers in different parts of the state. There has been a general spirit of unity to help each other, and he states that last night when the knowledge of this serious accident had spread among the people, prayers were offered in the homes of the wards for those who have had added to their already difficult plight, this sudden and serious misfortune. 15

At the time Harold was made stake president, his former mission president, John M. Knight, was serving as a member of the Salt Lake City Commission, responsible for public safety. Due to some controversy, Commissioner Knight was receiving quite a bit of public criticism. One of those critics was Elder Richard R. Lyman of the Council of the Twelve, who aired his criticisms one evening during a meeting in the Pioneer Stake, impugning the commissioner's integrity. "Oblivious of the source of these charges and of the consequences of speaking out, President Lee defended his friend [John Knight] in a public meeting by questioning the accuracy of Elder Lyman's charges. Anyone seeking evidence of Harold B. Lee's boldness and independence need only consider this astonishing incident. How many thirty-three-year-old men, with no powerful friends or relatives to support them, would publicly oppose a member of the Twelve Apostles? ...However, to him it was not a question of what was politic or popular. Still less was it a question of whether it would enhance or diminish his reputation. It was rather a question of whether he would remain silent while his mentor was wrongly attacked." 16

Not long after the above incident, Harold went to Commissioner Knight's office to discuss the matter with him. It happened that the recent death of another commissioner, John Lake, was mentioned, whereupon John Knight asked Harold if he would accept an appointment to that office if it were offered him. Harold responded that it was the furthest thing from his mind.

Unbeknownst to him, however, Commissioner Knight immediately set out to stir up interest and support for the young leader from the west side. Meanwhile, that same day, Harold encountered two others who also mentioned, quite casually, that they thought he ought to consider seeking the appointment to fill the vacancy. By that evening he was feeling that the Lord wanted him to consider it, and in spite of Fern's less than enthusiastic support, the next morning he began taking immediate steps to secure the appointment.

> Elder Lee's efforts to receive the appointment proved successful when the city commission unanimously designated him to fill the vacancy effective December 1, 1932. An editorial that appeared in Mr. Fitzpatrick's *Tribune* the following day set the tone for the new commissioner's relationship with the press and the public during his brief political career. "The commission is entitled to public commendation for its wise and happy selection," it read. "The *Tribune* extends its congratulations to the new commissioner and commends the remainder of the commission for an appointment so promising of sound public service." The editorial also referred to President Lee's youth, his vigor, his courage, and to his keen interest in public affairs, notwithstanding a lack of experience in politics. The editorial announcing the appointment, which appeared in the Church-owned *Deseret News*, elaborated on this interest.

Harold B. Lee's campaign picture
for Salt Lake City commissioner

CA. 1933

"He has been prominent in civic organizations, particularly those interested in building up and improving the west side of the city. He has been the leader in battles before the city commission for the maintenance of adequate public transportation for west side residents." The *Tribune* editorial also emphasized the new commissioner's connection with the city's west side, suggesting that this was the key factor in his appointment since his predecessor had been elected from that area. President Lee's ecclesiastical role in aiding the Latter-day Saints living on the west side further underscores the significance of the decision he and Fern made to put their roots down in that area following their marriage. 17

Resigning from his job with the Foundation Press, Harold entered into his new employment with characteristic enthusiasm and determination. Not everyone thought he had made a wise decision, yet Harold felt certain that the Lord's hand had been in his appointment. "Subsequent events demonstrated the soundness of this impression as Harold B. Lee's dual role as the president of the Pioneer Stake and a member of the Salt Lake City Commission representing the west side provided essential ingredients in the successful development of the welfare plan." 18

Harold wrote:

I entered upon my new work with considerable fear and many misgivings. Most of my close friends bemoaned my "entrance into politics" as disastrous to my character and standing. Then, too, I was entering the governing body of the city at a time when the finances and business affairs were in a precarious condition. While the demands of the people were the same as formerly, the available funds were the lowest since the inauguration of the commission form of government in about 1915. By the 15TH of December, the budgets had to be prepared, and immediately after my taking office I worked day and night in a study of the Departments of Streets and Public Improvements in order to make a fairly intelligent budget of the department's needs for 1933.

...The Department of Streets and Public Improvements employed more men than any other city department except the public safety, which was operated largely under civil service. I found that to be responsible for a half-million dollars annually in the management of the department required intensive study of the organization itself and the personnel. 19

Though Harold was now busier than he had ever been in his life, it seems obvious that he "was exhilarated by the challenging complexity of his new assignment...[developing] to a high degree his ability to keep many balls in the air at the same time and to do it with poise and grace. His duties as stake president were...especially demanding at this time as he and his brethren struggled to stem the tide of economic disaster that had engulfed their people.... In addition to all this, the new commissioner [was still teaching his] early-morning seminary class, "20 which had begun in 1931 when the Church organized a seminary at the then new South High School in Salt Lake City. And finally, "his family duties continued unabated as he fulfilled the needs of his wife and their maturing daughters, while taking care of the yard work and other chores around the home." 21

In the "small home on Indiana Avenue on the west side of Salt Lake City, where they had moved in 1928, the Lee family—Harold and Fern and their two little girls—continued to build their loving and exemplary relationships....

"The idealism of these parents immediately began to leave a lasting impression on their children, their friends, and their neighbors. They consistently demonstrated a simple joy and appreciation for each other and the absolute assurance that God was near and would bless their every pursuit." 22

Helen's childhood memories illustrate the loving relationship of this young father with his little girls: "Daddy...always had some endearing words to say to us as he tucked the covers tightly around us." 23 Harold "knew then, and later was to teach the entire Church, how important it was that children feel their father's love for them. It was through experiences such as this nightly routine that Maurine and Helen grew up knowing of their father's interest and concern for his little girls. Helen reflects even today on that important emotional foundation, saying, 'I have often thought about that expression of father love to us and ever will be grateful that love, security, and tenderness were planted deep in our hearts.'" 24

As his girls grew, Harold developed a rather interesting way of motivating them to greater effort—a form of modern psychology known as the "As If" principle. As Helen explained it:

> Whatever it was that he wanted us to become he told us that we were already. Because we loved him so much we tried hard to be what he thought we were, what he told us we were, so that we would not disappoint him. We didn't ever want him to find out that we really weren't as good as he thought we were. We always wanted him to be proud of us.
>
> For example, my sister and I started taking music lessons when we were very young. I played the violin and my sister, the piano. He would tell us that there was nothing grander than to have his little girls play for him and that together we made the most beautiful music this side of heaven. In reality, we were squeaking and squawking and playing many wrong notes, but he always made us feel that it was just the loveliest music he'd ever heard. The result was we'd practice when we really didn't want to do so, to perfect our music just for Daddy's sake. Finally, after we

had surmounted the initial obstacles, it then became an enjoyable experience for us and we were able to practice for the right reason. But the psychology had worked as he must have known it would. His desire to have musicians in the family was fulfilled, and our lives were made richer because of his wisdom and encouragement.

In our awkward, adolescent years he would tell us often that he was so proud of his beautiful, charming daughters. Well, I knew I was anything but beautiful and charming. My hair was "Dutch" cut, I wore horn-rimmed glasses which I hated, I was pudgy and overweight, and even had to wear corrective shoes. Yet, I reasoned, if Daddy thought I was beautiful, I must try very hard to be what he thought I was, because I just couldn't disappoint him. So every night in my prayers I asked God to help me become what my daddy thought I was already. 25

If he were ever disappointed in not having a son, Maurine and I never knew that. He made us think that having two little girls was just the greatest blessing he could have as a father. I've appreciated that attitude, because, of course, as we grew older we knew that he might have had some regrets. But if he did, we certainly didn't know it at the time we were growing up. 26

There was always an ice cream cone or some other treat when Daddy had finished his business for the evening. We frequently stopped at an A&W Root Beer stand, where Daddy would drive in, roll down his car window, and order, "Two and two." That meant he wanted two large mugs of root beer and two small ones. The half-sized mugs had the same handles on them as the large ones, and we took great delight in drinking from them. 27

As with his seminary students, Harold delighted in teaching his daughters the gospel of Jesus Christ. Since the girls were only fifteen months apart and grew up as constant companions, one facet of this was the teaching that sisters never quarreled with each other, but only loved one another. They were also taught obedience—not just "because" but "because their parents loved them enough to want only the best for them." It was no great step, then, to increase that understanding of love from parents to the infinite love of a kind, wise Heavenly Father, which Harold did when his daughters were quite young. As Helen put it, Daddy explained "that [Heavenly Father] loved us every bit as much as did our earthly father, and that He had the power to be with us wherever we were, wherever we went....

"...That lesson has never been forgotten and my understanding of my relationship with my Heavenly Father began in that early childhood [teaching]." 28

"Obedience and confidence in God," Harold declared later when speaking publicly of this teaching he presented to his daughters, "...are absolutely necessary to moral safety and spiritual well-being.... If confidence in God is established, love for him and obedience to him will follow. Then, and only then, can the teachings of the scriptures become live symbols to us." 29

Harold used the scriptures constantly in his own life, cherishing the words of God and the prophets. At an early age he taught his daughters to do the same. According to Helen:

Whenever we had a question as we prepared for a two-and-a-half-minute talk we were to give, or whenever anything was discussed around the dinner table requiring an answer, we'd ask, "What about this, Dad? What do you think?" He would reply, "Get out your scriptures, girls, and let's see what the Lord says about it." He would get his book, too, and have us turn to the right scripture and we'd read together what we needed to know. There were many times when I would think how much easier and quicker it would be if Daddy would just give us the answer. But I came to understand later that he was once again giving us a wonderful opportunity to learn important lessons. In so doing, he taught us that the scriptures were where we turn first for our answers. He didn't go to the intellectual, academic, or philosophical answers of men, or to the beautiful, lofty lines of poets. Those, he told us, were wonderful resources, but they were sought only after we had searched the scriptures and the spiritual essence was understood. These were keys to his profound knowledge of the scriptures, and he wanted us to know and love them, too. 30

It should not be inferred that only Harold taught his daughters, or that Fern had little impact upon them. In fact, the opposite is true. "Fern Tanner Lee was an example of everything that a marvelous homemaker and mother ought to be. She taught her two daughters all the homemaking skills which she had perfected. She was an exceptional cook and a most gracious and lovely hostess, serving with charm and warmth the many groups invited to her home. For all these qualities, she was constantly praised and encouraged by her appreciative husband." 31

Helen reaffirmed this, saying:

All during my growing-up years, whatever Mother did, whether it was arranging furniture or flowers, making a bed or ironing a shirt, Daddy would always say to us, "Now, girls, when you can do that just like your mother, you'll be the best there is." I can remember when she hung her wash on the clothesline outside (this was long before we had heard of automatic dryers), he would watch her work as he was doing his jobs out in the yard, and would say to us as we played about, "Just look at that—your mother even makes the washing on the line look artistic."

Lee family portrait: Fern, Maurine, Helen and Harold

CA. 1939–40

Courtesy of the Lee Family Collection

It was true. She would hang the white clothes together and then the colored pieces and then the dark items, very carefully and in perfect order. The long pieces were all hung together and the short ones were alongside each other. He reinforced the wisdom of our learning from Mother by this oft-repeated admonition: "You will never find any better example of anything that you will do as women when you grow older than that which is provided by your own mother. She is the perfect example. You just watch the way Mother does it!" 32

Life did not always go smoothly in the Lee home. Particularly as the girls got older and were seeking social acceptance, conflicts inevitably occurred. Nor did Harold always maintain his composure or instantly make wise choices. On one occasion, as was illustrated in the vignette at the beginning of this chapter, Maurine, whom Harold did call "his little harness-fighter," stayed too late at a party, sending Helen home without her. Both decisions were infractions of the Lee family rules, and Harold was irate. But, thanks to Fern's cool-headed guidance, as Helen tells it:

> Well, I don't know what happened because I didn't go back with Daddy and I wasn't on the scene, but when he arrived at the dance and found her and brought her back, she apparently came willingly and happily. Mother and I were greatly relieved!
>
> Through the wise handling of tense situations in this manner, discipline in our home never degenerated into the abrasive confrontations that are common today in too many homes. 33

Though Fern Tanner Lee was small of stature, quiet, and unassuming, she was the source of great spiritual strength in the Lee home and exerted profound influence on the life of her husband. In all respects he both adored and honored her, saying: "'The loftiest thoughts for which I have been given credit were first expressed to me by my dear wife.'" 34 Helen writes:

> Though she was quiet and unassuming in personality, [Mother's] inner strength was unquestioned as a powerful influence upon all who knew her. Her mind was filled with wisdom and her heart with empathy as she met my father's needs, as well as the needs of others around her. She had a remarkable sense of fairness. My father's personality was one of being very quick, moving ahead into a situation, making a decision and taking action promptly, regardless of whether the given situation was in Church work, employment, or in a family setting. He needed the influence of a wife who would say to him, as Mother would, "Now, dear, you need to think about this and you must not fail to look at the other side of the situation." She balanced him in this way.
>
> Mother also was his inspiration....
>
> There was a sweet relationship which existed between the two of them. He was always so kind and thoughtful of her needs, and the limited strength she had was always extended for him first, as it should have been. He was at the top of her list of priorities. 35

As the Lee children grew, "the family moved into a larger home at 1208 South Eighth West in Salt Lake City. President Lee worked hard to improve the home and its surroundings, proving his competency as a do-it-yourself man. Up early in the morning to work in the yard, and working late every evening he was free, he developed a lovely backyard that was used by his family and their many friends. He did all of the landscaping himself, installing a beautiful board fence, fish pond, pagoda, benches at strategic spots, and a brick fireplace for barbecues." 36

His daughter Helen recalls:

Daddy learned in his early years that if he was going to accomplish anything, he was going to have to move fast. And I mean that literally. His movements were always very quick, and I suppose that as he got busier and as his life became more complicated, he just had to move at top speed to get everything done—especially with a big yard to take care of. He'd come in from work, greet all of us, then upstairs he would go and change his clothes, wasting not a minute. In his old clothes, he'd start to cut the lawn before supper, while mother was still getting things on the table. It might be that he'd get a call—somebody wanted him to come and administer to him or somebody needed counsel or help. He would race back in, put on his suit again, take care of the administration or other business, come back, change his clothes again, work for a while, and then go off to an evening meeting. He wouldn't have had time to do all that if he moved at a normal pace. 37

As the Depression deepened, the needs of the Pioneer Stake members increased dramatically. By the end of 1932 the drain on the finances of the Church became more than the Church could stand, for a major portion of the people no longer had any income to tithe. The federal government had just launched a huge relief program, and many in the Church were turning to it. Yet Harold and his stake presidency had promised their members that if they would support the program of the Pioneer Stake, they would not need to turn to the federal government for assistance. Only, with almost no income coming into the stake from tithing or any other source, how were they to fulfill their promise? Harold describes the miraculous answer as follows:

At this critical juncture, we called a meeting of our bishops. They asked us what they were to do. As though moved by the Spirit of the Lord, President Child said: "We want you to see to it that every one of your people is taken care of. We don't know where the money will come from to pay the bills, but our people must be provided with their needs." I heartily seconded his instruction, but as we left the stake hall we wondered from where our help would come.

The answer came within the next two weeks. Through our efforts, our storehouse, with its entire personnel, was made a county auxiliary storehouse to serve our district and the government agreed to purchase all the produce we had on hand at regular prices. My appointment as city commissioner seemed to come at just the psychological time to give us prestige in accomplishing our objective. With the government purchasing our supplies garnered from the previous summer's effort, we were able to take care not only of those who came within the scope of the Reconstruction Finance Corporation, but all our worthy Latter-day Saints who were entitled to help from the Church. When the RFC discontinued its operations the next spring, we found we had between four and five thousand dollars in the bank and approximately two thousand dollars worth of produce in the storehouse. Certainly the Lord had "ordered" events for the succor of his children. 38

Under Harold's direction, by 1933 a forty-acre tract of land in the Pioneer Stake had been placed under cultivation as a vegetable and produce garden. All members who wished to participate did so with no cost except their labor, for which they received for their own consumption an ample share of all the garden produced. On another front, it was ascertained by the stake presidency that there was "a large pool of unemployed artisans—bricklayers, carpenters, masons, painters, and laborers—who wanted to work but who could not find employment. Again, President Lee's ingenuity found a way to match resources with needs. The result was the construction of the Pioneer Stake Gymnasium. The first step was to organize. T. T. Burton was appointed as the overall superintendent of the project, and Fred J. Heath was called to recruit and to direct the laborers. Much of the material for the gymnasium was obtained from old buildings that the stake workers demolished with the approval of their owners. What little money was needed for new materials came from a donation of the First Presidency, forty-five hundred dollars, and from the sale of surplus commodities realized from the operation of the stake storehouse. The workers on the gymnasium were compensated by receiving 'pay slips,' which could then be used to purchase food, clothing, and other commodities at the storehouse. When completed, the building had an appraised value of thirty thousand dollars. After its completion, an opening social was held in the building on June 16, 1933. Honored guests were President Heber J. Grant and Presiding Bishop Sylvester Q. Cannon, a native of the stake and a former president of, the Pioneer Stake." 39

Harold recorded:

The MIA organizations and the Primary were given charge of the activities of the gym, and from October 1933 through the winter, every night from six o'clock until eleven o'clock was programmed with activities involving the various groups, from Primary age to adult women and men. Bleachers seating four hundred people were provided, and it was no uncommon sight to see from four hundred to seven hundred spectators enjoying the evening's contests and sports. In many instances the recreation provided at the gym was the only recreation these people had enjoyed since the depression in 1929....

In 1934 we planned to further intensify its use. Our objective for the stake was "to provide fully for the spiritual, physical, educational, and recreational needs of every member of Pioneer Stake" ...All wards were put on a strict budget for all maintenance and organizational needs. All public dances in the stake were held in the gymnasium and participated in by all holders of stake budget tickets in order to control the character of the participants and to provide the highest standard of entertainment.

The building of the gym was a veritable inspiration; had it been started one month later, its success and the ultimate ridiculously low cost would have been jeopardized. 40

When Harold was appointed to the city commission, one of the things he agreed to do was run for the office again when the term of his predecessor, Mr. Lake, expired. Less than a year after his appointment, therefore, he found himself involved in his first political campaign. To get things going, he created a political organization out of his Street Department personnel. He writes:

My only hope to be successful in the election was to build my department into a political organization that could cope successfully with other political groups. To this end, I began the first of September to segregate my 250 employees into precincts and to hold meetings with them to become better acquainted, to outline plans, to define my position on various questions, to prepare them to answer complaints, and to meet opposition that might come.

In answer to those who declared that the Street Department was "not worth a damn" politically, we were successful in polling 13,336 voters in the primary election, to qualify the highest of the four winning candidates in the primary election. 41

The actual election, Harold said, "was a veritable nightmare, with each of the four qualifying candidates fighting for every advantage."42 When the *Salt Lake Tribune* attempted to make repeal of the Constitutional amendment prohibiting alcoholic consumption a part of the campaign, demanding a statement from each of the candidates regarding his position, Harold went to his old friend John F. Fitzpatrick, *Tribune* owner, to ask how he should word his statement. Though not LDS, Fitzpatrick knew of Harold's position as stake president and knew Harold could not endorse liquor. Nevertheless, Harold did feel that Prohibition was a bad law. Together the two men came up with the answer—that he was not satisfied with conditions as they were under Prohibition, and he certainly could not sanction the old saloon conditions of the past. This was sufficiently vague to confound Harold's enemies and at the same time sufficiently clear to please his supporters. For that and a host of other reasons, Harold won the election without difficulty and continued into his own term as a city commissioner.

While the high-profile nature of his department and his meteoric rise as a political force in Salt Lake City and elsewhere attracted it's share of criticism, Harold's reputation for sound, efficient, and honest dealings was never questioned. And he reciprocated the kindly feelings others had toward him. Of his work as a commissioner, he wrote: "My work brought me in contact with the leaders in every field, and I have formed friendships that wouldn't be possible otherwise. I have had the opportunity to see men at their best and at their worst." [43]

By the time of the election, Harold had also become close to the First Presidency of the Church, visiting with them frequently in their offices and seeking their counsel and advice. After the election, in which all of the presidency voted for him and wished him well, President Anthony W. Ivins, first counselor to President Heber J. Grant, told Harold: "'I would ten times rather a man would make a mistake while doing that which he thought was right, ...than to do right just for policy sake.'" [44]

That was advice Harold had been, and would continue, to follow.

Harold B. Lee and Commission
outside Salt Lake City and County
Building

CA. 1934

SEEKING THE WELFARE OF ZION

It was August, and the summer sun was just barely showing above the Antelope Range to the east. Yet already it was hot on the winding road through Sevier Canyon, and Harold B. Lee knew the day was going to be a scorcher. For the moment, though, he wasn't minding the heat. Instead, he was enjoying the beauty of the canyon—a rather sharp and colorfully arid contrast to the lush pine and quaking aspen forests they had passed through after climbing the Markagun Plateau to the east of Cedar City. He and Mark Austin had left St. George at 3:30 that morning, their destination Richfield, where they were to conduct an early morning meeting. But it had been a long drive, Mark had been asleep since shortly after their departure, and so Harold had been left alone to enjoy the grandeur and the solitude.

Out of St. George they had climbed north through Black Rock Canyon on U.S. Highway 91, and Harold had been pleased at the good condition of the paved road. Their nearly new automobile had also performed well on the long, steep climb, and by the time they had reached Cedar City, Harold had felt confident enough in the vehicle that he had turned east to begin another climb, this one on a gravel road that wound up several thousand feet in elevation before skirting around Cedar Breaks and stretching on northeastward across the mountainous plateau, finally winding down through a juniper and pinion forest and into the barely waking community of Panguitch.

There they had gassed up and turned north on U.S. 89, which was paved only in places, crossing the wide Buckskin Valley to Circleville and then following the twisted course of the Sevier River into and through Sevier Canyon, all the while paralleling the gleaming tracks of the Denver and Rio Grand Western Railroad. Once out of the canyon, Harold knew, it would be only a short distance through Joseph and Elsinore and on into Richfield, where his work would begin.

Four and a half hours, he thought as he glanced at his watch. Not bad, considering the rough roads over the mountain. Even better, they should be on time, perhaps a little early, and that was just how Harold liked it. Being late for anything was detestable, but to keep good brethren and sisters waiting was, in his mind at least, a sin. Which was why he had insisted on his and Mark's extremely early departure from St. George. Yes, it was inconvenient, but if these priesthood and Relief Society leaders could be expected to leave their farms, families, and businesses on a weekday for a several-hour meeting regarding the welfare relief of others, then the least he and Mark could do was be on time.

It had been nearly six months, Harold thought as the automobile sped past the steep, yellowed hills some were starting to call the Big Rock Candy Mountain; nearly six months since he had been called as managing director of the Church security or welfare plan and to oversee a committee of brethren whose assignment it was to implement and work out the plan's details for providing a system of relief for the whole Church. He had been called as managing director, President Grant had told him, because the Brethren wanted to take a leaf out of the Pioneer Stake's book—to do for the entire Church what he and his stake presidency had been doing for the Pioneer Stake.

But there were vast differences between organizing relief work in his stake and doing the same for the entire Church, Harold had quickly discovered, not the least of which was that he had no authority elsewhere such as he enjoyed in his own home area. From almost the first day he had encountered opposition, some of it severe, and some of it coming from very high up in the hierarchy of the Church. Yet President Grant and his counselors had fully and vocally supported and sustained him and had even placed Elder Melvin J. Ballard over the committee to give it credence. And so Harold had pressed forward, helping to divide the Church into regions and using the local priesthood and Relief Society leaders to work out, organize, and direct the various sorts of relief programs that might be best suited for their local areas.

In Provo the region leaders were promoting truck garden projects and acquiring an old sugar factory that could be converted into a cannery. In Nephi the local brethren were already in the midst of a wheat-growing project and were organizing a farmer's cooperative; Richfield's leaders were moving ahead to produce commercial fertilizer and get some lumber mills into operation; and the night before, in St. George, he had Mark had listened as the local brethren and sisters discussed their plans for growing beet seed and semitropical fruit. In May he had even accompanied Elder Ballard and others to Oakland, California, where the local regional directors had discussed organizing a storehouse to serve as a distribution point for Utah and Idaho produce.

It had also been in Oakland, Harold mused, where he and Elder Ballard had first encountered real opposition—at least opposition that was openly expressed in their meetings. Certain people there simply didn't think there was a need for the Church to become so involved in the relief efforts made necessary by the Depression. There had also been news articles in Salt Lake City inaccurately reporting the costs and value of relief work in the Pioneer Stake, and other critics both in Salt Lake and elsewhere were attacking Harold personally, calling him the boy wonder—a nice young man with no real experience to spearhead the vast, churchwide effort he was undertaking. Harold smiled at this, feeling thankful for the wisdom of the Brethren in installing Elder Ballard to oversee the work. Certainly no one would think to call Elder Ballard a boy wonder!

The opposition he and Mark Austin had been encountering of late, however, was more difficult to argue with, and so all morning Harold had been pondering it, wondering what it was the Lord would have him do. Since early summer there had been a gradual but marked upturn in business nationwide—so much so that many, including a good many Church leaders, were declaring that the Depression was at an end and that further relief efforts should be halted. Of course, no one really knew whether it was over or not. The upturn might indeed be permanent, which would give cause for the whole world to rejoice. Then again, it might only be a seasonal surge, leading people along in a vain hope that would end in another crash and further economic devastation. And that doubt alone, Harold had been thinking that morning, should be enough to keep Church leaders and members alike busy working for their own and each other's relief.

Of course that was a harder sell, as he and Mark had been discovering. There was real inertia among the ranks of the regional leaders, and this upturn was only giving them cause to spend more time doing less—

Harold had also been praying that morning, off and on for hours, pleading for inspiration regarding the welfare program and why it should be continued. There was no doubt that President Grant and his counselors felt it should; neither was there doubt about his or the other committee members' feelings and determination. But why were their efforts necessary, he had been asking the Lord that morning? What reason could he give the brethren that would satisfy their questions, their doubt?

Ahead of Harold the road forked to the left, a narrow track winding westward up Clear Creek Canyon and on over the low mountains to U.S. 91. He had gone that route once, he was thinking, and had found it rough but rather pleasant—

Abruptly Harold's musings about routes and difficulties stopped. In his mind instead, words were forming—words as distinct as though someone were speaking audibly. The words were also accompanied by the inner fire or burnings he had come to know were the witness of the Holy Ghost, and so Harold listened intently, knowing he was being taught by a voice from the eternities—given an answer to his pondered question.

"There is no individual in the Church," he was told, "who knows the real purpose for which the welfare program now launched has been intended. But hardly before the Church has made sufficient preparation, that reason will be made manifest; and when it comes, it will challenge every resource of the Church to meet it."

Harold trembled as the message burned into his mind and heart, for now he knew beyond doubt that the Church's welfare plan—the same that he and Mark and Campbell Brown and the others were endeavoring to implement and press forward—was God's will, God's plan. What really mattered, he suddenly understood clearly, was not what the economy might be doing, but what the Lord's anointed servants, the prophets of God, were saying. To those fountainheads of truth God would reveal his will, and thus his Saints would be preserved through an evil day that was certain to come!

Filled with emotion Harold drove on, for now he knew what to say to the brethren and sisters who had gathered at such personal sacrifice that morning in Richfield—and to the leaders of the Saints wherever else he might be sent throughout the world—1

Saturday, April 30, 1935, was a significant day for Harold B. Lee, for his heaven-directed life was impelled forward dramatically. He was not, however, relieved of any of his burdens, such as stake president, city commissioner, father, or husband. Rather a new responsibility was added, one that would consume his thinking and dramatically change his life's labor. On that morning he was invited to meet with the First Presidency "to discuss a Church welfare plan whose focus would be on self-reliance rather than on a direct relief, or a dole, formula.... [T]his turned out to be a half-day session with President Heber J. Grant and his second counselor, President David O. McKay. President J. Reuben Clark, the first counselor, was out of the city at the time but was aware of the meeting and had previously approved the purpose of it and also the assignment given to Elder Lee at the conclusion of it." [2]

Because it was a Saturday there were no calls expected, so the Presidency asked Harold to take his time and thoroughly explain the details of the welfare plan he had organized in the Pioneer Stake. Then they gave the young stake president their undivided attention.

Harold's record of that meeting reads:

> President Grant said he wanted to take a "leaf out of Pioneer Stake's book" in caring for the people of the Church. He expressed dissatisfaction with the then existent program of social service investigations. He said that there was nothing more important for the Church to do than to take care of its needy people and that so far as he was concerned, everything else must be sacrificed [so that] proper relief [could be] extended to our people. I was astounded to learn that for years there had been before them, as a result of their thinking and planning and as a result of the inspiration of Almighty God, the genius of the very plan that was waiting and in preparation for a time when, in their judgment, the faith of the Latter-day Saints

was such that they were willing to follow the counsel of the men who lead and preside in this Church. My humble place in this program at that time was described....

I left the First Presidency's Office about noontime with an assignment to work out a program of relief for the entire Church based upon my experience with the relief problem in the Pioneer Stake, where perhaps the greatest problem of unemployment in the entire Church was to be found. 3

Overwhelmed by the magnitude of what the Presidency had asked him to do, as well as by the burden of responsibility he was already carrying, Harold sat stunned in his car. Years later he described those first staggering moments of contemplation:

There I was, just a young man in my thirties. My experience had been limited. I was born in a little country town in Idaho. I had hardly been outside the boundaries of the states of Utah, Idaho, and Colorado. And now, to put me in a position where I was to reach out to the entire membership of the Church was one of the most staggering contemplations that I could imagine. How could I do it with my limited under-standing? 4

Feeling the same need that the Prophet Joseph had once felt to seek for wisdom and understanding at the hands of his Creator, Harold took the same course. Just as Joseph had gone into the woods to pray, so Harold started "his car and drove up City Creek Canyon, whose mouth is only a few blocks from the Church Administration Building. Driving through Memory Grove, which is near the canyon's mouth, he wound his way upward alongside the stream, which at that time of year would have begun to increase in volume as the snow on the high watersheds melted. Arriving at what was called Rotary Park, which was then the terminus of the canyon road, he parked his car."5

What was troubling Harold—causing him great consternation, in fact—was his worry over how to assemble and put in place an organization that could produce, churchwide, the same marvelous results that the organization he had put together in his stake had accomplished. How could he do it when he knew so few? Or when so few knew him? And how could he possibly determine which men and women had the genius for organization and administration that he knew they would need? With such questions plaguing him, Harold records that he got out of his car and:

> ...walked up through the trees, seeking a secluded spot, where I knelt in prayer and sought the guidance of an all-wise God in this mighty undertaking. I told the Lord to guide me to conclusions dictated by His will, and that, for the safety and blessing of his people, I must have His direction. As I kneeled down, my petition was: "What kind of an organization should be set up in order to accomplish what the Presidency has assigned?"
>
> Having sought my Heavenly Father, I sat down to pore over this matter, wondering about an organization to be perfected to carry on this work. There came to me on that glorious spring afternoon one of the most heavenly realizations of the power of the priesthood of God, that God had already revealed the greatest organization that could ever be given to mankind and that all that was needed now was that that organization be set to work. It was as though [someone was] saying to me: "There is no new organization necessary to take care of the needs of this people. All that is necessary is to put the priesthood of God to work. There is nothing else that you need as a substitute, and if you use it the temporal welfare of the Latter-day Saints will be safeguarded."6

Despite now knowing that the priesthood was to be at the core of the new organization, however, "the Church Welfare Program presented President Lee with monumental problems during the days when national economic devastation was most severe. Manpower, materials, finance, and organization were all independent challenges that required coordination and insight to manage. Besides the tremendous logistical problem, there was the awesome task of administering [a] new program in the face of criticism from those who felt that subsidy should be kept within the province of secular government."[7]

With customary zeal, however, Harold launched himself into the work, reviewing everything the Pioneer Stake had done and visiting with and seeking advice from people such as former U.S. Senator Reed Smoot, John M. Knight, his counselor Paul C. Child, Campbell Brown Jr., and a large number of others. Gradually, a report came together that outlined a preliminary program the First Presidency could consider. Harold also created a chart showing the various agencies he thought ought to participate in a churchwide relief program. His report and chart were submitted to the Brethren about June 1, 1935.

"When this report was circulated among the General Authorities for review and comment, some negative reactions were generated to...Elder Lee's proposals. These created uncertainty in the mind of President Grant, who hesitated in going forward. 'In the face of this indecision and opposition,' Elder Lee noted in his record, 'President McKay felt incapable of taking the initiative without the personal support and backing of at least one other member of the First Presidency.' Since President Clark was not available to get involved, Elder Lee's plan lay dormant with no action being taken on it. However, between June 1, 1935, when the plan was submitted and the October 1935 general conference, Elder Lee met periodically with President McKay to discuss welfare principles. As a result of these meetings, preliminary steps were

Illustration by Robert T. Barrett

taken toward establishing a Church welfare plan (originally called the Church security plan) when in September 1935 a churchwide survey was initiated to determine the welfare needs of the members of the Church. In the ensuing months, a close follow-up was made to insure that these data were gathered and submitted to Church headquarters. Also, at the general priesthood meeting on October 5, 1935, the First Presidency developed themes that became fixtures of the Church welfare plan as it was rolled out. The brethren, for instance, were admonished to get out of debt and to stay out of debt and to be faithful in paying their tithes and offerings. As to the latter, President McKay said, 'We have in the church one of the best systems in the world of aiding one another—the fast offerings. Our young people should be taught from their youth; our older people should practice it and set a proper example.'" 8

In February of 1836, Harold was again invited to meet with the First Presidency, this time in company with Campbell Brown Jr. The survey of the needs of the Church membership had been completed, and the two men were instructed to study the survey and, in light of its findings, submit a revised report for the consideration of the presiding brethren. Harold records:

> Working all the possible time, both day and night, it took about three weeks to study the survey statistics. I prepared a graph to show clearly the findings and, counseled by Brother Brown, revised, simplified, and extended my original report. On March 15, 1936, we read over the program carefully with President McKay. After the conclusion of the reading, he slapped the table with his hand and exclaimed: "Brethren, now we have a program to present to the Church. The Lord has inspired you in your work."...

At the general conference of April 6, 1936, another special meeting of stake presidencies and ward bishoprics was called and a statement was read from the

First Presidency by President McKay, embodying the recommendations and results of our report following a study of the Churchwide survey. Filled with emotion, Presidents Clark and McKay pleaded with the local authorities to cooperate with a program they could expect shortly to be given to the Church, they declaring that the Church was under condemnation if it failed to take care of the Lord's people. 9

Uncertain as to whether or not his role in the Church's welfare plan was over, Harold began to refocus his mind on his responsibilities as stake president and city commissioner. Nine days later, on April 15, 1936, Harold "was again asked to meet with the First Presidency. At that time, he was called to serve as the managing director of the Church security plan and to launch it churchwide among the organized stakes." Because this was to be a full-time job, it "entailed his resignation as a Salt Lake City commissioner. He was also advised at that time that a central security committee would be organized under which he would serve in a manner like a board of directors. Because of the sensitivities this central committee would create with the Presiding Bishopric, which historically had principal authority and responsibility for temporal matters, he was also told that a member of the Twelve would be designated as the chairman of the central committee so as to give it authority over any objection raised by the Presiding Bishopric or by priesthood leaders in the field. Soon after, Elder Melvin J. Ballard of the Twelve was designated as the chairman of the central security committee, with Elder Lee and Mark Austin as members. Within a few months, Campbell M. Brown, Stringham Stevens, Henry D. Moyle, and William E. Ryberg were added to the committee. Once this central organization had been put in place and the general and local leaders had been advised of its existence and of the scope of its authority and responsibility, [Harold] had a track to run on and, as the managing director of the churchwide security plan, was in a position to begin to implement the welfare program he [had been] so instrumental in formulating." 10

To give official impetus to the new plan, President Grant issued an official statement. The Church welfare program was established by prophets "'to set up a system where the evils of the dole will be abolished and where independence, thrift, industry, and self-respect can again be established among our people.'" 11

From that declaration, Harold and the others on the committee began presenting the three foundations of the new plan: 1. This was not a new program, but merely an incorporation of existing Church philosophy into a practical program of cooperation to meet the needs of Church members with financial problems. 2. The program would be implemented through the existing Church organization. And 3. All activities and projects helped the people to help themselves rather than providing a simple subsidy. Those receiving food and commodities were expected to work for them, if at all possible. In Harold's words:

> Every member of the Church gives what he is able to give and receives in return whatever he needs for the sustenance of himself and his family....
>
> There must be no idleness in the Church; we must learn the lesson of self sacrifice; we must master the art of living and working together; we must practice a greater brotherhood in our priesthood quorums. 12

With characteristic energy and enthusiasm, Harold pushed forward the work, setting up shop in an office in the Church Administration Building.

In just six days "the first of many regional meetings was held to establish the organization and teach the principles by which stake leaders could begin to oversee and care for their own needy members. Following this initial meeting, which was held in

Ogden, the pace was fast and furious."13 President Heber J. Grant attended the first few of these meetings, introducing Harold and thus giving him and the welfare program he was implementing the authoritative endorsement of the First Presidency.

From then on, Harold, "Elder Melvin J. Ballard, and frequently Bishop Sylvester Q. Cannon, the Presiding Bishop of the Church, were on the road almost every night to hold meetings. This effort was the first regionalization of stakes in Church history, although undistributed writings of President Clark mention the concept as early as 1933. It was a new organizational development that was ultimately expanded in 1967 with the appointment of Regional Representatives of the Council of the Twelve. Such geographic division appears now to be firmly entrenched in Church government, but it had its start with the welfare program in 1936, when there were 115 stakes in the Church, 110 of which were in the United States.

"A whirlwind tour around the Church in Utah (excluding Salt Lake City), Idaho, Arizona, and California was accomplished in an amazing fourteen-day period, these areas being organized into thirteen regions. Accountable leadership was installed, record systems were initiated, and education about the new plan was commenced. Although this was not recorded in Harold B. Lee's welfare journal, the Salt Lake region was also organized in 1936. It consisted of the following stakes: Salt Lake, Ensign, Bonneville, Granite, Wells, Pioneer, Cottonwood, West Jordan, North Davis, South Davis, Tooele, Oquirrh, Liberty, Highland, Grant, and East Jordan." 14

From that point forward, Harold and others of the committee, including Brother Mark Austin, found themselves traveling from one regional meeting to another almost constantly. In each of these meetings "a regional chairman and vice-chairman were appointed from among the stake presidents in attendance and instructions were given about how the program would roll out.... At some meetings, in addition to the usual instructions about welfare principles and organizational matters, there was discussion about production assignments that had already been given and about possible welfare projects. So, at a meeting held in Provo, Utah, on April 23, 1936, there was discussion about promoting truck garden projects and about acquiring an old sugar factory that could be converted into a cannery. At Nephi, Utah, on April 27 there was discussion about a wheat growing project and about the creation of a farmers cooperative. The next morning at Richfield, Utah, commercial fertilizer and lumber mill projects were considered while that evening at St. George, Utah, the local brethren talked about growing beet seed and semi-tropical fruit. May 1, 1936, found Elder Lee, Elder Ballard, and Bishop Cannon in Oakland, California, where there was discussion about organizing a storehouse to serve as a distributing point for Utah and Idaho produce." 15

From the beginning of these regional meetings it was debated among the Saints whether or not the welfare plan was inspired of God and whether or not the Saints were as required to live it as, say, the law of tithing. To answer them, Harold "often quoted from the 115th section of the Doctrine and Covenants: 'Arise and shine forth, that thy light may be a standard for the nations; and that the gathering together upon the land of Zion, and upon her stakes, may be for a defense, and for a refuge from the storm, and from wrath when it shall be poured out without mixture upon the whole earth.' Applying the meaning of that declaration, [Harold] rephrased the scripture to convey an immediate message: 'I have caused you to be organized into stakes of Zion that you might provide a defense, a refuge, and a protection for my people.'" 16

For too many doubters, unfortunately, this was still not enough. Finally, after nine years of arguing, Elder Marion G. Romney forcefully declared in general conference:

I believe I have heard almost all the objections which have

been raised against it, and also the labored arguments in justification for not living it. As I have listened to these objections and arguments, I have been painfully aware of the dull spirit in which they have been urged.... I believe I have made a rather complete study and I now testify to you that I do know beyond any doubt, by the same power that Peter knew that Jesus is the Christ, that the Church Welfare Plan in its inception was and now is inspired of the Lord; and that the great principles implemented by it are eternal truths, which the saints of God must abide if they are to purify and perfect themselves as the Lord has commanded. [17]

Nevertheless, this doubting of the program's inspiration or even necessity was something Harold ran into on a regular basis. It discouraged him, and Elder Ballard told him he was disappointed also, particularly that opposition continued among " 'a few in high places.' " [18]

It was after an August 1936 encounter with opposition to the plan, and Harold's ruminations on how to respond to such vocal critics, that he wrote:

[W]ith Brother Mark Austin of the General Committee, I had driven down to St. George and then back across the mountains to Richfield for an early morning meeting. At that time there was an upturn in business, so much so that some were questioning the wisdom of this kind of activity, and why hadn't the Church done it before now?

There came to me, in that early morning hour, a distinct impression that was as real as though someone had spoken audibly, and this was the impression that came and has stayed with me through these years: There is no individual in the Church who knows the real purpose for which the program then launched had been intended, but hardly before the Church has made sufficient preparation, that reason will be made manifest; and when it comes, it will challenge every resource of the Church to meet it.

I trembled at the feeling that came over me. Since that day that feeling has driven me on, night and day, hardly resting, knowing that this is God's will, this is his plan. The only thing necessary today is that the Latter-day Saints everywhere recognize these men who sit here on the stand as the fountainheads of truth, through whom God will reveal his will, that his Saints might be preserved through an evil day. [19]

By mid 1937 the welfare program was established and gaining momentum throughout the Church. Many "had recovered confidence in overcoming the desperation they had felt only months before. Thousands of Saints had risen from the valley of despair to the mountaintops of hope. Through thought, prayer, and experience, [Harold] had instigated a program that would convert dreams into reality. Much of his empathy and zeal to help the poor came from his own experience. In speaking to those who had known want, he said: 'I have loved you. I have come to know you intimately. Your problems, thank the Lord, have been my problems, because I know, as you know, what it means to walk when you have not the money to ride. I know what it means to go without meals to buy a book to go to the university. I thank God now for these experiences. I have loved you because of your devotion and faith. God bless you that you won't fail.' " [20]

To facilitate the welfare plan's various aspects of administration, in April 1937 a company was organized called the Cooperative Security Corporation, which handled the plan's legal and financial transactions. Later in 1937 the federal government passed the Social Security legislation. The Church, concerned that confusion might arise because of the similarities of the names, in April 1938 changed the name to the Church Welfare Plan.

Also at the April 1937 conference, "Presiding Bishop Sylvester Q. Cannon and his counselors were released and were replaced by LeGrand Richards and his counselors, Marvin O. Ashton and Joseph L. Wirthlin. Also, about this time, Henry D. Moyle was appointed as the chairman of the general Church welfare committee and Elder Melvin J. Ballard, John A. Widtsoe, and Albert E. Bowen of the Twelve were designated as advisors to the general committee."[21] These changes had a significant impact for good on the welfare plan, as well as on Harold's role as the plan's managing director.

It was also in 1937 that Harold was released from his calling as a stake president, presumably so he could more fully devote his energies to the welfare program.

With intermittent changes in personnel, this welfare organization provided the leadership for a literal explosion of projects and facilities during the ensuing years. By 1964, the Church welfare plan included hundreds of enterprises located throughout the United States. Among these were over five hundred farming projects that produced soybeans, peas, hay, beans, sugar beets, peanuts, pineapples, cotton, grapefruit, oranges, and other crops. There were also numerous canneries that handled and processed these crops, as well as ranches or farms that produced cattle, hogs, and sheep. Along with these projects, numerous storehouses were constructed, which warehoused and distributed the foods and other commodities the welfare plan produced. In the process, there were developed companion enterprises designed to provide job opportunities and to improve work skills. Early on, Deseret Industries was organized, whose purpose was to repair, renovate, recycle, and resell used furniture, clothing, and other commodities donated to the system. Toward this end, factories were established where these commodities were renovated or renewed. They were then marketed through Deseret Industries retail stores. This creative system provided gainful employment for numerous people, many of whom would otherwise have been unemployable because of advanced age or physical disabilities. There also grew up an employment arm of the welfare plan, whose object was to help train and place the unemployed or to upgrade the skills of those who sought to improve their status. Later as the plan evolved, it came to embody the concept of "provident living," which embraced every aspect of human life, whether physical, mental, emotional, or spiritual. All of this grew out of the initiatives that were begun during the depression of the 1930s and were based upon timeless principles enunciated and reinforced by prophetic inspiration.

Working under the direct supervision of the First Presidency, and later within the framework of the formal organization that came into being, Harold B. Lee was the key player in this extraordinary effort. It was he who, as the president of the Pioneer Stake, first demonstrated practically how the ageless principles of work, self-help, and cooperation could be applied on a large scale to help satisfy the economic wants of the people. It was he who, under assignment of the First Presidency, first designed the basic structure used to implement the goals of the Church security, later the Church welfare plan, and who formulated the basic job descriptions of the principal leaders. And it was he who, over the first formative years, provided the executive drive and acumen that overcame the initial inertia and opposition to the plan, established it on a firm foundation, and kept up the momentum as it continued to grow and strengthen. 22

In short, the various apostolic aspects of Harold's character and abilities, given premortally by the Lord and then molded under difficult but divinely directed tutelage in this life, had now become obvious to the leaders of the Church.

Before a churchwide welfare system existed the
enterprising Saints in the Pioneer Stake, led by
stake president Harold B. Lee, took care of its
members during the Great Depression (above).
(Below) Harold B. Lee with church leaders at the
Bishops' Storehouse created under his directorship

CA. early 1930s (above)
CA. 1940s (below)

Both photos courtesy of The Deseret News. Used with permission

8

A Life Forever Changed

"My goodness, dear, it's after ten!" Late in the evening as it was, Fern Tanner Lee was still at the sink, trying to keep up with the dishes that were being dirtied by the guests scattered through the home. "What has taken you so long to get home?"

"Oh, I'm sorry, Fern!" Harold's cousin, William Prince, was seated at the table with a half-eaten sandwich in his hand. "Harold asked me to tell you. After priesthood meeting he was asked to meet with Bishop Wirthlin." With a grin the man turned to look at Harold. "Sorry, old boy, but with all the ruckus around here, not to mention the great food, I forgot to tell her."

Harold, who had just stepped through the back door, returned the man's smile, though he felt sobered as well as exhausted. "Don't worry about it, Bill. Fern's used to me being late, and sometimes not coming home at all."

"That's the gospel truth," Fern chuckled. "A body would think that working for the Church would stabilize a man. All it's done for Harold is give him bags under his eyes and a sober disposition."

"Well, at least it hasn't made him gray!"

The speaker was William's wife, who had come into the room moments before. Harold, whose hair at forty-two contained not a speck of gray, also smiled at her, but he remained standing near the back door, uncertain of how he should proceed. As happened at every season of general conference, his home was brimming with guests who had traveled to Salt Lake City to attend the various sessions. This conference—April, 1941—was no exception. Not only were St. George residents William H. Prince and his entire family crowded into the Lee home, but Harold's first convert from Denver, Mabel Hickman, was also staying with them. At the moment it was the Prince children who were creating most of the din, though the adults were also having a hilariously good time.

Harold's youngest daughter, Helen, was also enjoying herself, bustling in and out of the kitchen with more food or empty plates, which she stacked beside the sink for her mother to wash. Maurine, his eldest daughter, was not in evidence, and Harold was just about to ask for her when the telephone rang.

With a quick dash, teenaged Helen grabbed the telephone and held it to her ear. Then, with a look of keen disappointment, she mouthed the words, "It's only Maurine," to her mother. All eyes were on her then as she nodded once or twice, giggled, but said nothing more than "Bye" as she hung up.

"Well?"

"Mar needs a ride home."

Fern sighed. "Very well. I'd better go now rather than put it off—"

"I'll go get her," Harold volunteered. "In fact, why don't the three of us go together?"

"But, Daddy—"

"Helen," Harold's voice was soft, though his eyes were flashing in a way that warned his daughter it was not the time to argue. She had seen that look before, and knew!

"Very well," she sighed, "but let's hurry, puh-lease! After all, we do have guests here!"

Moments later the three were in the car, Harold driving. "All right, Daddy," Helen said as Harold slowed for a corner, "why do all of us have to go get Mar?"

"That's right, dear," Fern added. "You obviously have something on your mind. Is this your way of getting us alone so you can tell us?"

Harold smiled. "Yes, dear, there is something I must tell you. This morning when I awakened, but before I arose, I received the definite impression that I would be named to the Quorum of the Twelve."

"Oh, Harold," Fern breathed, "are you sure?"

"The Twelve Apostles?" fifteen-year-old Helen asked incredulously, almost echoing her mother's question. "Oh, Daddy, what if it really happens?"

Fern, for her part, continued to look at her husband, her eyes filled with concern. She well knew that Harold received frequent impressions from the Spirit, and she knew just as well that those impressions had never failed to be correct. But, if this were the same—

"Daddy," Helen declared, obviously contemplating the impact such a calling would have on her father and their family, "Apostles don't ever get released, not until they die! That's a long time, for all of us!"

"That's very true, Helen; very true."

"Dear," Fern finally asked, still feeling anxious, "was the impression immediate?"

"I thought so," Harold replied quietly. "But then I sat through both sessions of conference today, and no one said a word. It was the same with the priesthood session this evening, leaving me to believe that I had misunderstood my early morning feelings."

"Go on," Fern requested when Harold paused, suddenly driving as though it was requiring all his concentration just to keep the vehicle on the road. "You were very late this evening, you know."

"Yes. As Bill told you, at the conclusion of the priesthood session President Clark, who was conducting, announced that

Bishop Wirthlin wished me to come to the stand for a moment to meet with him. I did so, we briefly discussed an issue pertaining to the welfare program, and then Joseph Anderson, who as you know is secretary to the First Presidency, came up and suggested that I step into the General Authorities room behind the pulpit. He also told me that President Grant was waiting there for me. Such a meeting is highly unusual, so of course I knew instantly that something was up—something more than a mere social visit."

Fern's eyes were suddenly filling with tears, which she tried desperately to hold back. "And...was your impression of this morning, correct?"

Harold stared straight ahead, his automobile now moving at little more than a crawl. "It was," he said bleakly. "I have been chosen to fill the vacancy in the Twelve caused by the death of Elder Reed Smoot."

"Oh, Harold—"

"Daddy, you're really going to be an apostle? Now?"

"It appears so, dearie."

"Wow! Wait until Mar hears about this!"

"What did you say?" Fern queried anxiously. "I mean, I'm certain you must have accepted, but how—"

Looking at his wife, Harold smiled. "I said, 'Oh, President Grant, do you really think I am worthy of such an exalted calling?'"

"And he replied?"

"Well," Harold responded softly, his voice trembling and filled with the weight of the burden he was suddenly carrying, "About all he said, was, 'If I didn't think so, my boy, you wouldn't be called.' And other than telling me I would be sustained in the morning, that was the end of our conversation."

And Fern Tanner Lee, knowing as well as her husband that in a brief moment he had been elevated to a place of almost unbelievable eminence in the Church, and knowing too that because of the call their lives had been changed forever, took his hand in hers and began, finally, to weep. 1

When Harold B. Lee awakened on the morning of April 5, 1941, he was forty-two years old and had been managing director of the Church welfare program for five years. "He had traveled about the Church many times. He had helped to organize the Church into welfare regions. He had stimulated, begged, pleaded, inspired, and wanted to scold at times, the leadership of stakes, some of whom [had] accepted the new program but many of whom were apathetic and skeptical and most of whom were slow to implement." 2

Now, as he lay in the early morning darkness pondering the work that lay ahead, and thinking too of what might be said in general conference that day to push the welfare plan forward, he was also thinking of certain conversations he had had with some of the General Authorities. They had been unsettling, and—

And that was when a powerful impression came upon him. "'Before I arose from my bed I received a definite impression that I would be named a member of the Quorum of the Twelve.'" 3

Harold had no way of knowing the sort of odds he faced in obtaining such a calling. Approximately three weeks before, President Grant had written that:

> ...we concluded...to wait for the return of Rudger Clawson, who is the President of the Apostles, before deciding on a man to fill the vacancy in the Quorum of the Twelve. It was quite remarkable the names that we had. I had asked the brethren for a first and second choice. There were ten of them and I am sure I had about twenty names. It is quite remarkable how many fine men there are in the estimation of the Brethren to fill the Quorum of the Twelve. 4

Three weeks later, however, the unanimous decision of the Brethren had been made, and so the Spirit of truth could speak to Harold's mind. On his way to conference that April morning, still

pondering his strange impression, Harold stopped in his office to
see if there were any matters of welfare business he needed to be
aware of. He then crossed the street and entered the Tabernacle on
Temple Square. There he sat through both morning and afternoon
sessions of conference without any of the authorities saying a word
to him about a future call. On Saturday evening he returned again
to the Tabernacle to attend the general priesthood meeting. Of
what happened there, he wrote:

> I was sitting in the audience attending the general
> priesthood meeting as the managing director of the
> Church Welfare Program. At the conclusion, President J.
> Reuben Clark, who was conducting the meeting, called my
> name out and asked that I come to the stand to meet
> Bishop Joseph L. Wirthlin. Bishop Wirthlin did have a
> matter of business to mention to me, but it was really a way
> to have me meet with President Heber J. Grant.
>
> When I arrived at the stand, Elder Joseph Anderson
> said that the President was waiting for me in the General
> Authorities' room. It amazed me, and I immediately
> sensed that there was something more than just a social
> visit that President Grant had in mind. It was then that he
> announced to me that I had been named to be elevated to
> the Quorum of the Twelve to fill the vacancy which had
> been created by the death of Senator Reed Smoot. [5]

According to L. Brent Goates, Harold B. Lee's son-in-law, Harold
"often retold to his family the conversation of that precise
moment. After learning of his appointment, he said: 'Oh,
President Grant, do you really think I am worthy of such an
exalted calling?' The plain-spoken President replied simply. 'If I
didn't think so, my boy, you wouldn't be called!'" [6]

Concerning his own feelings about that moment, President
Grant declared:

After the priesthood meeting (at general conference), I had a little talk with Harold B. Lee and told him we had decided that he should fill the vacancy in the Quorum of the Twelve Apostles. He was overwhelmed and shed tears. I feel sure that we shall be very happy with his work. 7

Harold returned home quite late, only to find his home "brimming with guests, a customary condition at conference time. Harold's cousin, William H. Prince, and his entire family were visiting from St. George. Also, Mabel Hickman, a long-time friend of the family, whom Elder Lee had been instrumental in converting in Denver twenty years before, was staying with the Lees." 8 Finding a typical festive mood in the home, with the usual noisy atmosphere that accompanies many guests, Harold wondered how he would find a quiet place to inform his wife and daughters of what had transpired. Helen remembers:

My father returned from priesthood meeting quite late, an hour or so after the time when the meeting would have concluded. Mother and I were busy with dinner preparations for the next day, endeavoring to make our company comfortable and happy. My sister had gone to visit a friend for the evening.

When Dad came home Mother explained to him that Maurine had called and that she needed someone to go and pick her up at her friend's house, and asked if he would do so. He agreed to go and then said: "Mother, you and Helen come with me." This seemed unusual for him to request that all three of us go to pick up my sister. It was late and Mother still had much work to do to prepare for the Sunday dinner, but because of his serious manner and insistent voice, we didn't question his desires further. We left what we were doing and went with him in the car.

As soon as we got into the car with him he said, "There

is something that I must tell you." Very quietly and obviously more subdued in manner than I ever remember my father being before, he explained to us that following the priesthood meeting, President Grant had detained him and in privacy had informed him that he was to be named the next morning as the new member of the Council of the Twelve. I was then fifteen years old and was fully capable of understanding the impact of this calling and what it would mean in his life, as well as in the life of our family. It was a very sobering but choice moment.

He then said, "Now, we'll go and pick up Maurine, and we'll tell her about it." As could be readily appreciated, with all the guests filling our home, he knew that this was the only place that he could share this momentous news with us without the possibility of interruption by others, and without arousing their curiosity. He then added: "When we return, you girls come up with us to our bedroom and we'll have our prayer together."

We did as he suggested, cherishing those sacred moments together. Of course, no explanations could be made to our house guests, so we tried to go on about our business as usual and make preparations for bed and for the following day. There was a message when we arrived home for Dad to phone President J. Reuben Clark, Jr., and after he made that phone call we had our prayer together. 9

Of course everyone in the Lee household, including Fern, who had been too ill to attend the previous two days of conference, attended the Sunday morning session. Harold, who had not slept at all the night before, did not look well, and several people remarked about it. As President Clark read the names of the General Authorities to be sustained, Mabel Hickman noticed that "Sister Lee leaned forward 'with both hands on the back of the

Harold B. Lee as a newly appointed apostle   CA. 1941

Courtesy of the Lee Family Collection

bench in front of us, and the knuckles of her hands were white with tension.'" 10

After his name was read out as the newest apostle, and after all the Twelve had been sustained, Harold was invited to take his place on the stand, "'at the foot of the ladder,' as he expressed it— 'a member of the Twelve.'" In the afternoon session he "was called to address the conference and enjoyed a remarkable peace that overcame all fright and fear that I had anticipated." 11

Harold had thus been "elevated to a place of eminence reached only by a select few. It placed him within a small circle of men who, under inspiration, chart the earthly destiny of The Church of Jesus Christ of Latter-day Saints. And, it put him in the chairs, so to speak, which in the normal course of events would lead him to the prophetic office President Grant then occupied. That, in turn, would invest him with vast authority as to people, property, and programs all around the world. Yet, with that would come correlative responsibilities of crushing weight as the master of all would become the servant of all. In this process, Elder Lee would discover a fine irony—that the modest living allowance provided for General Authorities...was less than the salaries earned by some Church staff personnel. This reality would serve to underscore the dominant spiritual aspects of the apostolic calling as compared to those of a temporal nature." 12

At that time Elder John A. Widtsoe wrote a tribute to Harold that proved to be prophetic. He declared:

> He is full of faith in the Lord; abundant in his love of his fellow men; loyal to the Church and State; self-forgetful in his devotion to the gospel; endowed with intelligence, energy, and initiative; and gifted with eloquent power to teach the word and will of God. The Lord to whom he goes for help will make him a mighty instrument in carrying forward the eternal plan of human salvation.... He will be

given strength beyond any yet known to him, as the prayers of the people ascend to the Lord in his behalf. 13

When he arose before the conference to speak for the first time, Harold said:

> Since nine o'clock last night I have lived an entire lifetime in retrospect and in prospect.... Throughout the night, as I thought of this most appalling and soul-stirring assignment, there kept coming to me the words of the Apostle Paul, "Let us therefore come boldly unto the throne of grace, that we may obtain mercy, and find grace to help in time of need."... Therefore I shall take the word of Apostle Paul. I shall come boldly unto the throne of grace and ask for mercy and his grace to help me in my time of need. With that help I cannot fail. Without it I cannot succeed. 14

That Sunday afternoon, April 6, 1941, was a time to be remembered. Newspapers sent photographers, flowers and telegrams poured into the Lee home, and dozens upon dozens of neighbors, friends, and family dropped by to express their delight in Harold's calling. He wrote:

> In the days to follow I was able to do little else than to receive telephone calls and letters of congratulations from many friends on my appointment as a member of the Council of the Twelve. It was pleasing that many of these were from those who were not members of the Church, with whom I had associated in politics or in business. 15

Several years before, President J. Reuben Clark had begun keeping a watchful eye on Harold, encouraging him, counseling him from time to time, and simply being his friend. That watchful friendship now intensified. On Tuesday, April 8, Harold recorded:

I went to lunch with President Clark, where he gave me careful and detailed explanation of the procedures on Thursday, where I was to be ordained an Apostle in the temple and accept a charge from the President of the Church as to my duties, obligations, and responsibilities as a member of the Quorum of the Twelve. 16

The next day, Wednesday, President Clark called Harold on the telephone, once again discussing the same issues so the new apostle would be prepared. Finally, on Thursday morning, Harold was escorted into the "upper room" of the Salt Lake Temple.

No picture or description of the room could have prepared him for the impact the experience would have upon him. The mystique that has built up around the room over the years because of frequent, veiled references made to it and to things that have taken place there, cannot fail to create a sense of wonder, or even awe, in one who enters it for the first time. Aside from this, the actual appearance of the room conveys a clear visual impression of its purpose, its historical significance, and the reason why it bears the name "council room." Arranged in a sweeping semicircle are twelve large easy chairs, facing the west side of the room, and so positioned that each member of the Twelve seated there can see all the others. Facing this semicircle is a desk, behind which, against the west wall, are positioned three other matching, upholstered chairs intended for the First Presidency. To the right and south of the First Presidency's desk and chairs, adjacent to the semicircle, stands a second desk for the use of the secretary. The only other pieces of furniture in the room are a third desk, standing against the south wall beyond the semicircle of chairs, which holds scriptures and reference books, a small bookcase in the southeast corner of the room, a movable altar used during prayer circles, a sacrament table with an upholstered stool for use by the one offering the kneeling sacramental prayer, and an organ with its

President Heber J. Grant (center)
with counselors J. Reuben Clark (left)
and David O. McKay (right)

CA. 1941

bench, used to accompany the singing, which stands in the northwest corner of the room. It would not be long before Elder Lee's skill at the organ would earn him the role of "official" organist for the meetings of the Council of the First Presidency and Quorum of the Twelve, a role in which he would serve for almost thirty years, and which he would relinquish to Spencer W. Kimball only after he became a member of the First Presidency. On the walls of this unusual room hang portraits of all the former presidents of the Church, as also a portrait of the martyr Hyrum Smith, and three paintings of the Savior depicting him calling his disciples at the Sea of Galilee, on the cross, and at the tomb standing before Mary after his resurrection. The heavy carpeting in this isolated room, which produces a quiet hush on it, and the furniture, arranged as explained, create an atmosphere conducive to careful and deliberate council by the apostolic brethren who direct the worldwide affairs of The Church of Jesus Christ of Latter-day Saints. The imposing presence of the portraits and paintings described conveys the impression that all the deceased modern prophets, as well as heaven, are looking down and listening in on the deliberations going on there." 17

Once all had been seated, Harold in the chair at the far northern end of the half-circle of his apostolic brethren, the bearded and beloved prophet, President Heber J. Grant, and his counselors, in slow, measured tones, delivered much the same apostolic charge as had been delivered by the Three Witnesses to the first apostles called in this dispensation. Afterward, "with quiet humility, [Harold] accepted the charge without qualification, and then shared things of a personal, sacred nature." 18

Once he had finished, one of the Brethren placed a chair in the center of the circle and invited Harold to come forward and be seated. The other members of the council and the First Presidency then surrounded him and placed their hands on his head. In the blessing that followed the ordination, President Grant said:

I say unto you, avoid the very appearance of evil, seek foremost and at all times for the advancement of the work of the Lord. Give your thoughts not to the ordinary things of life, but to things that are of great importance, and that are concerned with eternity.... We say unto you that above all other things, "obedience is better than sacrifice and to hearken, than the fat of rams." Humility is the key to the guidance of the Spirit of the Lord, and may that spirit of humility that you possess today, that spirit of humility when you had the impression that you might be called to be an Apostle, be ever with you, and the power and spirit of the priesthood of the apostleship shall be yours to withstand the temptations and allurements of life. [19]

Afterward, Harold wrote of the experience:

I attended my first meeting in the Salt Lake Temple with the First Presidency and the Council of the Twelve. I was ordained an Apostle and set apart as a member of the Council of the Twelve by President Heber J. Grant, with his counselors and the eleven members of the Council assisting. Before the ordination I was given a charge by each member of the Presidency in which they stressed important matters pertaining to activities of General Authorities. [20]

That evening a dinner in honor of Harold and Fern was held in the home of Elder Stephen L. Richards, which was attended by all the First Presidency, the Twelve, and their wives. Both officially and socially, Harold had "once and for all time" been placed "in a select circle of distinction from which he would never be removed, except by death or misconduct. Throughout the remainder of his days, he could look forward to returning...again and again, to counsel with his brethren, to report his activities, and to be renewed in his spirituality and in his resolve to serve with diligence and discipline until the end of his life. This continual, unending routine, laden with the diverse joys and traumas of the conflict between light and darkness, has been called the 'imperious mandate'.... [A]nother distinguished name had been added to the select list of special witnesses of the divinity and mission of the Savior, Jesus Christ, and...the newest apostle had been set on a path whose tortuous and testing course could lead him ultimately to the prophetic office." 21

Yes, much in the life of Harold B. Lee had changed, yet his lifestyle remained the same as it had been for years. Of a truth, he had long before given his life to the Lord, an indication of which was his decision to set aside a promising political career, as well as an ordered and easygoing family life, in order to accept the call of the Brethren to organize the welfare program. Yet what an appropriate training that call had been for the tremendous responsibility he had now assumed.

9

FAST-FOOTED FOLLOWER
OF PROMPTINGS

"Elder Lee, how would you like us to proceed?"

Newly ordained apostle Harold B. Lee glanced at his former bishop and counselor in the Pioneer Stake Presidency, Charles S. Hyde, and from him to Leo J. Muir, current president of the Northern States Mission. Actually, he himself had no real idea of how the three of them should proceed. All he knew was that the Spirit had impressed upon his mind the need for them to go to Lafayette, Indiana, where young Theodore M. Burton, a former member of the Pioneer Stake and the son of a dear friend, lay near death. Now that they were in Lafayette and approaching the hospital, however, all he was feeling was that they needed to hurry.

Praying for inspiration, Harold found his mind drifting back and focusing for a moment on the reorganization of the New York Stake, which he had been assigned to put into effect only a few days previous.

From the beginning he had been inclined toward calling as the new stake president the young bishop of the Manhattan Ward, Howard S. Bennion. The trouble was that a good many of the locally prominent leaders had raised questions about Bishop Bennion because of his relative youth. Their concerns had raised doubts in Harold's mind, and even by late evening he had been unable to come to a decision.

Early the next morning, however, as he had awakened, the Spirit of the Lord had rested upon him in a remarkable manner, and he had known without doubt that Bishop Bennion was to be the new stake president—this in spite of the objections that had been raised. A little later, as he had sat in a meeting with the man whose name had been most often mentioned by the local brethren as the "best choice" for the office, that man had made a sarcastic remark in a setting where no such remark ought to have been made. It was thereby reaffirmed to Harold, very conclusively, that not only was the man in question not to be the stake president, but that Bishop Bennion was to receive the call. And so it had been done.

But what did that have to do with now? he wondered as President Muir pulled the car into the hospital parking lot. Why had his mind been directed to that most recent experience? There must be some connection, of course, for the Lord never trifled with his thoughts. So, again he began praying—

Harold had been in the mission home on Sheridan Avenue in Chicago, trying to use wisely a forced layover on his return rail journey from New York to Salt Lake City, when President Muir had informed him of young Theodore Burton's extremely serious illness. Apparently the young man, who was in Lafayette working toward a Ph.D. from Purdue University, had undergone an appendectomy the previous June. A postoperative infection had caused his diaphragm to rupture and the infection to spread into his body cavity. Then had followed several operations that had unsuccessfully sought to locate the source of the infection. By mid-September and Harold's arrival in Chicago, Theodore had lost so much weight that he was practically skeletal, and the doctors had given up hope. Nevertheless, they had decided on a final surgical procedure, intending to remove some ribs so as to provide access to the chest cavity for a flushing procedure that might eliminate the infection. It was at that juncture, President Muir having heard within the hour from the young man's father back in Utah, that Harold had felt the impression to take the two men and hurry the ninety miles to Indiana to give him a blessing.

"About all I can tell you, brethren," he finally replied as they exited the car and started on a fast walk toward the hospital entrance, "is that I have the constant impression that we need to hurry."

"That doesn't surprise me." The older Charles S. Hyde, along with a surprised President Muir, was already struggling to keep up with Harold's rapid pace. "You've always been in a hurry, Elder Lee!"

Harold chuckled. "That's because I always feel behind, Charlie."

"Maybe." Charles glanced at President Muir. "The other thing I've noticed about our young and fast-footed friend, President, and this during years of serving with him, is that he goes so far using his mind to analyze situations and strive to come to decisions, and in that he is like most other good men. But then come these impromptu flashes of inspiration or revelation from the Lord, and in a heartbeat he is off on some totally and completely unexpected tangent—that other men would have missed altogether because they are not so in tune—and miraculous results always follow."

"Charlie—" Harold called back, obviously hearing the entire monologue.

"I'm not patronizing you, Elder Lee. Believe me, I'm not. I'm stating a fact that's as true as can be. President, when these flashes of inspiration hit him, he follows them without fear or hesitation. He did it when I was his bishop; he did it when he was my stake president and I his counselor; he did it as we worked together on the welfare plan; and now that he's an apostle he's probably doing it even more. People around the Church are starting to call him a seer, and this is why! He 'sees' things others don't."

"Thank you, Elder Lee." President Muir was surprised when Harold held open for him the hospital door. "I should have held it for you."

"Nonsense," Harold responded amiably. "You know what the scripture says. It's better—"

He paused, smiling at his two companions. He felt certain they were both thinking he was referring to the verse: "And whosoever will be chief among you, let him be your servant." But not feeling worthy to equate himself with any sort of greatness, the young apostle concluded instead: "It is better to be a door holder—"

At this all three men chuckled as they entered the hospital. "I just..." Abruptly, Harold's attention was riveted elsewhere. "Wait a minute, brethren! Say, there! Excuse me, Sister! Excuse me! Is that Theodore Burton you have on that gurney?"

Surprised, the Catholic nun Harold was calling to halted to look back at the three men hurrying down the hall toward her.

"Is that Theodore Burton?" Harold repeated as he drew closer.

"Why, yes, it is," she responded as Charles Hyde and President Muir gave each other knowing glances. "How did you know that? Who are you, anyway?"

"We're friends from his church," Harold replied kindly as his pace quickened. "Where are you taking him?"

"To the operating room," the nun answered, suddenly defensive, "where he is scheduled for immediate surgery."

Seconds later Harold stopped at the gurney, where he looked down into the emaciated, sallow face of young Theodore M. Burton. "Hello, Theodore. I'm Harold Lee, this is Charles Hyde, and this is Leo Muir. Charlie and I used to be your neighbors. Do you remember us?"

"I...I...do, Brother Lee. Did...my father send you?"

"In a manner of speaking, yes." Harold smiled tenderly. "Would you like us to give you a blessing?"

"I would...very much!"

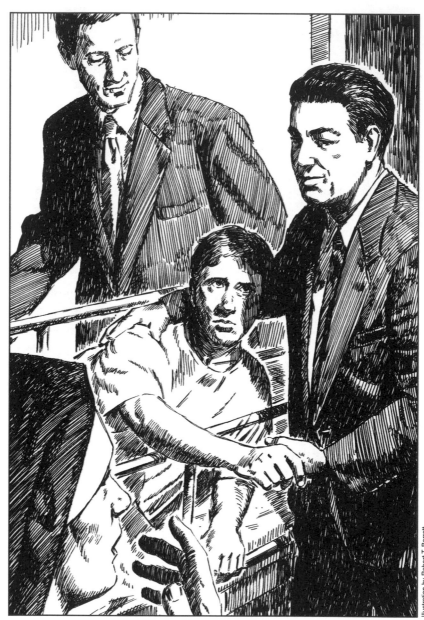

Harold's smile grew as he turned again to the nun. "Sister, we would like to perform one of our church's ordinances for Theodore before he goes into surgery. May we help you in returning him to his room?"

"But…the doctors are waiting—"

"This will only take three or four minutes." Again Harold smiled. "And it is very important in our faith that this ordinance be performed."

"Oh," the nun was nonplused but clearly unable to resist Harold's charm, "very well. But you must hurry, and no matter what you do, I will not leave his side!"

"That's just fine," Harold responded as he and his companions grabbed the gurney. "Why don't you lead the way, Sister, and we'll follow."

Moments later Harold was introducing himself, Charles Hyde, and Leo Muir to a surprised Minnie Burton, Theodore's young wife, who had remained in the room praying after her husband had been wheeled away to surgery.

"Very well, Charlie," Harold said once the nun had stepped back near Minnie Burton, "why don't you anoint, and then I'll seal it and pronounce the blessing."

Charles Hyde nodded, pulled a small vial of consecrated oil from his pocket, and proceeded to perform the ordinance. Harold then laid his hands on the young student's head, Charles and President Muir followed suit, and Harold sealed the anointing and then began the blessing.

"Brother Theodore," he declared, his voice low but filled with authority, "your work on earth is not yet finished. Therefore, we command you to get well. We command your spirit to take over the healing processes that must occur in your body, and say to you that you will now begin to recover. Through you we pronounce a blessing upon your doctors, those who are about to operate, and bless them that they will know what to do in order to restore you to health—"

The blessing continued until Harold no longer felt the whisperings of the Spirit giving him utterance, whereupon he closed the blessing in the name of the Lord Jesus Christ. As the three brethren then visited for a moment with young Theodore, Harold could not help overhearing a conversation ensuing between the Sister and Theodore's wife, Minnie.

"This wasn't right," the nun was saying, *sotto voce*.

"Why, what do you mean?" Minnie asked, surprised.

"I mean it wasn't right for you to invite those Mormon priests to come today and administer the last rites to your husband! I believe he might have lived until tomorrow, perhaps even until the day after. But now he knows he is going to die, and all hope is gone!"

"But you didn't understand," Minnie explained. "Their blessing was to give him life, not death."

For a moment the Sister eyed the young woman narrowly. "My dear," she finally observed, "it is well to have faith, but you must face up to reality. Your husband cannot live, and you will only hurt yourself further by keeping up an impossible hope."

With that she stepped to the gurney, and without another word or glance at Harold and the others, wheeled Theodore once again from the room. 1

One of the interesting aspects of being elevated to a position of public prominence is being required to deal with the numerous acquaintances—both new and former—who flock like moths to the flame. Like "filings to a magnet, many seek to connect themselves with a person in the public eye, whether to bask in reflected glory or merely to express support and congratulations. The phenomenon, while flattering to the one experiencing it, carries the deadly danger of attributing the public attention strictly to personal qualities rather than to the prominence of the new position. It was a danger of which Elder Lee was fully aware and with which he struggled with notable success throughout his ministry." 2

In fact, in the beginning of his ministry Harold felt terribly inadequate. His first assignment, two days after his ordination, required him to accompany Elder Charles A. Callis to a stake conference being held in the Riverside Stake, which was next door to the Pioneer Stake over which Harold had presided. Of his experience there, he said, "'I had extreme difficulty expressing myself.... Things I said seemed to lack spirit and enthusiasm.'" 3 In Vernal, Utah, a week later, his experience wasn't much different. "'Somewhat disappointed at my difficulty in gaining the freedom of speech necessary for a satisfying feeling.'" 4

These feelings continued for a month or so until, when he delivered the baccalaureate address at Brigham Young University on June 1, 1941, he experienced a sense of freedom in his speaking and felt satisfied that the Lord was pleased with his efforts. So, what had happened to bring about this change? Harold knew that his calling was to be first and foremost a special witness of the Lord Jesus Christ in all the earth. Since his youth he had held firmly to a continually growing testimony of Jesus Christ, the truthfulness of the restored gospel, and the prophetic calling of Joseph Smith and the other modern prophets. Suddenly, though, it seemed to him that it wasn't enough, not if he was to be a special witness of Christ in all the earth. A few days following his call to the apostleship he was asked to give a radio talk on Easter Sunday. This apparently provided the impetus for a soul-searching experience. Of it, he said:

> I locked myself in one of the rooms in the Church Office Building and took out the Bible. I read in the gospels, particularly the scriptures pertaining to the death, crucifixion, and resurrection of the Lord, and as I read, I suddenly became aware that something strange was happening. It wasn't a story I was reading, for it seemed as

though the events I was reading about were very real, as though I were actually living these experiences. On Sunday night I delivered my humble message and said, "And now, I, one of the least of the apostles here on earth today, bear you witness that I too know with all my soul that Jesus is the Savior of the world and he lived and died and was resurrected for us."

I knew because of a special kind of witness that had come to me the preceding week. Then someone asked, "How do you know? Have you seen?" I can say that more powerful than one's sight is the witness that comes by the power of the Holy Ghost bearing testimony to our spirits that Jesus is the Christ, the Savior of the world. To that, I bear testimony. 5

Very quickly Harold's position put upon him the responsibility of performing temple marriages, or sealings, an activity that would occupy an ever-increasing amount of his time. This happened not only because his youthfulness made him popular with the young people of the Church, who sought him out in ever-increasing numbers, but because he was so spiritually discerning, meaning that frequently things were said while under the impression of the Spirit that had a profound effect upon the hearers. His own opinion of his counsel given under such circumstances was that it "focused on mutual love and consideration, obedience to the commandments, and cleanliness of thought, word, and action in marital relations." 6

Nearly two weeks after his address at BYU, Harold was called into the office of President Clark. There it was made known that the First Presidency had approved the appointment of Marion G. Romney, one of the new Assistants to the Twelve, as assistant director of the welfare program. Harold was then asked to continue as managing director, supervising Elder Romney's labors.

Harold felt that this decision of the First Presidency was "'an excellent move.'" Until the day Harold B. Lee died, his bond of friendship with Marion G. Romney was among the most meaningful companionships men enjoy in mortality." 7

For the next several years, Harold's principle duty when he was not traveling but was at Church headquarters was administering the welfare program. "The far-flung and rapidly burgeoning welfare projects created vast and ever-changing problems of administration. It was big business with farms, ranches, fruit orchards, dairies, processing facilities, manufacturing plants, and distribution centers to oversee. The supervision of accounting practices and personnel policies, added to the ongoing process of recruiting and training local welfare leaders, were constant challenges." 8

In spite of the increasing load of welfare, Harold was gradually given additional responsibilities. These included:

> the chairmanship of the music, general priesthood, and servicemen's committees. In addition, he continued to serve as the managing director of the General Church Welfare Committee; as adviser to the general board of the Primary Association; and as a member of the publications, garment, and expenditures committees.
>
> He continued to enjoy music and often, when visiting wards and stakes, would surprise the members by offering to render his services on the piano or to act as organist. 9

Then, too, Harold found himself constantly involved in counseling and comforting members who came to his office; setting apart newly called missionaries; speaking at graduations, funerals, and sacrament meetings; performing marriages in the temple; giving priesthood blessings to the troubled, ill, and infirm; and serving on the boards of various Church-owned businesses. And on almost every weekend of the year, while others were enjoying their leisure after usually far less strenuous weeks, he was on assignment somewhere or other across the earth, conducting stake conferences, interviewing sometimes dozens of brethren and sisters, and making the required changes in their stake organizations.

All these things took their toll, so that, "like life itself, [he] soon found that service in the Twelve was a mix,...there were happy times, and there were sad times,...there were sweet and peaceful experiences, and there were stressful experiences.... Yet, for Elder Lee...there was a certain exhilaration in getting out into the field to mingle with the Saints, to teach them, and to bear testimony to them, which was renewing to mind, body, and spirit." [10]

Harold's first assignment out of Utah was to conduct a stake conference in northern Arizona. This was in August. He drove down because there was no rail service to the area, and serious car problems along the way required him to hail down a motorist who pushed him twenty-eight miles to the next town. When offered, the man refused compensation. The repairs were quickly made, and the assignment at the stake conference fulfilled. It took Harold until Tuesday night to drive back to Salt Lake City, traveling with Oscar A. Kirkham, a Scout executive who had been counseling in northern Arizona. As they visited back and forth, Harold was impressed with Brother Kirkham's numerous faith-promoting stories. In his journal, at the conclusion of the journey, he wrote that Brother Kirkham was a likely candidate to fill the vacancy in the First Council of the Seventy created by the death of Rulon H. Wells. A few weeks later, during the October general conference, Elder Kirkham was sustained to that very calling.

Two days after returning to Salt Lake City, Harold "experienced another conspicuous first when he was asked to lead the Council of the First Presidency and Quorum of the Twelve in their prayer at the altar in the upper room of the Salt Lake Temple. This was a ritual to which he attached great significance. He frequently attested to the spiritual power generated by these prayers, bringing solace, healing, and comfort to those remembered. Often through the years he would add names to the prayer list...confident that through the exercise of faith and the power of God, miracles could occur in the lives of men and women." 11

And miracles did occur! Constantly! The incident dramatized at the beginning of this chapter, for instance, occurred in September, 1942, hardly a year after Harold's ordination. What happened in Indiana is best told by Theodore M. Burton:

> Brother Hyde anointed me with consecrated oil. Then those three men placed their hands on my head, and Elder Lee, as mouth, sealed the anointing and gave me a blessing. I don't remember all he said, but one idea stays in my memory. He did not bless me to get well as the others had done. He commanded me to get well and said that my work on earth was not yet finished. He commanded my spirit to take over the healing process and, through me, blessed the doctors who were about to operate that they would know what to do to restore me to health. 12

Despite the Catholic Sister's dire predictions to Theodore's wife, Minnie, six weeks after Harold's blessing, Theodore was discharged from the hospital to return to his home and his studies. And not quite twenty years later, "the earthly mission for which Theodore M. Burton's life had been spared emerged when, on October 8, 1960, he was sustained as an Assistant to the Twelve." 13

As he experienced these things, or heard later from people who had experienced them under his ministerings and then wrote to thank or inform him, Harold began to keep a file which he labeled, simply, "Miracles." From it come the following:

> one young college coed wrote... "To have an apostle put his arms around you and cradle you like a little child and bless

you was like nothing I could imagine. I got a glimpse of Christlike love....

Sonya Watts Burnidge described the unforgettable vision she had at age 17 when she saw the Savior standing near to Elder Lee who as an apostle was speaking at a stake conference in Idaho. She wrote to Elder Lee, describing her experience, and received the following reply:

> Undoubtedly such as you saw was given to you because of your worthiness and preparation for it. If you will guard it sacredly and continue to live worthily, the Lord will continue to bless you with the inspiration of his Holy Spirit.

One man told how he had attended conference and "prayed that someone would tell me how to repent. As [Elder Lee] stood and addressed the audience, [he] stated, 'I won't give my prepared talk today because someone here wants to know how to repent.'"

Countless stories were related by grateful mothers who had sought a maternity blessing at Elder Lee's hands and were later able to bear children. Over a dozen [that he knew of] named their sons after him. 14

In another account, written by Paul E. Reimann:

> Since [16 January 1836 (*History of the Church*, 2:374)]...when a man has been ordained an Apostle, he is given all the keys of the holy priesthood, but those keys of authority to preside over the Church remain inchoate, or dormant, until and unless he becomes the senior Apostle. He does, however, as an Apostle, exercise immediately all the powers of a prophet.
>
> I was personally acquainted with President Harold B. Lee when he was president of the Pioneer Stake, and along with many others, I was very fond of him. In 1940 I was a

member of a group of young lawyers who wanted to have him nominated for the position of governor of Utah. He graciously declined and stated that he had dedicated his life to the service of the Lord. At that time I was convinced that someday he would become one of the Twelve Apostles. When he was called to be an Apostle, my wife, Maybeth, and I were very happy. At that time I believed that someday he would become President of the Church.

Elder Harold B. Lee was called to the apostleship on 6 April 1941. Not long thereafter, he telephoned me at my office and told me he wanted me to do some special research for him involving Church history. He asked me how long it would take me to do it. I estimated two weeks. He told me he had to have it in three days! When I said I did not believe I could possibly obtain that information for him within three days, he said to me, "Paul, if you will go into your inner office and close the door so you will be alone, and kneel down and ask the Lord to guide you, he will guide you and inspire you so that you will have that information for me in three days."

His statement reminded me of Naaman, the leper, who hesitated when he received the message from the prophet Elisha to dip himself in the Jordan River seven times.

I did exactly as Elder Lee had counseled me to do. After praying alone, as I arose from my knees, I felt the instant inspiration. Instead of proceeding as I ordinarily would do as a lawyer, I was inspired to go immediately to the Utah Historical Society. Arriving there, I was impressed to go to a volume that was not published by, or for, the Church. I walked to the very stack where the volume was located and took it out and found, within seconds, the information Elder Lee had requested. My steps could not have been in a more direct path if I had been given a detailed map on where to find this material.

In fulfillment of the promise of Elder Harold B. Lee, a prophet of God, I was able to write up that information and present it to him at his office within two days instead of three.

This experience has given me indisputable evidence that Elder Lee became a prophet when he was ordained an Apostle of the Lord. 15

On October 1, 1941, Harold received a call from Stake President Spencer W. Kimball of Safford, Arizona. A disastrous flood on the Gila River had caused wide-spread damage in his stake among members and nonmembers alike, and so he was calling Harold to discuss tentative plans for relief. Two weeks later Harold and Marion G. Romney arrived to do what they could to assist Stake President Kimball. He, meanwhile, had gone forward to assist his people, many of whom had been financially ruined by the flood.

This was the first major test of the welfare plan in a disaster situation. Therefore, the attention of the whole Church was riveted on the Gila Valley. Articles in the Church publications kept the Saints everywhere advised of what was going on there. Three main figures stood out in this glare of publicity: Elder Lee; ...Marion G. Romney; and the young, energetic stake president, Spencer W. Kimball.... [W]ithin two years, he would be called to the Twelve to take his place in the circle at the right hand of Elder Harold B. Lee. There for twenty-seven years this pair would sit, side by side, as they slowly moved up in apostolic seniority toward the prophetic office, which both were destined to fill. Their leadership styles present an interesting study in contrasts that stand out against the background of the Gila Valley flood.

On the one hand was Elder Lee, the consummate plan-

ner and delegator, whose genius was chiefly responsible
for the development of the Church welfare system. He had
the capacity to formulate plans of broad scope and to
marshall the energies and the talents of numerous people
to bring his vision to fruition. As he stood in Duncan, there
were at his command vast resources, developed in large
part through his skill, which could be called upon to alleviate the suffering of the Gila Valley Saints. On the other
hand was Brother Kimball, whose chief role in this disaster
was to lift the morale of the people and to set them to
work, fighting off the flood and repairing the damage once
the wasting waters had subsided.... [Q]uietly, persistently,
and deliberately over the years, Elder Lee would put in
place an intricate system of correlation and coordination
in the Church whose impact and importance would survive
him and would influence the direction of the Church for
decades. He would also revamp the headquarters machinery
of the Church to introduce more modern methods of
preparing and distributing instructional and other materials
and of facilitating public communications. If Harold B.
Lee was more adept at designing and building an intricate
vehicle, with all the planning, delegation, and follow-through
that entailed, Spencer W. Kimball could demonstrate
novel and daring ways to drive it. 16

The evening of his return from visiting the flood-ravaged area of
Duncan, Arizona, Harold received a call from President Don B.
Colton of the Salt Lake Mission Home asking that he come to the
temple the next morning and speak to the newly called missionaries
concerning the temple endowment. He accepted the assignment,
called President McKay about how he might proceed, and then
spent most of the night in preparation. The next evening he
recorded, "Enjoyed greatly my study and discussion with the

missionaries in the temple on the significance of the temple endowment. It seems my presentation had the approval of the temple presidency and President Colton." 17

This presentation became another part of Harold's ministry as he thereafter met weekly in the upper assembly hall of the temple with new missionaries, helping them to prepare spiritually for their service.

Speaking again of prophetic gifts, while in Arizona, Harold had uttered before the assembled Saints a remarkable prophecy, promising them that "if they would work together and apply the principles of the welfare plan, out of their crisis would come great missionary success with the nonmembers of the Church in that area, and their own prosperity would increase beyond what they had known before the flood." 18

The following year, as Harold was driving through the area with President Clark, they went to Duncan, Arizona, where the Saints had been so devastated. In his journal, Harold recorded:

> They recalled our meeting with them when I promised them that as a result of the flood they would gain more than they lost. It was reported by Brother Payne, the work director, that with the exception of three, all the others were already better off than they were before the flood— also they had been counseled to stay with their farms instead of going to the mines and all had stayed but one, and he had returned after one month. 19

Concerning a stake conference in Mancos, Colorado, Harold declared:

> At this conference I received a rather remarkable demonstration of the power of prophecy in the ordination and setting apart of Elmer Alphonso Taylor, former second counselor in the stake presidency, as the new bishop of the

Farmington Ward. He received a blessing that his crippled foot and leg would not hinder his work as bishop and that because of his humility in accepting this new appointment he would be given such influence with his family that not one would go astray, and all would marry in the temple and all would be a credit to any community in which they lived. He had a family of six girls. A remarkable spirit was in the meetings, many people being in tears as they sang the closing song and bid us good-bye. 20

It took seventeen years and a great deal of heartache for this prophecy to reach its literal fulfillment. Five of the Taylor daughters married in the temple when they matured; sadly, one did not. But within seventeen years this daughter had divorced and married again—the second time in the temple.

This spirit of prophecy, as well as other spiritual gifts and manifestations such as the halo or aura of light about his head that was seen by many, rested upon Harold with ever greater frequency as he grew in years and in the power of the Spirit.

Shortly after his apostolic call, because so many of the younger members of the Church were involved in World War II, he was given the unique assignment of preparing a series of Sunday evening radio talks that were to be called "Youth and the Church." This series, which was broadcast over the CBS radio network, lasted several months and gave him a unique opportunity to involve his wife and daughters in one of his apostolic duties. His daughter Helen explains:

> My sister and I were then in our late teens, so Father was very much interested in our reactions [to what he intended to say]. He was very much aware of the kind of problems we were facing at that particular time in the history of the world, and we regularly discussed the things that he was going to talk about. He always had three talks that he was

working on. He was putting the finishing touches on the one that he was to give the coming Sunday, then one for the following week that would be in a rough draft form, and then a third one that he had just begun outlining. He would bring scripts home that he was working on, read them to us, and we would discuss them at the dinner table in a free exchange of ideas. We'd say, 'Oh no, Dad, you can't say that. It just isn't like that,' or else 'You'll have to say that differently.' Then we would all go with him each Sunday evening to the Tabernacle where he gave these talks. Such experiences drew us closely together. 21

At the conclusion of his first talk, entitled "True Patriotism—an Expression of Faith," the phone rang almost instantly in the broadcast booth. "It was President Clark calling from his home to congratulate Elder Lee on the content and delivery of his message."22 Later these talks were published in book form, first under the title *Youth and the Church*, and some time afterward expanded as *Decisions for Successful Living*.

By April, 1942, World War II was making life more and more difficult for people throughout the world. Besides ravaging both Europe and the South Pacific, following Pearl Harbor there were sporadic attacks on the west coast of the United States. The conflict also had a heavy impact upon the Latter-day Saints, altering plans, imposing burdens, and creating anxieties. For some, its impact was devastating. "'Talked with President J. Reuben Clark,' Elder Lee wrote on December 10 [1941], 'and he just advised me they had heard definitely that their son-in-law, Mervyn Bennion, had lost his life at Pearl Harbor.'" 23

But there were other impacts that were equally severe. When it is remembered that in January of 1942 the last group of missionaries before the end of the war was sent out, Harold and thousands of other Latter-day Saints were required to register for the draft, and even in Salt Lake City streetlights were turned off at night and windows shrouded, it is not surprising that the June 1942 conference had to be canceled entirely and the April conference scaled down to just members of stake presidencies. The Church, along with almost all the western world, seemed to be in full retreat.

Because of the decreased attendance, and no doubt acting under the spirit of inspiration, the First Presidency determined to hold the Sunday morning session of conference in the fourth-floor assembly room of the Salt Lake Temple. The meeting turned out to be remarkable in many ways. Harold recorded his feelings about it by writing:

> Today in the upper room of the Salt Lake Temple was held one of the most spiritual meetings of this generation and certainly the most impressive meeting I have ever attended. The meeting commenced at 10:00 A.M. and ended at 4:30 P.M. The first part was the regular Tabernacle broadcast of the "Church of the Air" address by Stephen L Richards and radio addresses by President David O. McKay and Elder A. E. Bowen. At 12:30 P.M. the sacrament was administered to all those present by the Twelve Apostles. Many of the brethren wept as the sacrament was passed to them by the Twelve. Our joy was supreme in thus serving this people. In the next four hours, forty-five of the brethren bore testimonies, and in that time there was hardly a moment when tears were not in the eyes of the listeners. Testimonies of miraculous healing, raising the dead, divine guidance, power of cleanliness, and rewards for keeping the commandments of God were borne. President McKay testified that many of our loved ones were present in the meeting. 24

One other unusual aspect of this powerful 1942 temple gathering of the priesthood was that it seemed, from that day, that the tides of war began to shift in favor of the United States and the rest of the Allied Forces. While Harold's above account does not specifically mention the war, he was no doubt aware that the Lord had declared that those being called to his order of the priesthood "should have power…[t]o put at defiance the armies of nations… [and] subdue principalities and powers" (JST, Genesis 14:30–31). Extrapolating from that to two different congregations, Harold taught:

> There are two things that, when fully applied, would save the world. The first is to put the full might of the priesthood of the Kingdom of God to work, and the second is the powerful teachings of the gospel of Jesus Christ. 25
>
> We talk of security in this day, and yet we fail to understand that…we have standing the holy temple wherein we may find the symbols by which power might be generated that will save this nation from destruction. Therein may be found the fulness of the blessings of the priesthood. 26

By 1945 the shift that had begun following that remarkable session of the April 1942 conference had resulted in victory for the Allies and relative peace being restored to the earth. And thus the Lord's work was enabled once again to go forward.

In the meantime, unfortunately, there were other kinds of trials that had to be endured. In November 1943, Harold was called upon to help make one of the most difficult decisions of his life — a decision that "deeply shocked and saddened many, particularly the First Presidency and the Quorum of the Twelve. Following a Church court that the Twelve held in the temple, Richard R. Lyman, one of their number [and the man who had set Harold apart as a high councilor], was excommunicated from the Church for violation of the Christian law of chastity. Elder Lee recorded, 'It was a most saddening experience, with most of the Twelve in tears as Brother Lyman was asked to leave the meeting and shook hands with each brother in parting those sacred premises and that choice companionship for the last time.'

"The members of the Quorum of the Twelve slowly shuffled out of their council room, still dazed and bearing the deep hurt of the first excommunication of an Apostle in thirty-eight years.... It was not until the following general conference in April of 1944 that the vacancy was filled with the call of Mark E. Petersen." 27

Despite these apostolic activities and difficulties, Harold remained very much a family man, with family responsibilities. In that aspect his strenuous weeks and long conference weekends, as well as the almost constant travel by rail and automobile, were very difficult for him. Truly his heart was never far from his wife and daughters—now students at the University of Utah. He often told them that the longest days of his life were the ones immediately preceding his return home from his far-flung travels on the Lord's errands.

Except for having a husband and father who was a member of the Twelve, the Lees were quite normal and looked forward to the rare occasions when they could do normal things. For instance, they gathered together one evening and celebrated the paying off of the mortgage on their home by burning the document. Harold then consecrated and dedicated the home to the end that the Holy Ghost might always be there.

Most Christmas seasons were celebrated as a family, and Harold always reserved New Year's Day for special celebrating— for this was his mother's birthday, and he knew relatives would be calling. For many years the Lee home was the focal point of that celebration.

Because Harold did not involve himself in recreation as such, his recreation became his gardening and yard work, in which he was a "do-it-yourselfer." He acquired his skills growing up on the farm where it was impossible to pick up the phone and hire a specialist for repairs. In fact, he actually preferred to do such work himself, and his gardening provided the one outlet he enjoyed from the constant demands of his calling. For instance, he "describes his labors over the Memorial Day holiday in 1942:

> This being declared a holiday I arose early and spent until the early afternoon gardening around the yard and cutting the lawns and trimming up the trees. The rains have made things very pleasant and the warm weather seems to induce a fine growth of shrubs. I did some studying and preparing for my conference tomorrow and rested, although I fancy my family were somewhat chagrined that I did not pay more heed to the celebration of the holiday. In the evening we drove to the cemetery and visited with my mother and sister Verda. 28

There were also more difficult family issues, such as in 1945, when Fern "showed signs of a heart strain that caused rapid beating, exciting an extreme nervousness. Because Sister Lee's health was always fragile at best, [Harold] often assisted his daughters with the housework. Many are the diary entries in early 1945, for example, that reflect his evening activities at home: 'Spent the evening helping Fern with her house cleaning;...the girls and I went through the house and cleaned the living room rug and readjusted the furniture.'" 29

After the passing of Elders Rudger Clawson and Sylvester Q. Cannon in 1943, Harold returned from a tour of the Northwestern States Mission to find an invitation for him to visit privately with President Grant. At the President's home they spent a delightful hour together, discussing the two men who had been nominated to fill the vacancies—Spencer W. Kimball and Ezra Taft Benson, whom Harold had first met at the Oneida Academy when they were only boys.

At the hour's conclusion, as Harold rose to depart, an extremely tender scene ensued—one that seemed to set the tone for the remainder of his life. In Harold's words:

> When I started to leave, President Grant pulled me down
> and kissed me and commended me for the "wonderful
> work" he said I was doing. I told him that there was
> nothing more I desired than to please him and my
> Heavenly Father. [30]

ON THE LORD'S ERRAND

"What do you think, Harold?"

"Yes, Elder Lee, what do you think? There is no doubt that you can win. In fact, we are persuaded that you have a better chance than any other man in the state."

For a moment Harold's eyes remained on the floor, his mind racing as he evaluated the remarkable proposal he had just been made. Behind his desk, David O. McKay, second counselor in the First Presidency, sat silently, his eyes on the junior apostle while a slight smile creased his pleasant face.

Following the weekly report meeting with the other General Authorities, Harold had been on the fifth floor of the Church Administration Building having his photograph taken when one of President McKay's staff had handed him a message marked urgent, requesting that he report immediately to the Office of the First Presidency. Uncertain about what might be wrong, but fearing the worst, Harold had arrived to find in President McKay's office a delegation of four men, headed by W. W. Seegmiller, who were insisting that he file his candidacy for U.S. senator in preparation for the coming election.

These four were not the first to approach him concerning a possible political campaign. For the past several weeks there had been an almost continuous stream of visitors to his office in the Church Administration Building, inquiring, enticing, cajoling, even pleading. But these men, having first approached President McKay, were certainly the most official delegation he had encountered.

Harold knew President McKay would not tell him what to do—not with President George Albert Smith in Mexico. He also knew from previous discussions that both Presidents Clark and McKay felt inclined that he should accept the proposal. That being the case, what was he to do?

This wasn't the first time since becoming a member of the Twelve three years before that he had been asked to return to politics. Ever since he had won his city commissioner seat so handily back in the '30s, influential people had been talking about his possible candidacy for governor of Utah or else the United States Senate. Back in 1944, in fact, President Clark had informed him that leaders of the Republican Party in Utah wanted him to head their ticket and would give him the choice of which office he would prefer running for. When they had asked the First Presidency for their approval before approaching Harold directly, President Clark had come to Harold, asking what he wished to do.

"President Clark," Harold had responded at that time, "the only terms under which I would even consider such a matter would be if the First Presidency were to call me on a mission to become a candidate."

"Are you certain, Harold?"

"Absolutely!"

President Clark had smiled. "Then perhaps now is not the time. As a presidency we feel the need for your services in the Twelve and with the welfare program. Besides," he had continued with a wink, "there is no certainty you could be elected, with the strong New Deal sentiment extant here in Utah—"

That was then, however, and this was now—May 29, 1946. The political climate had shifted considerably during the past two years, and a person such as Harold, with his conservative leanings, would almost certainly take the Utah election for the United States Senate. Everyone seemed to know that. And being a U.S. senator would give a man some remarkable experiences, Harold knew, not to mention political clout—

"It has a nice ring to it, don't you think?" It was almost as though W. W. Seegmiller had been reading his mind. "Senator Harold B. Lee. I know I like the sound of it!"

"Harold," J. Bracken Lee, a nonmember who was no relation to Harold and who was currently serving as mayor of Price, Utah, added, "we know that you have George D. Keyser's support , and we are here to inform you that Bishop Hunt of the Catholic Church has now offered his wholehearted support of your candidacy. In fact, you are the only candidate in which he places unlimited confidence and for whom he will actively campaign."

"He is very kind," Harold responded, his mind racing. He knew Bishop Hunt, all right—knew him as a good friend. During his years as a city commissioner, Harold had made it Sunday morning policy to clear fresh snow first from streets around area churches and even to help clear their parking lots if his men got there in time. Of course, as a stake president he had seen such a need for the LDS buildings in the Pioneer Stake, and it had been a simple matter to institute a snow-removal policy covering all churches, Mormon and non-Mormon alike. Bishop Hunt was one who had been particularly grateful, and in the years since, he and Harold had enjoyed many pleasant conversations. No doubt, he would indeed support Harold in such a race.

As for George Keyser, another non-Mormon who was a prominent Mason in the city, it was more of the same. A fine friendship had developed between them, too, during Harold's days as city commissioner, and it continued. What Brack Lee, W. W. Seegmiller, A. V. Watkins, and Harry Clarke didn't know, however, was that George was one of the many who had already come to see Harold—

in private. There, he had offered his support should Harold run. But he had also offered Harold advice "as a dear friend." That advice? To stay out of politics and to put all his energies into the calling which had his heart and soul—that of an apostle and special witness of the Lord Jesus Christ!

Harold almost smiled with the remembered joy of hearing George Keyser urging him to remain committed to the Lord. It was incomprehensible to him how such good men had rallied to the support of his beliefs through the years, even when they themselves were not so theologically persuaded.

"Elder Lee," A. V. Watkins, Republican leader for Utah County, spoke up, "we need a man of known and unimpeachable integrity to run against Abe Murdock, who as you know is extremely vulnerable in that area. None of us can think of anyone who is better qualified than you."

"He's right, Harold." This was Harry Clarke, another of Harold's trusted friends. "But solid integrity isn't the only issue that makes you so attractive to us. You have demonstrated time and again your remarkable skills in leadership and organization; your conservative thinking is as purely refined as the gold in Fort Knox; and you have the rare ability to see to the heart of every issue presented before you—"

"More importantly," W. W. Seegmiller interrupted enthusiastically, "you actually care about your constituents, Harold, each and every one of them. Their welfare rather than your own is your top priority, and there's hardly a person in this state who doesn't know it."

"In other words, Harold," J. Bracken Lee concluded, "we want you as our candidate not because you can win, which we believe you can, but because every one of us would breathe easier and sleep better at night knowing it was you rather than Abe Murdock who was representing us in the Senate."

Harold smiled, thinking of how quickly such compliments might go to a man's head. Again he glanced at President McKay, who was idly tapping his pencil eraser on his desktop, the slight smile still on his face. What was this great servant of the Lord thinking, Harold wondered? Was he smiling because he believed that Harold would accept? Or was he smiling because he believed Harold would not, and would therefore prove himself a dolt. Of course Harold couldn't tell. All he knew with certainty was that neither of the counselors in the First Presidency could—or would—make a final decision regarding his candidacy without hearing President Smith's opinion. And President Smith could not be reached before the filing deadline! Therefore, this issue was now up to him and him alone—

"Gentlemen," he said as he looked from one to another of the four men, "you, and everyone else who is supporting you in this proposal, have done me a great and unbelievable honor. I cannot thank you enough, and I feel humbled more than at almost any other time in my life. But as it stands today, I cannot accept."

"Harold—"

"Hear me out, please." Harold looked intently into the eyes of each of the men. "You spoke moments ago of my integrity and other supposed gifts or qualities. If any of that is true, then because of personal covenants I made both recently and long ago, my life is wholly and completely in the hands of my Lord Jesus Christ and the First Presidency of my Church, whom I firmly believe represent him. If these three men unitedly tell me to run, then I will do it. Otherwise, I am not interested, for with every fiber of my being I have covenanted to wear out my life in apostolic service, at their direction, among the Saints."

"President McKay?" W. W. Seegmiller pleaded.

"Without the affirmation of Presidents Smith and Clark," President McKay intoned solemnly, his smile finally gone, "I cannot give Elder Lee such formal direction."

"But President Clark is available, and he agrees with us! Surely two out of three—"

"If either of us were the President of the Church," David O. McKay interrupted, now smiling again, "then I'm certain two out of three would be good enough for Elder Lee. But because we are not, we have no authority to speak as a quorum and cannot give Elder Lee the counsel and direction he quite appropriately seeks."

"And there is no way you can make contact with President Smith?"

Somehow President McKay made his smile appear sad. "Not before next week. I wish I could, but he is completely *incommunicado*."

Harry Clarke looked pleadingly at his friend. "So your answer, Harold, is final?"

"It must be, Harry. Otherwise, none of the qualities you have praised me for can be true."

"Very well!" W. W. Seegmiller now rose to his feet. "You know this means your political career is over?"

"I do."

J. Bracken Lee chuckled as he abruptly stood, leading the other two to do likewise. "Well, Harold, I don't know if that's so or not. Never's a very long time. Neither am I certain that all of your goodness must hang on just one decision. To me, that seems harsh. What I am certain of is that no matter what you might have decided today, you'll never find me doubting you or your word. I tell you, Harold, as disappointed as I am in your decision, it's a real pleasure to know a man whose integrity isn't blinded by his ambition!"

With that, he and the others shook hands with Harold and a still-smiling President McKay and departed. As it turned out, W. W. Seegmiller had been right about one thing. Harold was never again approached with secret enticements to include national politics in his apostolic mission. 1

It would seem natural to assume that a call to the holy apostleship would mean the man thus called had learned the necessary lessons, passed the prerequisite tests, and would be sufficiently ready to serve the Lord without much further refinement. If that has ever been the case, it certainly wasn't so with Harold B. Lee. From the first day of his call his refinement continued in a variety of difficult ways, and it was apparent to many that the Lord was preparing him for much more. Today we know that "much more" was to become the Lord's Anointed—prophet, seer, revelator, and President of The Church of Jesus Christ of Latter-day Saints. With that in mind, his training as an apostle presents an interesting study.

At least part of the difficulty Harold faced was his relative youth. As junior apostle he was at least twenty years younger than the man seated next to him. And though he would remain the junior member of the quorum for only a short time, he still encountered some interesting difficulties that included what he perceived as an apparent lack of respect.

For instance, not long after his call, Harold had the following experience in front of the Twelve and the First Presidency:

I attempted to make a somewhat detailed report of my three-week visit to the Texas-Louisiana Mission, but was stopped by President Grant, who said if everyone were to take as much time we would be here two days. President Clark and President McKay and Stephen L Richards all expressed regret that I had not been allowed to complete what to them had been a very proper and desired report. I was greatly humiliated. 2

Because of his relative youth, Harold was also given some of the more strenuous and difficult assignments. Mission tours, for instance, required tight schedules, extensive travel, irregular and oftentimes inadequate meals, and constant changes in sleeping accommodations. Harold did many mission tours. Each stop meant not only public meetings—held with missionaries, members, and non-members alike—but also private interviews conducted with each missionary. Additionally, there were priesthood blessings to confer on the many who requested them, local leaders to counsel in their responsibilities, and media and government representatives to deal with.

Stake conferences, of which Harold averaged about three a month, required him to travel just as much as did mission tours, with the same constant inconveniences. The fixed meetings he was required to attend at such conferences "included welfare, priesthood leadership, and general sessions held over Saturday and Sunday, interspersed occasionally with special missionary and youth sessions. Aside from these meetings, he was usually heavily involved in between them, counseling with leaders and members, giving priesthood blessings, interviewing prospective missionaries, and setting apart officers. Because in the early days of his ministry, only members of the Twelve could ordain or set apart stake presidencies, bishoprics, high councilors, and patriarchs, it often happened that brethren from adjoining stakes would travel to the place where the conference was being held so Elder Lee could do it. This meant that from the time he arrived in a stake, usually about noon on Saturday, until he left Sunday night or Monday morning, he was on duty practically all the time with little opportunity to rest or to eat. When he did eat, it was usually a sumptuous meal that the sisters had lovingly prepared to fete him, which ordinarily included their most delectable and caloric dishes. Thus occupied and stuffed, sitting down during most of two days, it is little wonder that early in his ministry Elder Lee developed stomach problems. These would stress him intermittently throughout the remainder of his life and would even contribute to his comparatively early death at age seventy-four." 3

An assignment to visit the Hawaiian Islands immediately prior to the end of World War II provides yet another example of the difficulties he regularly faced. Because Harold was to be the first General Authority to visit the islands since the Japanese attack on Pearl Harbor, and because submarine warfare by the Japanese was still a threat, Harold began his assignment by receiving a blessing from his sixty-eight-year-old, ailing father before traveling by train to San Francisco.

> What might seem like a luxurious vacation to us today was in fact an arduous one-week journey by sea in an ancient steam freighter filled with a cargo of milk cows, trucks, tractors, and produce. In addition to the cargo there were twenty-four passengers, comprising as motley an assembly of human beings as the mind could conceive. The accommodations were anything but comfortable, Elder Lee's cabin consisting of a 10 x 12-foot space he shared with five others. Each had a cot and a small wooden locker. Boxes served as chairs when they could be found, and the toilets and washroom were on the upper deck.
>
> The old freighter *Maunawili*, built in 1921, lumbered out of the San Francisco harbor at eleven o'clock in the morning on July 6, 1945. Engine trouble developed at about fifty miles out to sea, and the ship limped back to port..., thus wasting the entire day. After a two-day delay for repairs, the ship finally cleared the bay at 9:00 P.M. in a heavy fog, requiring the captain to sound the horn every few minutes as a safety precaution. Not surprisingly, Elder Lee recorded in his journal, "I had some peculiar feelings at the thought of the trip away from the Mainland for the first time in my life." 4

On Sunday an impromptu worship service was held on the ship, which was attended by nine of the passengers. Harold wrote:

" 'Seldom could one meet a less religious group than those who are on this ship. With vulgarity, profanity, and gambling, they, by every breath they draw, seem to defy the principles of truth, and it seems as though we are casting pearls before swine.' " 5

For several days after his arrival in Hawaii, Harold traveled about the islands with President Ralph E. Wolley and President Wolley's son-in-law, visiting historical sites, giving blessings, and conducting meetings. One particular occasion stood out—a meeting at the leper colony at Kalaupapa—which was attended by twenty-nine of the fifty-two members enrolled there. In his journal, Harold wrote:

All of them were in pitiable condition with eyes blinded, fingers eaten away, face and arms and legs mutilated. Yet they are carrying on faithfully every phase of the Church, including priesthood work, Sunday School, M.I.A., Relief Society, ward teaching, genealogical, and missionary work. The branch president made a brief report of their work, and Brother Kailemai, a counselor and chairman of the Genealogical Committee, bore testimony and in behalf of the Saints there expressed appreciation for our visit to them.

When they sang to us, "Come, come ye Saints, no toil nor labor fear," and bore their testimony of what the Church meant to them, one of them turned to us, representing the visitors and the authorities and said: "If we had to choose between having the leprosy and being here with the gospel of Jesus Christ, or being well and whole, off the island, without the gospel of Jesus Christ, we would choose to be here as lepers so we could enjoy the blessings of The Church of Jesus Christ of Latter-day Saints."

I then spoke to them briefly and extended the love of the presiding Brethren, and as an Apostle of the Lord I

Harold B. Lee in Hawaii

CA. 1945

blessed them that they might remain true and faithful; and we closed with singing, "We Thank Thee, O God, for a Prophet." The four girls in the colony under twenty years of age arrived just at that point from a picnic excursion to the north of the island. Their faces looked old and terribly disfigured. 6

Despite such difficulties and even dangers, and despite the fact that he was frequently required to be away from his family for extended periods of time, the above experience indicates the faith and joy Harold found in "counseling with the young missionaries, mingling with the Saints, visiting new places, and feeling the thrill of the Holy Spirit working through him." 7

As his ministry began, Harold was constantly being reminded that he was an apostle of the Lord Jesus Christ, and having been called to the ministry for the balance of his life, was therefore responsible, first and foremost, to minister. It was vital, therefore, in Harold's thinking, that he honor the presiding stewardships of the First Presidency and the President of his quorum, and he made it his goal to never give any of them cause for concern. As an example, though it is uncertain how many times before 1946 that Harold was approached concerning running for political office, his answer remained the same. "I told [President Clark] that the only terms on which I would even consider such a matter would be that the First Presidency were to call me on a mission to permit myself to become a candidate." 8 And two years later: "I told them [the draft committee headed by W. W. Seegmiller] that I would not run unless the First Presidency told me to do it." 9

Had there been any doubts regarding Harold's commitment to his apostolic mission, no matter the personal cost, these episodes silenced them forever. Throughout his lifetime of service, evidence would pile upon evidence until all who knew him, and a vast number who didn't, would acknowledge that he had indeed been raised up by the Lord to represent him upon the earth.

Nevertheless, Harold was not a "yes man," and he was not afraid to speak his own mind, even when that differed from the opinions of others of his brethren. As an example, since the days of Brigham Young, General Authorities seem to have been of two minds regarding an issue some have called spiritual transparency or spiritual integrity 10 — the question of whether to hide up in one's heart, or to share with others by way of joyful testimony, spiritual or faith-promoting experiences. Harold had strong feelings regarding this issue, which he expressed in a quarterly meeting with the First Presidency and the Twelve in the Salt Lake Temple on April 5, 1944. These feelings were "summarized in his diary when he expressed the hope that 'we would never discourage the relating of faith promoting experiences in testimony bearing.' This was prompted by comments he had heard expressing the contrary view. It was difficult for Elder Lee to understand this attitude, given the aim of the Latter-day Saints to be led constantly by the whisperings of the Spirit. This was a reality for him. Seldom did a day pass but that he received spiritual direction from the Lord. It was his lifeblood. And the thought that he should not mention these faith-promoting experiences in bearing testimony was incomprehensible. Therefore, whenever the circumstances were appropriate, Elder Lee never failed to share spiritual direction or insight he had received. In doing so, he bolstered the faith of many who, seeing how the Lord had revealed to him, were anxious to receive similar spiritual direction. In this practice, Elder Lee emulated the Prophet Joseph Smith, whose repeated testimonies about heavenly visitations and other extraordinary phenomena have provided spiritual nourishment for generations of Latter-day Saints." 11

By 1945 Harold had already moved up three chairs in the Council of the Twelve and was being referred to by the First Presidency as the dean of the younger apostles. These were, in order beneath him, Spencer W. Kimball, his boyhood acquaintance

Ezra Taft Benson, and Mark E. Petersen. Then, on May 14, 1945, Harold experienced for the first time as an apostle the passing away of a prophet, seer, and revelator of the Lord. As soon as he received word, he took Fern and went to his beloved President Grant's home to pay his respects. Sister Augusta Grant and her family invited the Lees to kneel with them in prayer, and then the new widow asked Harold to offer it.

"The following morning, a special meeting of the Council of the Twelve was held where the funeral arrangements were discussed and where Elder Lee was assigned to prepare a tribute from the Twelve to the prophet." 12 What transpired in that meeting so affected Harold that many years later he used it in teaching youth leaders in the Church. He began by asking:

Have you ever thought what a great experience it is to witness the calling home of a prophet of God? I have witnessed several. After the passing of President Heber J. Grant, each of us of the Twelve were called in the late afternoon by President George F. Richards, who was the senior member of the Council of the Twelve in the city. We were told that President Grant had just passed away and that there would be a very important meeting in the Church Office Building at nine o'clock the next morning at which we were all expected to be in attendance. With great expectations and with great heaviness of heart, we were all there. And as I looked around the circle, there was no one standing at the head of the table. President McKay had moved down, standing between President George F. Richards and Joseph Fielding Smith. President Clark had gone way down the row and was standing between Charles A. Callis and Albert E. Bowen. That was his place of seniority. There was no First Presidency, because the prophet had been called home.

We sat around the table and President Richards, with great feeling, said: "Now you understand that in the absence of President George Albert Smith, who is in the East and is now returning home, that we should get things underway for plans for the funeral service. I think none of you will suppose that I am presumptuous in taking the responsibility of calling this meeting. And I suppose that therefore I have the right to conduct it in any way that I see fit. Now it is rather awkward here with Brother McKay and Brother Clark sitting down here in our midst. President Clark and President McKay, get up and come here to the head of the table, and President Clark, you take charge of this meeting."

And as they stood up and walked to the head of the table, I could see the emotion of that moment. We recognized, as we saw a transition taking place, there was no politics after the passing to fill a vacancy. It was the Lord's way and his will, and the smoothness and the ease with which it was done brought about an amazing transformation. 13

"On the following Monday, May 21, 1945, the First Presidency was reorganized. Of this first experience with the succession process, Elder Lee wrote, 'It was a day long to be remembered.'" 14

All of the apostles, including the two former counselors to President Grant, had been asked to come fasting. Dressed in white, they met in the temple and prayed, after which George Albert Smith briefly spoke. Under his direction each of the others then spoke, going in order of their seniority. Each declared his feeling that there should be no delay in organizing the First Presidency, and every one of them felt that George Albert Smith, as senior member and president of the Council, should be named as the President of the Church. Harold wrote, "'There was a rich outpouring of spirit, and love was freely expressed.'" 15

President George Albert Smith (center)
with counselors J. Reuben Clark (left)
and David O. McKay (right)

CA. 1945

Church Archives, The Church of Jesus Christ of Latter-day Saints

The new Presidency was officially reorganized when George Albert Smith was ordained and set apart by George F. Richards, with all the Twelve assisting. President Smith then chose President Clark and President McKay as his counselors, and set them apart. George F. Richards was sustained and set apart as the new President of the Council of the Twelve. President Smith was seventy-five years of age when he was ordained, having served previously for forty-one years as an Apostle. He felt comfortable in retaining President Grant's former counselors as his own, since they had been leading the Church for the past eleven years. 16

This was the first of four times Elder Lee was to witness this formal transfer of prophetic authority to a new president of the Church. The fourth and last time, of course, was when in July 1972 he was ordained, in the same manner, as the eleventh president of the Church, with Spencer W. Kimball acting as voice in the ordination. On each occasion, he was struck by the simple, orderly way in which the transfer of such vast authority was effected, without dissent or controversy, and without any divisive "campaigning," which often accompanies changes in ecclesiastical or other leadership. 17

During the October 1945 general conference the new First Presidency was sustained by the membership of the Church. They also sustained Matthew Cowley as the newest apostle, setting him apart to replace President Grant in the quorum. In just three years Harold had moved from twelfth to eighth in seniority and was now instructing his less-senior brethren in the very things President Clark had once explained to him.

The four junior members of the Council of the Twelve enjoyed a close relationship with Elder Lee in many ways. They could relate better socially and administratively to

Harold B. Lee accompanies the quartet
comprised of apostles (from left) Mark E. Petersen,
Matthew Cowley, Spencer W. Kimball
and Ezra Taft Benson

CA. 1945

Deseret News. Used with permission

him, their families were the same age, and they tended to look to him for guidance because of his experience. They also had some moments of relaxation together, one of which proved to be highly entertaining to all of the General Authorities and their wives at a Lion House social. Elder Kimball arranged a program of singing and stunts, and Elder Lee accompanied Elders Kimball, Benson, Petersen, and Cowley at the piano while they performed as a male quartet. Elder Lee pronounced the performance a success and said in his journal that their act "went over very well." 18

As the end of the war loomed near, Harold and the rest of the Brethren had "moved promptly to prepare for the changes that event would produce. Elder Lee convened a meeting of the military relations committee to consider the steps to be taken to help returning servicemen smoothly reenter civilian life....

"When this meeting was held, it was uncertain how long the war in the Pacific would last. The Japanese were fighting tenaciously and apparently had the will and the resources to continue the struggle into the indefinite future. It was under these circumstances that Elder Lee received [his] assignment to go to the Hawaiian Islands to hold a series of meetings with members and missionaries and to check on the LDS servicemen's facilities at Honolulu." 19

When the atomic bombs dropped on Hiroshima and Nagasaki brought an abrupt end to the war, a new era was ushered in for the world and for the Church. Having been appointed chairman of the servicemen's committee, Harold was now concerned for the orderly demobilization of all members of the Church who had served in the military and their smooth return to civilian life. In September 1945 he received the assignment to go to Washington, D.C., to confer with government officials—and on the way to conduct a stake conference and install a new stake president in Chicago.

A week later Harold was conducting a stake conference in New York, but in between he had been in the nation's capital. "There, with the assistance of J. Willard Marriott, he was able to confer with various government officials, including the Chief of Chaplains. 'Found them very cooperative,' he reported. On the twelfth, Elder Lee spent the day with Ernest L. Wilkinson, a future president of the Brigham Young University, who was then a counselor in the stake presidency and a prominent Washington attorney. At the request of the stake presidency, Elder Lee agreed to hold a meeting with priesthood leaders that evening. He was surprised to find that it convened in the cultural hall instead of in the adjacent, air-conditioned chapel. He was even more surprised when, during the meeting, he was asked to keep his voice down so as not to disturb the organ recital in the chapel. The incident, while inconsequential, reflects an attitude that was prevalent at the time, an attitude that relegated priesthood functions to a subordinate position in the Church's order of priorities. In the years ahead, through the revolutionary correlation program, Harold B. Lee would play the major role in altering these attitudes." 20

After participating on the way home in the dedication of the Idaho Falls temple, which was dedicated by President George Albert Smith, Harold returned to immediate involvement in the October general conference in Salt Lake City, focusing his remarks then and later in various stake conferences and other meetings on how the welfare plan could be put to significant use now that the war was over. As he explained, the most critical and serious welfare problem the Church was facing had to do with the Saints who were struggling to survive the devastation the war had wrecked in Europe. Of course, the Church had begun providing assistance immediately, and now the Brethren decided to send one of the Twelve to Europe to oversee and coordinate the work there.

At first Elder John A. Widtsoe, a Norwegian and the only native European in the Twelve, received the assignment. But when a sudden illness made his going impossible, the assignment went to junior member Elder Ezra Taft Benson. Some thought Harold should go, but the First Presidency felt he was needed at home to coordinate the relief efforts for the European Saints on this end and to deal with the gathering flood of returning servicemen and women.

After a farewell dinner in President Clark's home to honor Elder Benson, who would be in Europe indefinitely, the junior members of the Twelve and their wives all went to the airport to bid him fond farewell. Within a short time he was established and sending home reports.

> Thus, working in tandem, with Elder Lee directing affairs at home and Elder Benson on the job in Europe, the two [boys] from the Oneida Academy, now grown to apostolic maturity, were the key figures in a modern drama not unlike the ancient one when Joseph fed Israel from the granaries of Egypt.
>
> It is significant to see the tender regard this pair had for each other as they worked through the various phases of this drama. When it was first announced that a member of the Twelve would be assigned to go to Europe, Elder Lee felt it would not be "T" Benson because of his large, young family. Then when the call came, he lent every support to Elder Benson, assisting him in his preparation to leave.... and providing advice and support to the family after his departure. When Flora Benson became ill while her husband was away, it was Elder Lee who gave her special blessings for her health and peace of mind. 21

Elder Benson's assignment in Europe would keep him away from his family from January 1946 until December 17 of that same year.

In addition to his duties with the serviceman's committee, because these servicemen and women were now returning and reuniting with loved ones, during 1946 Harold ended up performing 196 temple sealings. None of them was more significant for him, however, than the one he performed on June 24. Of that day he wrote, "'I had the glorious experience of sealing my own baby daughter, Helen, to L. Brent Goates.... It was the greatest experience of my life.'" 22

The following November, while on an assignment in Mesa, Arizona, Harold sat in a lonely motel room and penned his now busily married daughter the following:

> This is intended to be something of a birthday letter to my "youngest" from a sentimental old Dad who is lonesome for his lovely daughter. So far as I can recall this is the first time in your life that you will be spending your birthday and Thanksgiving away from us, and...away from your home on those days.
>
> As with every day of your life, you can never relive any part of it except in memory and if any day be wasted or misspent, that day becomes only one of regret or remorse. To live one's life to the fullest then becomes a daily responsibility for which you need the constant guidance of divine powers to avoid the pitfalls that make for long detours back onto the path of safety and truth. Too many adopt the philosophy of the old preacher "unless you are in desperate need, your prayers just ain't got no suction." One who has understanding realizes that we are always in great need of spiritual help. So it was that the Master taught:
>
> "Blessed are the poor in spirit who come unto me, for theirs is the Kingdom of Heaven."
>
> The "poor in spirit" are the spiritually needy who daily lean on and trust the arm of the Lord.
>
> To me your birthday, always on or about Thanksgiving Day, has always seemed most appropriate. I thanked God

Helen and Brent Goates

CA. 1946

for my baby when you came twenty-one years ago and I have thanked him for you every day since. From babyhood you have possessed strong opinions and a will. Well do I remember your childhood efforts to make it an obedient will, and my prayer for you today is, as always in the past, that your will be made subservient to that which is right. As the depth of your thinking has been revealed on many occasions when you have furnished us keepsakes of your thinking, I have gloried in the unfolding of the life of my own daughter. When you made the greatest decision of your life thus far, in choosing your life's companion, somehow I had complete assurance that you had chosen well. My own way would have been to have urged greater deliberation, but perhaps the times justified the means and I accepted your decision with thanksgiving.

There lies yet ahead greater joys and, yes, greater anxieties than you have yet known, for remember that great love is built on great sacrifice and that a daily determination in each other to please in things that are right will build a sure foundation for a happy home. That determination for the welfare of each other must be mutual and not one-sided or selfish. Husband and wife must feel equal responsibilities and obligations to each other. Two of the things that today strike at the security of modern homes is that young husbands have never sensed their full obligation in supporting a family and young wives have side-stepped the responsibility of settling down to the serious business of raising a family and making a home.

Your being with Brent now should prove a blessing to both of you. Together you can dream dreams and together you can work and sacrifice to make your dreams come true. With all my love to you and Brent and wishing you much joy on your birthday, I am, Your loving daddy, Harold B. Lee. 23

The next June 11, 1947, following their simultaneous graduations from Brigham Young University, Harold again had the sweet privilege of sealing a daughter in eternal marriage, this time his eldest, Maurine, to Ernest J. Wilkins of Prescott, Arizona.

> In the fall of 1947 Maurine's husband commenced his studies at Stanford University in Palo Alto, California, his course designed to lead to a doctorate degree in Romantic languages. Maurine's parents, always concerned and helpful, went to be with them as they settled into new housing. While in California, the parents learned of the birth of their first grandchild on September 9, 1947. Helen had given birth to a boy, later named David Brent Goates, but forever afterward known by his Grandfather Lee as "Skipper," meaning, the captain of Elder Lee's kingdom. 24

In July 1948, following a series of extremely stressful assignments, as well as nervous tensions brought on in March by the difficult birth of Maurine's first child, Alan Wilkins, Harold took his family for a relaxing week on the upper reaches of the Weber River. He "and Fern, accompanied by Helen, Brent, and grandson David, spent a relaxing week at the Thousand Peaks Ranch. Intermingling hikes with horseback riding, visiting, reading, snoozing, and leisurely study, the apostle was able to revive his energies for the full season ahead. Especially pleasing to Elder Lee were the carefree and spontaneous antics of his grandson [Skipper]. There was a special bond between him and the boy, both resembling each other so much in both appearance and temperament....

"Two weeks after returning from the ranch, Fern accompanied her husband to San Francisco, where he held a series of welfare meetings. They then stayed on in nearby Palo Alto for eleven days, helping the Wilkinses move into a larger home. 'Cleaned the house on Waverly to be occupied by Maurine and Ernie,' wrote Elder Lee on August 4. The next day, he 'bought a crib for Alan,' and the day

Maurine and Ernest Wilkins

CA. 1947

Courtesy of the Lee Family Collection

after that found him 'house cleaning.' He was still at it three days later when he noted optimistically, 'beginning to see the end.'" They returned home "with the satisfying feeling that their 'little family' would be comfortable and happy." 25

Despite his grueling schedule and relentless responsibilities, Harold remained very much the family man, particularly enjoying his new status as "Grandpa." Neither was he above a little light-hearted ribbing of his dear Fern about now being married to a "Grandma." Home would be an important source of solace and rejuvenation, for his apostolic responsibilities stretched endlessly ahead to days that would be made endurable only by his rock-solid testimony and his love of being out among the people.

Harold and Fern gained great joy
as a "Grandpa" and "Grandma"

CA. 1956

THE GIFT OF REVELATION

Elder Harold B. Lee was concerned. Something was troubling Oscar W. McConkie, president of the California Mission, and Harold had no idea what it was. Now, as he sat waiting for the meeting with this particular group of missionaries and others to conclude, he thought back over what had been accomplished thus far on his eighteen-day tour of the mission.

He and President McConkie, whose son Bruce R. McConkie had been called in 1946 to the First Council of Seventy, had started their tour in Blythe, California, near the Colorado River on the east of the Salton Sea. There they had met with both members and missionaries, found a thriving branch, and Harold had dedicated a new chapel on Sunday, March 16, 1949.

Beginning in that first area Harold had grown increasingly impressed with President McConkie's leadership abilities. Widely known as Judge McConkie, this outstanding mission president had retired after a legal career of many years that had concluded with a term on the bench in the Third Judicial Court in Salt Lake City. Now he manifest a dynamic and powerful pulpit style which Harold admired, speaking with authority and conviction. He was uniformly kind to members and missionaries alike. He displayed a marked deference toward the visiting apostle, which Harold felt evidenced a very real depth of humility. Finally, and this is what Harold appreciated and enjoyed most, President McConkie had a great mastery of the scriptures, and his spiritual sensitivity was everywhere evident. He not only knew how to hear, he knew how to follow the whisperings of the Spirit.

One thrilling experience President McConkie had related during their travels together, however, continued to replay itself in Harold's mind, making him wonder. During Bruce's early childhood the McConkie family had lived in Monticello, Utah—a small town in the southeastern corner of the state that had, for the most part, remained wild west, with horses, cattle, rustlers, and attitudes similar to what they had been in the 1880s.

As President McConkie had sat reading on his porch one day, he found himself springing from his chair and racing toward the field—this in response to a spiritual prompting he had received to get up and run. He didn't know why, but he had no hesitation about obeying. As he reached the field he found young Bruce, his foot caught in a saddle stirrup, being dragged over the rough ground by his frightened pony. President McConkie's prompt response to the spiritual whispering had doubtless saved the boy from serious injury and maybe even death.

More than being thrilled by this account, Harold couldn't get past the feeling that there was more to it than the saving of a young boy's life. Somewhere there was a greater purpose behind President McConkie's experience, though at the moment it seemed to be hidden—

Hidden, too, was the cause of President McConkie's concern. Over nearly eighteen days together, the two of them had spoken of many things—but not that. So Harold had waited, knowing that when the time was right he would know, and then he could do whatever might be possible to ease this wonderful mission president's mind.

From Blythe the tour had returned to Cathedral City and

Hemet, California, not far from Palm Springs, where meetings had been held. Returning to the coast, they had held meetings in Carlsbad, San Juan Capistrano, and Laguna Beach. At Laguna Beach they had also visited President George Albert Smith, who was staying at a home owned by the Church while overcoming the effects of a mild stroke. They had given President Smith a blessing before traveling on.

Moving southeasterly, they had held meetings in Brawley, in the heart of the Imperial Valley, where many of the Mexican farm laborers were beginning to join the Church. Traveling into Arizona they had held meetings in Ajo, Prescott, and Cottonwood. At Prescott, Harold had been impressed by the production of a group of young missionaries who had dedicated themselves to doing just as their mission president had instructed—in every possible way.

Back in California they'd held more meetings in Needles, Barstow, and Death Valley. While driving to Death Valley, President McConkie had told Harold about a vivid dream in which Satan had appeared to him. After thinking about it, Harold had interpreted the dream by relating his experience as a young stake president with a woman who had been possessed. The evil spirit in her had said to Harold, "You are the head of the Church," which of course Harold had denied. President McConkie, after hearing Harold's account, had remarked that he thought the evil spirit was not speaking of what then was, but of what Satan knew would one day be. Harold thought the same was true of President McConkie's dream.

The tour had then wound down with meetings in Ridgecrest, Mohave, Bakersfield, San Luis Obispo, the one just concluding here in Santa Barbara, and a final meeting on the morrow that would be held in Ventura. After that Harold would go home— ending a journey of over a month during which he had not once seen his family. Still, he had been privileged to meet with numerous small but thriving branches and to visit with and occasionally interview a corps of dedicated missionaries who, motivated by their president, had learned to rely on the promptings of the Spirit in their work. There had also been delightful testimony meetings with the missionaries when they had shared their own spiritual and faith-promoting experiences, including accounts of several converts who had been foretold in dreams of the coming of the missionaries to their doors.

Better than most mission presidents, President McConkie had used Harold to inspire and motivate his mostly young charges. Besides encouraging discussions and conversations, after each meeting the president had lined the missionaries up so that Harold could go down the line, shaking hands and sharing a few brief words with each of them. Though exhausting, Harold had enjoyed this activity, and now as the meeting in Santa Barbara was ending, he geared himself up for the process once again, praying fervently that the Lord would make known to him the very things he needed to know and say to each elder and sister.

It took about an hour for Harold to greet and briefly visit with each missionary there in Santa Barbara—an hour during which President McConkie busied himself nearby but never under any conditions intruded on the private conversations. This, of course, was a part of Harold's apostolic task, and Brother McConkie's respectful distance was further evidence of the mission president's humble deference to the office.

Outside the chapel at the mission car, Harold was just starting to climb in when he stopped, straightened, and nodded toward one of the missionaries who was passing by. "Oscar," he said quietly, "why haven't you sent that elder home?"

For a moment President McConkie only looked at him. Then without a word he climbed into the car, started the engine, and drove out onto the roadway. "You know, Elder Lee," he finally said, "for two weeks you and I have rarely been apart. There hasn't been a day in that time that I haven't witnessed God speaking to you, and through you. As for myself, I have prayed about various things

I felt each of the groups needed to hear, asking the Lord to inspire you. Well, time and time again you have addressed those very topics. But this with our young elder? This is different, and I want to explain why.

"Some time ago I interviewed that elder and uncovered his unrighteous behavior—"

"His sins."

"Yes, Elder Lee, his sins. I knew immediately that he should be given a dishonorable release and sent home. But you see, Elder Lee, I haven't wanted to do it. I love that young man every bit as much as I love my other missionaries, perhaps even more. He is my responsibility—he was my responsibility when he committed his transgressions, as a matter of fact—and so I determined that it was my responsibility to save him, to work him through his repentance and bring him back to where he could at least conclude his mission honorably.

"The thing is, I haven't made much headway with him; neither have I had any peace about my decision. Nevertheless, I determined to say nothing to you about him; neither have I mentioned the situation to the Lord. I decided, simply, to wait, knowing that if my determinations for the young man were in error, the Lord would allow you to 'see' the situation clearly."

Harold nodded soberly. "Your problem, Oscar, is that you have a king-sized heart and an incredible amount of ability."

"Yes, perhaps," President McConkie acknowledged quietly, "but no right to oppose the will of the Lord. Elder Lee, I am a witness that God has indeed made you a revelator and a seer! I thank him for the wonderful work you have done thus far in my mission, and before this day is over I will write my children and bear them my witness to the divinity of your apostolic calling. My prayer and desire is that they will each sustain you with as much fervor as do I—"[1]

In January 1947, Harold was assigned to accompany Elder Charles A. Callis to Florida, where the two apostles were to organize the first stake in the southeastern part of the United States. Elder Callis, now elderly and a widower, had served for many years as mission president in the South, was extremely beloved of the people, and had lived for the day when the membership would be strong enough to sustain a stake of Zion. "He seemed to look upon the event as a fitting capstone to his ministry and was as happy and as excited as a child as preparations were made to depart." 2

Traveling separately, Elder Callis met Harold and Fern in Jacksonville, Florida, where the first in a series of unusual events occurred. While the Lees stayed on the banks of the St. Johns River at the palatial home of Brother and Sister Archie O. Jenkins, who had been re-activated by Elder Callis' personal missionary efforts, Elder Callis asked if he might stay in a sparely furnished apartment adjacent to the Jacksonville chapel. In that apartment he and his wife had stayed many years before while he was serving as the branch president, and he desired to relive some of his cherished memories of their life together.

"It was a bittersweet time for the aged apostle. Elder Lee noted that when Elder Callis heard a rendition of 'O My Father' at one of the meetings, 'he broke into tears, saying, "Take care of your wives, I haven't mine. She is gone."'" 3

Harold wrote:

> I had the impression, and so expressed myself to Sister Jenkins, that Brother Callis wanted to die and had wished it could take place in that room, by himself. He had us drive him to the old chapel and to the home where his twin sons were born and died. He seemed to be reliving these experiences for the last time. 4

The interviews, the choosing of a stake presidency, and the meetings with the Saints all went beautifully. After Harold's principal talk in the morning session, during which Elder Callis seemed to have suffered a mild heart attack, the venerable apostle grew quickly stronger. During the afternoon session he felt strong enough to speak and did so, paying a moving tribute to Sister Callis and declaring to the assembled Saints that she and others who had labored as missionaries in the South were there in attendance. He also prophesied that there would yet be other stakes in the South and that some of the younger members would live to see a temple built for their area. That night Harold and Fern departed for St. Augustine, and Elder Callis, in apparent good health, asked that arrangements might be made for his return journey to Salt Lake City.

The next day, as the Lees drove toward Miami, a highway patrolman stopped them to deliver a message. Elder Callis, they were told, had died suddenly the night before of a heart attack. Immediately, Harold reported the death to President McKay, asking if the funeral might be held there, as that was the wish of the Saints. President McKay agreed, and services in Salt Lake City were planned for later. Of what followed, Harold later said:

> I was the one to conduct Brother Callis' funeral service in Florida. It was a sorrowful trail that I had followed. I loved Brother Callis. My heart was tender. In the quiet of my hotel room I shed some tears; I tried to prepare. Finally the day came. It was Thursday, January 23, 1947. The funeral was to start at 10:00 A.M. in the Jacksonville Ward Chapel....
>
> As the first two speakers concluded it was now about a quarter to eleven, and as the song was being rendered, before the president of the mission and I then were to conclude the service, a Western Union messenger arrived with a telegram for me. When I opened it, it was a message from the First Presidency requesting that I read it at the service. I arose to read it and I suddenly found myself overwhelmed with some kind of a great feeling that I couldn't

quite understand. It wasn't sorrow, because I had conquered that in those two days preceding. And then I began to think, "This is Thursday." What was it that I felt? Suddenly when that telegram came it was as though I was just as close to the Council of the Twelve and the Presidency as though they had walked in and taken their seats on the stand behind me. Up to that time I had felt so much alone, with such a heavy responsibility. Twelve o'clock in Florida meant it was 10:00 A.M. in Salt Lake City, and knowing the way the Council meeting is held, at 10:45 A.M. every member of the Twelve and the First Presidency would be dressed in temple clothing surrounding an altar in the place nearest to heaven on earth. And I said, "Now I know what is happening. They have offered a prayer for me, and this is the answer. I am receiving the answer of the prayers of the First Presidency and the Twelve."

When I returned home, my first question to President George F. Richards was: "Brother Richards, in your temple meeting last Thursday do you remember whether or not at the prayer at the altar there was a prayer offered for me particularly?" He thought a moment and said: "Yes, Brother McKay led us. And he prayed that the Lord would bless you down there all alone so that you would feel the strength of the Presidency and the Council of the Twelve to be with you." I said: "I received it in one of the most dramatic experiences of my life."

I was taught by that experience how important it is to receive the prayers of the faithful. 5

In the April 1947 general conference, Henry D. Moyle, long-time chairman of the welfare committee and Harold's dear friend, was sustained as the new apostle to replace Elder Callis. With five members called more recently than he, Harold could no longer be considered one of the junior members of the Twelve.

Interestingly, just a few weeks later the Brethren decided to form a second stake in the South, in part fulfilling Elder Callis' prophecy. Now (2001) there are dozens of stakes in the area, and temples that serve the Saints in the South have been built in Washington, D.C.; Atlanta, Georgia; Memphis and Nashville, Tennessee; Orlando, Florida; Dallas and Houston, Texas; St. Louis, Missouri; Raleigh, North Carolina; Louisville, Kentucky; Baton Rouge, Louisiana; and Birmingham, Alabama.

As with Elder Callis, though he was an apostle of the Lord Jesus Christ, neither Harold nor his family were spared the normal vicissitudes of mortality. On May 9, 1947, Harold's father, Samuel Marion Lee Jr., passed quietly away. He had been ailing for some time, and Harold had spent many long and sleepless hours at his bedside. His death came shortly after a blessing of comfort given by Harold and President J. Reuben Clark.

> Harold B. Lee loved his father fervently. That love was demonstrated by the way he lived and by the treatment accorded to his parents. The son could never forget how they had sacrificed to raise a large family under stressful economic conditions and how they had scrimped to keep him in the mission field. In turn, the parents idolized the son who had more than achieved the "big things" they anticipated for him when he entered the mission field. 6

Fern's health also continued to be quite frail, and frequently Harold and his daughters were called upon to carry her burdens. On one occasion earlier on she had been hospitalized for the removal of several tumors—which fortunately proved to be nonmalignant—from her abdomen.

> "She was colorless throughout the day," wrote Elder Lee the day of the surgery. During the next twelve days,

the harried husband haunted the hospital at every opportunity, anxiously monitoring his wife's recovery. "Fern miserable with gas pains," he wrote the day following the operation. Thereafter, he watched carefully for any change in her condition, whether for better or for worse....

The next Sunday, the crisis ended. "Fern was like one released from prison," wrote Elder Lee...after bringing his wife home from the hospital. "Everything seemed beautiful and lovely to her," [though] [s]everal weeks of convalescence lay ahead. 7

In fact, when you combine the pressures that accompany a typical life with those heaped upon the presiding brethren of the Church, "the crucible of service through which the General Authorities are called upon to pass daily is an indication of their keen reverence for the sacredness of their callings.... Working under pressure and fatigue seemed Harold B. Lee's lot throughout his ministry, almost as if there were not enough time to accomplish his life's mission. He described one Sunday as follows:

I arrived in Los Angeles at 7:15 A.M. and was met by the stake presidency, who drove me to the Huntington Park Chapel, where I met with them until the high council came at 9:00 A.M., and through the general sessions, which were held at 10:00 A.M. and 6:30 P.M., with a priesthood leadership meeting in the afternoon and a fireside after the evening meeting. Ordinations and missionary interviews entirely filled up the day until 10:30 P.M., with hardly time for a sandwich. 8

Not surprisingly, Harold suffered from chronic migraine headaches, which were no doubt aggravated by his relentless travel schedules, improper eating habits, and constant lack of sleep. Unfortunately, he usually had no choice but to simply work through them. For instance:

> I left at 8:30 A.M. on the Western Pacific train for
> Sacramento, California, to attend the regional meeting of
> the Northern California Region and the Sacramento Stake
> conference. I suffered from one of the worst headaches I
> have had for a long time, but I managed to make some
> preparation for my meetings and to study the reports. I
> arrived in Sacramento at 3:45 A.M. 9

Harold was not alone in his plight. By 1948 the Church was
expanding dramatically, with 170 stakes worldwide that required
rigorous effort by the Brethren to ensure regular visits. In
February, for instance, President McKay and six of the Twelve were
absent from their weekly temple meeting, being scattered across
the globe from Canada to the South Pacific. "They were all feeling
the pressure, and a rash of illness came upon them. By April, three
of the Apostles were sidelined because of heart ailments. At their
weekly meeting, with only seven assembled, word came that Elder
Benson had been diagnosed as having had a heart attack, though
not serious. Then the Twelve learned only three weeks later that
Spencer W. Kimball had suffered a heart attack in Arizona, and
cardiograph tests revealed a marked weakness in his heart. One
week later Elder Kimball had another heart attack, and Elder Lee
went to bless him and to take a message to his son who was serving
in the New England States Mission. President McKay was in the
hospital with a heart attack when Elder Lee returned from the tour
of the mission." 10

Not surprisingly, with all the traveling there were also occasional accidents. On one occasion Harold was driving Marion G.
Romney's new DeSoto through Arizona en route to a stake conference when he "hit a farmer on a small tractor who had pulled into
his driveway without any signal and had failed to see the approaching automobile as he crossed in front of [it]."11 Fortunately, nothing

but the DeSoto seems to have been injured.

Harold, as we all do, also struggled with personal traits. Like his mother before him, Harold was forthright and plainspoken. Now, with the ever increasing pressures, his other ancestrally bequeathed nemesis—a hot temper—became more of a problem. Once, when Marion Romney brought up a tongue lashing Harold had given a member of the welfare committee, Harold replied that it was only a "burst of truth." To this Brother Romney replied that he hoped "such would not 'burst upon him.'" [12] Chastened, Harold acknowledged his error, and he was ever trying to put his temper behind him.

> Whenever he detected that same tendency in one of his own posterity, he attempted to "nip it in the bud." With one Little League grandson he entered into a pact that if Grandfather provided him with a new fielder's mitt, it could only be worn if he did not allow his temper to take control in the game. When his temper flared, the mitt was to be returned to Grandfather until there was evidence that control had returned. An understanding Elder Lee often had the mitt as much as did his grandson. [13]

On the other hand, wise priesthood leaders and others usually knew where they stood with Harold, who "seldom failed to teach a lesson regardless of the time, the place, the circumstances, or the person involved. He took every opportunity to plant an idea, or to stimulate faith, or to lay a remonstrance upon someone, whether gentle or firm. He seldom, if ever, engaged in small talk. What he said had meaning and purpose.... It was not uncommon for him to speak 'over the heads' of an audience to a specific person or persons. This reflected an interesting aspect of Elder Lee's makeup. There were few leaders of his day more plainspoken than he. Yet, if the circumstances required it, he could be indirect and remote, accomplishing a desired result by finesse and adroit maneuvering rather than by direct speech. Occasionally, he would induce obedience by his silence." [14]

Illustration by Robert T. Barrett

Periodic breaks in the routine as well as a sense of humor also helped Harold maintain equilibrium. "A lighthearted moment occurred shortly before Elder Lee left for Richland, when two women and a man from California came for counsel. They 'needed someone to teach them about revelation they have been receiving,' he wrote. Then added, 'Apparently I did not qualify.' " 15

While touring the New England Mission in 1948, Harold found himself counseling missionaries who were facing considerable opposition from intellectuals within and around New Haven, Connecticut, the home of Yale University.

> Some felt that those who worked in an intellectual community such as this ought to alter their proselyting methods. Elder Lee disagreed. He taught that conversion comes through the Spirit and that missionaries should approach their contacts at that level. At the same time, he urged that those who worked among people of high intellect and training should be sure of their facts and the doctrine but should not aim merely at intellectual assent. Spiritual conversion was the goal. Yet, he realized that not all converts would receive a spiritual witness by the Holy Ghost. As to these, he counselled a patient acceptance of a secondary testimony, based on the witness of others, confidently awaiting the time when the primary testimony, imparted by the Holy Ghost, would come.... Still, he was quick to acknowledge that either kind of testimony was valid. (See Doctrine & Covenants 46:11–14.) 16

In the fall Harold traveled with Fern to Western Canada where he conducted two stake conferences, between which he met with President George Albert Smith to release E. S. Wood as president of the Cardston Temple. Shortly thereafter came one of Harold's many learning experiences with his longtime mentor, President J. Reuben Clark, one that proved more difficult than usual to handle. Though Harold loved President Clark deeply, when the older man once intruded on his sense of dignity or independence, Harold's feelings were ruffled. The incident began when President Clark "criticized Elder Lee for having gone to the hospital to visit one of the Brethren. He asked whether Elder Lee didn't realize that people go to the hospital to recuperate and should not be intruded upon. The criticism did not set well with Elder Lee, especially because he had been asked to go there. Later in a meeting President Clark said something that Elder Lee interpreted as a criticism of the extent of his participation in a discussion. These incidents caused Elder Lee to become withdrawn in his attitude toward President Clark, something that the older man sensed. To clear the air, President Clark invited Elder Lee to his office, where he mentioned the negative attitude toward him he had detected. 'He pleaded that there be no coolness between us,' Elder Lee wrote. 'He said it wouldn't be long before the younger brethren would rise to the leadership of the church and he must do all he can to see that there is unity.' This bridged over the misunderstanding that had developed between them, a misunderstanding that, if left to fester, could have created a serious rift in their relationship. As it was, the effect of it was to bring the two men closer together and to promote a greater sensitivity in their relationship." 17

Harold undertook two mission tours in 1949—the California Mission in the spring and the East Central States Mission in the fall. He was exhausted before going on both of these tours, but more so the tour of California. He wrote: "'I seem weary and hardly in the mood; but I am hoping to feel better as the visit progresses.'" 18 Harold's companion in California

was the mission president, Oscar W. McConkie, Sr..... He was a man of deep spirituality, learned in the law and the scriptures, who spoke with authority and conviction.... Such spiritual sensitivity was something with which Elder

Lee could readily relate. This, and President McConkie's perceptive knowledge of the scriptures, provided the grist for many enlightening gospel conversations between them during the course of the tour. 19

It was at the end of this tour when the incident dramatized at the beginning of this chapter took place. Less than a month later, Harold "spent several hours with two of President McConkie's sons, Bruce R. McConkie and Oscar W. McConkie, Jr. Elder Lee rode with them from Salt Lake City to Richmond, Utah, where he had a stake conference assignment. This incident, taken with his recent tour of the father's mission, gave Elder Lee insight into the McConkie family he had not had before.... Twenty-two years later, Harold B. Lee, as the president of the Church, would call Bruce R. McConkie to the Twelve, the only man he would call to that position during his short tenure." 20

In 1950, Harold took the only extensive trip he would ever take with Elder Henry D. Moyle—a three-week journey that would take the apostles by train to Washington, D.C., and then to Florida on Church business. "*En route* to Washington, they held a stake conference in Chicago. 'It was an enjoyable experience to be with Brother Moyle,' wrote Elder Lee, 'and I appreciated his wise counsel and able address.' They travelled to Milwaukee Sunday evening, where they dedicated a new chapel, and the next day went with David M. Kennedy, a member of the Chicago stake presidency, to look at an experimental dairy farm. Although he was a suave and successful banker, David Kennedy was no novice when it came to cows and farms since he was born and raised in the small, rural town of Randolph, Utah, where these things were a way of life. So, in talking with the Brethren about this dairy farm, he spoke with a voice of authority and experience, as he would speak authoritatively in the future about international finance and diplomacy when he became the United States Secretary of the

Treasury and later the United States Ambassador at large. Still later, these skills would qualify Brother Kennedy to serve as a special assistant to the First Presidency, advising about matters of international diplomacy, as the Church mounted a major, global missionary effort." 21

In Washington, D.C., Harold and Elder Moyle met with the chief of the Bureau of Internal Revenue and his staff attorneys, successfully negotiating a tax exemption for Deseret Industries facilities in California. In New York they examined the possibility of purchasing an expensive chapel site. "Predictably, during the discussions, the Brethren inquired about the status of the welfare plan in the area. Elder Lee expressed 'considerable anxiety' about the lack of enthusiasm for welfare work in the stake. This quality, or the lack of it, almost became a litmus test for Elder Lee and his associates in welfare in determining the qualifications of a person to serve in key positions of leadership." 22

After flying to Jacksonville the two apostles drove to Deer Park, near Orlando, where the Church had acquired large acreages of ranch and farmland. In charge of this development was Heber Meeks, President Lee's close friend and former president of the Southern States Mission. "'It is a pioneer venture of great magnitude,'" wrote Harold about the Florida ranch, "'which, when completed, will have about 180,000 acres of the best ranch land in Florida.'" 23

"After holding a series of meetings with leaders and members in Jacksonville, [Harold] finally succumbed to the urging of Elder Moyle to join him in a favorite pastime—deep sea fishing. Driving to the Atlantic Coast nearby, they rented a boat and, with a pilot who knew the waters, were taken to an area where success was likely. 'Enjoyed the thrill of landing a great sail fish,' Elder Lee wrote excitedly." 24

On that triumphant note, Harold and Elder Moyle boarded the train for home, Harold using the time *en route* to prepare for future assignments, especially a commencement address he had agreed to give at one of the high schools in Ogden. Upon his arrival Harold learned of the death in Clifton of his cousin Irvin Davis, whose family had pleaded that he speak at the funeral—a request he honored. He noted:

> There were about 250 in attendance, ...and [it was] one of the most satisfying visits I have made back home in meeting and renewing acquaintances with old friends. 25

"Although he never lived there after his marriage, and returned only sporadically for occasions like this, Elder Lee never seemed to lose the feeling that Clifton was home. This was the place where his roots had been planted and, despite his far-ranging travels, would always be the place where he seemed to feel more in touch with his past and his life's purpose." 26

As the years of his first decade as a member of the Twelve rolled by, Harold constantly witnessed the preservation of his own life, the workings and manifestations of the Holy Spirit in his speaking and other assignments, and other clear evidences that the Lord was watching over and prospering him in his apostolic work. Yet new medical disclosures seemed to be just as constantly threatening. "He had developed a major digestive disorder, ultimately leading to severe ulcers in the years ahead.... Compounding his own physical problems were his wife's frailties. He...spent his fifty-first birthday in the hospital with her, she having suffered a bowel hemorrhage three days earlier." 27 "Perhaps it was through his own battle for health that he was able to sharpen his understanding of and empathy for others." 28

Another peculiar and trying aspect of his work, which was occasionally repeated under various circumstances, was revealed by Harold when he wrote:

> I spent this Saturday afternoon cleaning up the yard, and

while at work I had a visit from a man who came to tell me about the condition of his wife, who about six weeks ago gave birth to her sixth baby. During the last few days she had developed a peculiar attitude in quoting scriptures and repeating messages from spirits, etc. He requested that I go to their home and administer to her. I arrived there and had a most unusual experience. As I sat beside her on the couch, she turned to me with a cynical smile and asked: "Do you know who you are?" I said: "Yes, I know; who do you think I am?" She replied: "You're the great physician; you're the head of the Church." When I tried to counsel with her she said: "Oh, no, you are not going to send me from this world." I had the distinct impression that she was in the power of an evil spirit and was impressed to rebuke the spirit and cast it out by the authority of the Priesthood. I trembled like a leaf and my hair seemed to almost be as pin pricks. I learned that a man who had been excommunicated for plural marriage had come to their home to sell insulation, and that she commenced to become irrational from the time he came to the home. 29

But for the most part, as his ministry continued, the Saints continued to pour out to him their love for his service.

Sister Nemelka, from a faithful German convert family in the Pioneer Stake, wrote to Elder Lee telling how her son, Nephi, [had] been reclaimed from inactivity. His first ray of hope had come, she said, when he read in Elder Lee's book *Youth and the Church* the chapter on repentance titled "The 'Successful' Sinners." 30

And:

A man who had protested his innocence for eighteen years since President Lee's high council in Pioneer Stake had

Harold B. Lee

CA. 1950

excommunicated him, came to him in 1950 and confessed his sins. After being malicious and vindictive toward Elder Lee all these years, falsely blaming him, he came on this occasion and said that "he had the assurance at the last general conference of the Church that Elder Lee was an authorized servant of the Lord." [31]

"As he traveled to all corners of the Lord's kingdom, Elder Lee always bore an assured testimony of the gospel of Jesus Christ. He inspired missionaries, members, and leaders, and spent many hours counseling with young people. He [also] lifted his voice in eloquence to comfort the forlorn and bereaved." [32] Thus, Harold continued forward, moving ever toward his ultimate mortal calling.

> In the decade from 1943 to October 1953, ten vacancies were created in the Quorum of the Twelve, caused either by death, by calls to the First Presidency, or, in the case of Richard R. Lyman, by excommunication.... These departures and their replacements advanced Elder Lee in seniority in the quorum so that in October 1953 when Elder Richard L. Evans was called to the Twelve, Elder Lee was its second ranking member, junior only to President Joseph Fielding Smith. President Smith and the members of the First Presidency, David O. McKay, Stephen L. Richards, and J. Reuben Clark, who were also senior to Elder Lee in the apostleship, had an average age of over seventy-eight years. Since Elder Lee was then fifty-four, the perception that he would one day be the president of the Church was even more pronounced than it [had been] in 1941 when...[he had been] the newest member of the quorum. [33]

A SPECIAL WITNESS
TO THE WORLD

Brother dos Santos looked carefully around the room in the missionarios' home where, he had been told, a few families in Londrina gathered weekly to worship the Lord Jesus. Though he was slightly uncomfortable and highly nervous, this being his first time to attend, he was nevertheless feeling good. All four of these gringos, these wonderful Mormon missionarios from the United States, had now called him "brother." Such an honor had to make a man feel good, and it was all Brother dos Santos could do to keep from smiling.

Yet he did not smile. He dared not, when such a serious and important thing was about to happen. It might be, in fact, the most serious and important thing that had ever happened to him or to his son, and when he thought of it his breath almost fled away. In another moment, he and his family were going to see—and actually meet if the missionarios were right—an apostle of the Lord Jesus Christ. This great man, about whom he had heard only a little, was nevertheless supposed to be the same as the mighty apostles of old: Peter, John, Paul, Andrew, James and the others, about whom he read to his family from the Bible at night! Brother dos Santos did not know if this were actually true, but the American missionarios had never deceived him yet, and doubtful as it seemed, in this great thing they might also be right. The man who was coming might actually be a true apostle of the Lord Jesus Christ! Thus the nervousness within him continued to grow.

For years Brother dos Santos had thought the apostles were long dead and gone and that God had ceased his work among men, at least until the two prophets mentioned in the eleventh chapter of Revelation would be sent to prepare the way for the Lord's second coming.

In fact, the small man thought with a little embarrassment, when the two tall gringo missionarios had first clapped at his door and he had seen their neatly groomed appearance and felt the aura of importance that seemed to surround them, he had thought for a moment that they were the two very prophets the ancient ones had written of.

They had claimed no such distinction, stating humbly that they were mere missionarios—representatives of The Church of Jesus Christ of Latter-day Saints. They had introduced themselves as Elders Richard R. Tolman and Darryl M. Jensen, from America, and for a tiny moment Brother dos Santos had looked with envy upon their tall frames and fine apparel. Yet not for an instant had these two acted like wealthy and important young gringos. Instead, they had willingly stooped their heads and entered into his humble home, made themselves very comfortable in spite of the poverty of Brother dos Santos and his family, and then in the common language of the Brazilian people, which they seemed to speak with ease, they had conversed about the Lord Jesus and his message of love for all mankind.

Such talk had been good, of course, and Brother dos Santos had been duly impressed with their knowledge. But until Elder Tolman had lifted little Joviniano and placed the child in his lap, paying no attention to the boy's dead legs but instead laughing and playing with him as if he were whole, Brother dos Santos had not known for certain that the two were men of God. But when Joviniano, whose name meant "young boy" and whose real name was Alderacy, had laughed and smiled in return, then he had known. Joviniano, who had been given no strength in his legs since birth, was a child of God who seemed able to sense goodness in people, and without hesitation the child had given his heart to Elder Tolman.

The boy had just as quickly given his heart to Elder Jensen, leaving Brother dos Santos with no choice but to believe with certainty that these missionarios were truly men of God—sincere young men who wished only good things for their Brother dos Santos and his family—and who taught them only good things from the written word of God.

As the days had passed, the missionaries had clapped often at his door. If he was not at home, but was working in the coffee warehouse that loomed next to his small house—unloading the fifty-kilo sacks of coffee beans from trucks that arrived from the fields, carrying them from one place to another in the warehouse on his head and loading them into other trucks that would take the beans away—then the missionarios would play with Joviniano and his other children, or answer the many questions he had left with his good wife for them to answer.

Brother dos Santos did not understand why it was that his wife had no questions of her own. She accepted all the missionarios told her without hesitation and tried to do exactly as they asked from that moment on. For him whom they called Brother dos Santos, however, it was a little more difficult. While he believed the missionarios readily enough, at least about most things, he felt that he should take all of it to God for his own witness before acknowledging his belief. And a man certainly couldn't light a candle and drop to his knees seeking understanding from God if he had not ordered all the facts most clearly in his mind. And so he asked questions; and when he was not home from his work, his good wife asked them for him .

Thus, despite his wife's desire to be baptized into the missionarios' church, Brother dos Santos himself was not yet so certain. Yes, it did seem to be the right and proper thing to do; and yes, the two tall young men from America were most certainly men of God. But did that mean there were no other men of God than among the Mormons? Did it mean that every religion other than theirs was not the true faith? Surely the power of God was in all churches, especially among those who believed in the Holy Bible, for God would certainly honor those who lived as the Holy Book told them to live.

Of course, no one of any church had been able to put strength into the long-dead legs of little Joviniano. No one wished even to speak of it. Instead, he was made to feel evil by those other men of God just for asking. But, his mind argued with him again, if this great man who was coming was truly an apostle—

A few days ago had come his family's last visit with the missionarios—at least for a little period of time. They were going, they had declared, to Bauru, in the state of Sao Paulo.

"But, why are you going so very far away?" Joviniano had asked anxiously. "I am afraid that you might not come back."

"We'll come back, Joviniano, we promise! But we must go." Elder Tolman gently tousled the boy's hair. "You see, we are going to meet with an apostle of the Lord."

"An apostle?" Brother dos Santos' wife had questioned in wonder. "A real apostle?"

"That's right." Elder Jensen smiled. "His name is Elder Harold B. Lee. In fact, we will be returning with him here to Londrina. Elder Lee will be speaking to a public gathering in our city—"

"Father," Joviniano interrupted excitedly, "didn't the apostles of our Lord Jesus heal many people? Isn't that what you read to us from our Holy Bible?"

"Yes, my son, it does say that. But—"

Now Joviniano's face glowed with hope. "Then when the apostle comes to Londrina," he said enthusiastically, not noticing that his father was endeavoring to tell him something else, "I'll ask him to bless me, and then I'll be able to walk!"

And so now it was a few days later, Brother dos Santos thought as he continued to look around the room in the missionarios' rented home while he waited for the apostle's appearance. The missionarios had gone to Bauru and had spoken of little Joviniano with this apostle, and wonder of all wonders, he had replied to them, "Faith like that does not go unrewarded." Then while the apostle and one other had been delayed and then flown from Bauru to Londrina in an old DC-3 of Verig Airlines, his own two missionarios and several others from the United States, including the apostle's wife, had come to Londrina by train.

And because his missionarios had come to the town before the apostle, he, Brother dos Santos, with his family, had been told that on this night they might have the privilege of seeing the great man bless little Joviniano.

This was the thing that was causing Brother dos Santos to wonder and perhaps even to fear. What if it was true that the apostle was more than a man of God? What if it were true that he really was an apostle of the Lord Jesus Christ, with all the powers of those ancient great ones? Certainly little Joviniano expected he would be the same. So, too, did his good wife expect it. And the way his own heart was pounding, the small man acknowledged to himself, perhaps he, too, believed—far more than he was willing to admit.

What, then, did that mean? Brother dos Santos shook his head, trying to clear it. All along Elders Tolman and Jensen had been saying to him and his family that their church was more than a fine church of God. All along they had been saying that it was actually the Lord Jesus Christ's very ancient Church, brought back to earth in modern times by Jesus and his holy angels. All along they had been saying that their church, alone among all the other churches in the world, had authority to perform ordinances that would take a man and his family back to God. All along they had

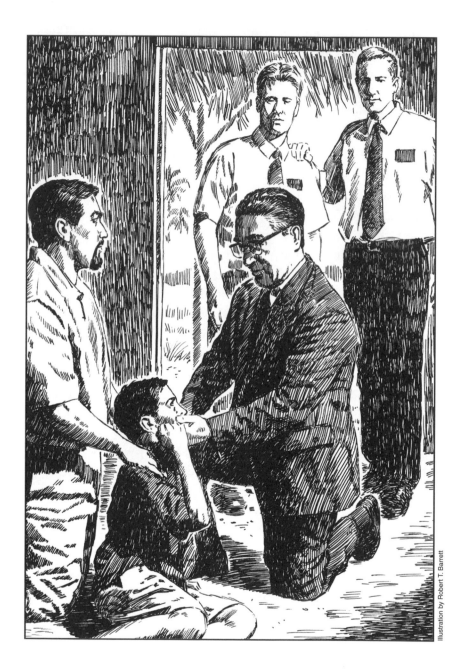

Illustration by Robert T. Barrett

been saying that the gifts of the Lord Jesus' Church had also been restored—the gifts of baptism, healing, and all the other mighty miracles—and of course the gift of the Holy Ghost, which could fill a man's heart with fire and teach him the truth of all things.

Brother dos Santos believed in the Holy Ghost, for from time to time in his life he had felt that great fire and knew that it was from God. For instance, when he read to his family of the Lord and his apostles out of the Holy Bible it had come; and, as they said it would, when the missionarios read to them out of their Book of Mormon, or when they all knelt together in prayer and prayed that a testimony might come to himself, Brother dos Santos, it had come also—

At that moment the door opened and his two missionarios entered the room, smiling and shaking hands with the people who had gathered. They were quickly followed by several other gringos who were all dressed very much alike, and they also were smiling and reaching out to shake hands with those in the room. Brother dos Santos was impressed and smiled with the joy of being near these good people.

But when the American with dark wavy hair and glasses—the man who, somewhat like himself, was not so very tall—led his frail but smiling wife through the door and into the room—then the heart of Brother dos Santos began to burn with a wonderful heavenly fire that was like nothing he had ever felt, and even his tears began to flow. Then he knew that God was with these people! What was more, then he knew that the blessed Lord Jesus had returned in modern times as the missionarios had told his family and now had sent one of his true apostles to Londrina—a great and good man who held within himself the power and authority of God to bless and heal his son! [1]

The second decade of Harold's service as a General Authority began with health problems—his own and those of President

George Albert Smith. Early in 1951, after an extremely busy week-end during which he had installed three new stake presidencies following a major stake division, Harold wrote: "'I finished the day very weary from my exertions.'"2

His weariness, caused by serious health problems and "aggra-vated by a throbbing sinus infection, hung on so tenaciously that on the first weekend in March, Elder Lee was excused from attend-ing a stake conference in Idaho Falls, Idaho. It was the first time in ten years he had missed a stake conference assignment because of illness. Three weeks later, on March 26, as he returned to Salt Lake City from a stake conference in Rexburg, Idaho, Elder Lee was stricken with a sinus attack so severe that it put him in bed for several days.... [W]hile convalescing from this attack...he wrote, under date of March 30, 1951: 'The word from President Smith continues to be discouraging and hope for his recovery has been abandoned.'"3

Four days later, on his eightieth birthday, President Smith passed quietly away. Under the direction of David O. McKay, who as the senior apostle now presided, general conference was changed to Friday and Sunday, with President Smith's funeral to be held on Saturday. Then on Monday a solemn assembly would be convened where a new First Presidency would be sustained by the membership of the Church.

Following the last session of conference on Sunday, April 8, 1951, the Twelve met in the council room in the Salt Lake temple. There, Joseph Fielding Smith nominated David O. McKay to be President of the Church. His nomination was seconded by Harold B. Lee. President McKay then startled everyone by nominating Stephen L. Richards as his first counselor and J. Reuben Clark as his second counselor—though President Clark had served for six-teen years as first counselor to the two previous presidents. Harold's record of the day displays his shock:

President David O. McKay (center)
with counselors Stephen L. Richards (left)
and J. Reuben Clark (right)

CA. 1951

Church Archives, The Church of Jesus Christ of Latter-day Saints

Sunday night, after a dinner at the home of Elder Henry D. Moyle, Brother Moyle and I went to visit President Clark and found him humble, yet loyal to President McKay. He assured us that he would...try his best to be a good counselor, despite the humiliation that was inescapable, as his family and others would seek for an explanation as to why a change in the order of counselors. 4

The next day in the solemn assembly President Clark delivered a masterful acceptance speech, affirming that "performance, not position, should be the governing criterion in evaluating Church service." 5

As the Church moved forward under President McKay, no one could foresee the dramatic changes that were about to take place. Up until the early 1950s, the Church had been rather small and intimate. The General Authorities

went out every weekend to attend stake conferences and stayed in the homes of the local stake leaders. They knew the children in the homes by their first names and remembered them when they came to Church headquarters or went to college. Travel was to the outer perimeter in the East to attend conferences in Washington, D.C., and New York City, but predominately the weekend trips were to California and the Intermountain West, where the stakes of the Church were strong.

General conferences were also more intimate then in some respects than in more recent years.... There were no television cameras to make the speakers feel they were 'on stage.' When the First Presidency spoke, their words were not beyond recall or correction, if later desired, before being distributed in Church publications. The informality of that day is gone now in today's different world and

Church. Microphones and cameras follow the President of the Church wherever he goes. Conference has become a media spectacular along with all that it has ever been as an outlet of spiritual guidance for a wayward world.

While there is an obvious gain from the media coverage, which permits Saints in distant places to actually see their President address them, there is sometimes a loss in his opportunity to speak freely. 6

To understand why, it must be understood that in 1950, membership of the Church in the United States was announced as 926,700. Only 34,251 Saints were in all of Europe; 23,965 in the South Pacific; 2,089 in Australia; only 283 in Asia, with no Saints living in the Philippines; and only 1,936 in all of Latin America, not including the 5,915 Saints in Mexico. These figures show the infancy of the missionary effort outside the United States and Canada, where only 8.7 percent of the Church's population resided. Of course, migration to Zion also had helped to keep these figures so low. 7 By 1956 the population of the Church would reach 3.1 million. 8

President McKay's vision as his presidency began was of a vast and rapidly expanding Church that would literally cover the globe. To that end he launched an ambitious worldwide travel program for himself, making "three lengthy trips to Europe during which he selected sites for temples in Bern, Switzerland, and London, England. On his third European tour he dedicated the temple in Bern, which underscored his message that the Church was international in character, that new members should remain in their native lands, and that all the blessings of the Church, including temple blessings, would be made available to all. During this period, President McKay also made a lengthy trip into Africa, and South America and Central America; and another separate lengthy trip was made into the Pacific, during which he approved the site for a temple in New Zealand." 9 Following this trip to New Zealand, the prophet announced that all missions in the Church would be visited by a General Authority once each year. Insofar as it was possible, it had also been determined that on their travel assignments the Brethren would be accompanied by their wives.

He also set in motion programs chaired by the Twelve and other General Authorities that would more thoroughly unite the Church as a body. Harold, who had long overseen the Church welfare program, was given additional responsibility when he was called to the executive committee of the Church's board of education. This placed him in a position where his influence on Church education would become dramatically noticeable.

For instance, Brigham Young University "experienced a phenomenal growth during the 1950s and 1960s. The main figures contributing to that growth from among the ecclesiastical leaders were President Joseph Fielding Smith and Elder Harold B. Lee. Working as a team, they were heavily involved in every aspect of the work that caused the emergence of Brigham Young University as a major American institution of higher learning.

"Elder Lee's involvement in this growth was a matter of personal satisfaction, given his background in education. And to have become involved in it at the threshold of that growth repeated, in a sense, his pioneering involvement in the development of Church welfare and later in the development of Church correlation and the restructuring of the Church's headquarters organizations." 10

There were also significant changes being made to the welfare program—along with much reevaluation.

President McKay believed some midcourse adjustments in the program were necessary. There was concern about the heavy, continuing welfare "assessments" that were imposed by the general welfare committee. There also was concern about the increasing number of complaints from LDS businessmen who protested against the sale of welfare commodities in the open market in direct competition with them. And there was a sense in some quarters that there had been an undue proliferation of welfare projects, beyond what was strictly necessary for the care of the needy, especially because the dire conditions of high unemployment and economic depression of the 1930s no longer existed. 11

Though aspects of these changes distressed Harold, as well as President Clark and Elder Romney, they willingly submitted to President McKay's directions. It was 1957 before President McKay vindicated the faith of these men and the work they had done during the previous two decades. During the first session of April conference, according to Harold, President McKay, "'for the first time during his presidency, made reference to the welfare program, extolling its leaders and declaring that its methods had been tested and proven sound.' Elated by this unexpected praise, Elder Lee went to the prophet to thank him for it. 'I told him that I felt as though the welfare program had gained a reprieve and that I had relived the feelings I had in the beginning when I was almost daily in his office as he directed me.'" 12 It was finally clear that President McKay had no intention of scrapping the program, but only of redirecting its growth to fit more worldwide needs.

In 1953 the stresses of his calling once again caused Harold's health to fail. Seeing this, President Clark and President Joseph Fielding Smith intervened to cancel his assignments and insisted that he go away for a week of rest. Taking Fern, he headed for California—but stopped in Cedar City to instruct a new stake presidency in their duties, dedicated the new Westwood Ward chapel in Los Angeles, gave a talk to the workers involved in the building of the Los Angeles Temple, and pronounced a blessing on a brother who approached him for that purpose. Finally he found the time to rest—for a night and part of the next day! Then his secretary called to announce assignments to conduct a stake conference in Panguitch, Utah, and Oahu, Hawaii. "My promised vacation was immediately ended," he wrote, "'as we began to keep the telephone busy making arrangements to leave Balboa.'" 13 Thankfully, someone back in Salt Lake City had become aware of this development and interceded. Quickly Harold was notified that his assignment in Panguitch had been canceled and that he was authorized to take Fern and leave immediately for Hawaii. Since the assignment on Oahu was two weeks away, this meant he would get his vacation after all.

Setting sail on the *Lurline* they traveled in style, enjoying a comfortable stateroom and other amenities comparable to a modern cruise ship. "The casual ambiance aboard ship had a soothing effect on the apostle. He settled into an unstructured routine, sleeping as long as he wanted, walking the decks for exercise, reading and writing when the urge came, and in between, gazing at the sea and the marine life that abounded there. On the last night aboard ship, the Lees joined other passengers at the traditional Captain's Dinner, a formal affair with 'paper hats and balloons to spice the occasion.' Harold Lee had not enjoyed such carefree frivolity since his school days. And, the fact he was on assignment from his leaders, was insulated from all telephone calls and visitors and had no meetings to attend or sermons to deliver, removed any sense of guilt or self-reproach." 14

Nevertheless, when he learned that the ship would stop at Hilo before going on to Oahu, Harold's thoughts were again for the welfare of the Saints he had been called to serve. Thus he wrote in his diary:

We regretted that we did not know soon enough...to have notified our missionaries there so that we could have the day with them and our Saints in Hilo inasmuch as we would be there from 8:00 A.M. to 6:00 P.M. In our prayers

...we asked the Lord to alert them somehow to our coming so that our day could be profitably spent with them.

The following entry, April 26, 1953, reported:

As we saw the crowd assembled on the pier, we noted a distinctive group of about fifty whom we recognized as our Latter-day Saints. Our prayers had been answered. They greeted us with a profusion of flower leis and took us to a priesthood and Relief Society meeting in our branch. 15

Despite the fact that he was well known as a tough-thinking pragmatist, this event again dramatizes Harold's deep spirituality—the quality he felt most clearly defined his ministry as an apostle of Jesus Christ. Wherever he went, the gifts of the Spirit followed and were manifest through and around him. As ever, he enjoyed hearing and receiving accounts of these and other spiritual happenings. For instance:

Elder Lee was impressed by stories told [in Hawaii] about how the Saints had been blessed during the devastating tidal wave in 1946, "when 35-foot waves washed away a number of buildings at the waterfront, leaving one lone building which had housed some of the missionaries." A sister also told how she had been washed to sea, but was saved by clinging to a door, and who testified that her temple garments had protected her body from mutilation by sharks. And later in Honolulu, Sister Mary Kaliki told Elder Lee how the tidal wave had receded when she "commanded" it "to spare her home." Such stories confirmed the tradition of Polynesian faith that Matthew Cowley had shared with Elder Lee and the Brethren. 16

As the growth of the Church continued unabated, and as the responsibilities and stress of their work grew ever more burdensome to the General Authorities, in June 1953 President Clark appeared one afternoon in Harold's office to brainstorm some ideas or impressions he had been receiving relative to the supervision of the increasing numbers of wards and stakes in the earth. His idea was to appoint three men in each region of the Church who could train and motivate stake and ward leaders within their respective regions and who would then report periodically to the Twelve. "In this we see the germ of several ideas that, in the years ahead, would become incorporated in the organizational structure of the Church, the concepts of regional training and supervision, of priesthood coordination and correlation at the general level, and even of area presidencies who would oversee groups of regions, and their constituent stakes, wards, and missions. In instances such as this, we also see the dynamics of Church growth and supervision at work, within the general framework of the priesthood, directed and controlled by apostolic authority." 17

Later in 1953, Harold officiated at a stake conference in Calgary, Alberta, Canada, where N. Eldon Tanner was sustained as stake president. It is "an interesting commentary on the fluid nature of leadership" in the Church that within ten years N. Eldon Tanner "would be catapulted into the First Presidency where he would have supervisory responsibilities over Elder Harold B. Lee, the apostle who called him as stake president. These leadership roles would, of course, be reversed in 1970 when Elder Lee became President Joseph Fielding Smith's first counselor, with Brother Tanner as the second counselor, and in 1972 when President Lee became the president of the Church." 18

And as he worked to speed and facilitate the growth of the Church, Harold continued to grow in spiritual prowess. "Through the years much inspiration had come to [him] in dreams. On February 24, 1954, he recorded in his journal a dream which predicted President David O. McKay's physical condition during his last years as President of the Church. The entry stated, 'I had an

Deseret News. Used with permission

Harold B. Lee and N. Eldon Tanner
became close friends as they served
together through the years

CA. 1973

ugly dream last night about President McKay, whom I saw very thin and emaciated, so much so that I carried him in my arms.'

"This became fact as President McKay was unable to walk in his last years of life. Many times Elder Lee and the other General Authorities carried him into the Tabernacle at general conference and other meetings which he desired to attend." 19

In the spring of 1954, Fern fell and fractured her hip, but because of low blood pressure she was not immediately operated on. This, and the fact that her health was frail anyway, gave Harold some serious concerns. In April, however, after being prayed for in the Thursday prayer circle of the Twelve in the temple, Fern underwent the delicate surgery. Harold wrote: "'The love and faith of the First Presidency and the Twelve and Bishop Wirthlin was never in greater evidence. Fern has undoubtedly been [blessed] by the wonderful prayers and faith offered by so many.'" The next day he added: "While seated in the tabernacle, in the closing service of conference, I seemed to have been bathed in Heavenly peace which assured me that the Lord had given my beloved Fern back to me." 20

Despite occasional setbacks, Fern's recovery was steady. When he was in town Harold spent long hours in the hospital with her, which wearied him and brought on a nervous stomach disorder. "In this condition, he drove to Pocatello, Idaho...for a stake conference. While there, he suffered a severe attack of sinusitis which was temporarily alleviated by a blessing given by the local brethren. Indeed, he felt so much better the next day after returning to Salt Lake that he cancelled an appointment...for...tests." 21

On April 20, Harold brought Fern home from the hospital. There, he placed his mattress on the floor near her so he could care for her during the nights. A few days later his own problems flared up again, and a week after Fern's return home, Harold underwent sinus surgery. This, and minor follow-up surgery a few weeks later, seems to have brought about a significant improvement in Harold's health—a blessing he had most fervently prayed for.

Then came the next assignment from the First Presidency—a literal bombshell. In May 1954, President McKay informed Harold that

> the Presidency had decided to have one of the Twelve visit the Orient, including Japan, Korea, and probably Hong Kong, as well as the Hawaiian Islands. They had decided, President McKay said, to send Elder Lee and he wanted Sister Lee to accompany him. He asked Elder Lee to obtain a medical opinion as to how long it would be before Sister Lee could walk without crutches. After additional X-ray studies, which proved that the bone was knitting properly and that the steel plate splicing the break was in proper place, they informed President McKay that Sister Lee could safely be off her crutches within two months or any time after June 15. Progress in Sister Lee's recovery came rapidly after this goal was set. 22

On June 15, Harold commenced his regular summer lecture series at BYU for seminary and institute teachers. Quickly, however, he encountered opposition, as some senior members of the Religion Department faculty objected to giving credit because Harold didn't have a Ph.D. Nevertheless, for the five weeks of the course he persisted with his daily lectures, even attending with other brethren who were assigned by the First Presidency to give different perspectives. The highlight of the series, at least for Harold, came at the concluding banquet—a spiritual event that went into his "miracle" file and was later shared with many. On one such occasion, after describing the grueling summer, he declared:

> [Afterwards] we had a banquet, something like the one we had tonight.... At the conclusion of the banquet one of these seminary teachers took me aside. He came with glistening tears in his eyes and was almost trembling. He said: "Come

over here in this corner, Brother Lee. I have got to tell you something. My wife and I were sitting over there at that table. We were looking over into this corner. Suddenly there appeared the faces of the Prophet Joseph Smith and Brigham Young. I thought, Isn't that marvelous to see the pictures of those two men together? As I watched, that picture faded; it wasn't there anymore. I turned to my wife and said, 'Did you see that picture?' She replied, 'I didn't see anything.' But, even though there is no picture there now, Brother Lee, it was there. I saw it. I wasn't dreaming."

"I'm not surprised," I said. "Aren't you aware of the fact that all through our summer course we have been quoting from the words of the Prophet Joseph Smith and President Brigham Young? Why wouldn't they want to be here? Where else would they rather be on such an occasion than to be permitted to come here at the conclusion of this great seminar where you are going out to influence 150,000 youth from all over this Church? I wouldn't be surprised that they are very close, to let their spirits attend such a gathering. Perhaps most haven't seen them, but have no doubt that they were here. Heaven isn't a million miles away. It's here."

To the young people with whom he was sharing this experience, Harold concluded by saying:

Yes, the Savior, too, is in our midst. His eyes are upon us, but we can't always see him. But the day can come when we could see him. It isn't the Lord who withholds himself from us; it is we who withhold ourselves from him. And if we were living completely worthy, we could see him and have a personal visitation and we would have the assurance, even though we couldn't see him, that he was there, walking, talking, listening, aiding, directing. Make no mistake—this is his work. 23

Once the summer lecture series was over, Harold could focus on preparing for his and his wife's journey to the Orient. Fern had continued to mend, though slowly, and was not feeling anywhere near as well as she or Harold had hoped. Under those circumstances they met with the prophet.

> On July 26, President McKay gave blessings to Elder and Sister Lee for the visit they were assigned to make into the Orient. He blessed them with good health, with safety in their travels, with an awareness of the problems of their mission, with an ability to interpret the conditions in each country, and with the power to impress government officials as they met them. To Fern he gave a blessing and promise that she would return greatly strengthened in her body. 24

Of their departure from the Salt Lake railroad station on August 3, Harold wrote:

> Dr. LeRoy Kimball has been most considerate and attentive in providing us with medicines and our last "shots." Maurine prepared dinner for all our family but I didn't get to see Helen's little ones. They didn't seem to realize just how much I wanted to see all my little ones before I left. After family prayer we found many friends at the depot waiting to say "good-bye" to us. 25

Over the next nine weeks Harold and Fern traveled over 20,000 miles—by rail to San Francisco and then by ship to Honolulu, where they spent two days in meetings. Then on they went by ship again for eight more days before disembarking in Yokohama, after stormy weather and seasickness. After clearing customs they were taken directly to the Eighth Army Base where they were greeted by the commanding general and other hosts. "After the usual pleasantries, [Harold] was outfitted with army clothing and insignia that would enable him to visit army camps as a VIP with all the privileges normally accorded to a major general." 26

For the next five weeks Harold and Fern toured many of the towns, cities, and military bases in Japan, Korea, China, Taiwan, the Philippines, Okinawa, Guam, and Wake Island, speaking to both members and investigators, conducting interviews, and establishing or setting in order what minuscule Church organization existed at the time. While not on a sight-seeing tour, they still saw many things of interest, including the horrible damage inflicted by the bombing during World War II and the smoke from the campfires of the North Koreans across the DMZ (the Lee's tour was made during the Korean conflict). In Seoul, South Korea, Harold "was interested to learn that of over two thousand Korean clan names, the four predominant ones were Kim, Yi, Chang, and Lee. His name, therefore, opened many doors and provided the grist for many friendly conversations. Given his name, it seems altogether fitting that Harold B. Lee was the first General Authority of the Church to visit Korea." 27

Arriving back in Salt Lake City on October 3, the next afternoon Harold became the concluding speaker at general conference. His topic, at President McKay's request, was to report on his and Fern's recent tour of the Orient. Typically, he focused first on that which was most dear to him—the miraculous recovery and physical strengthening of his wife, who only six months before had lain ill in the hospital. Continuing his theme of miraculous interventions and gifts of the Spirit, Harold then broadened his message to include those where he had traveled.

To you, President McKay, before the body of the Church today, as a humble servant whom you sent out into the Far East to check on affairs there, to visit our boys in military service, our scattered Saints in that far-off land, I come back to you testifying, as the Master told the disciples to

Both photos courtesy of the Lee Family Collection

Harold B. Lee visits the American servicemen in Korea   CA. 1954
and spends time visiting Saints in the Pacific isles

testify to John, the miraculous power of divine intervention is out there, which is one of the signs of the divinity of the work of the Lord.

We have seen one "nigh unto death" raised miraculously during this visit. We have seen the hand of the Almighty stay the storms and the winds, and overcome obstacles that otherwise would have made impossible the fulfillment of our mission. We have passed through danger-ridden country only a few hundred miles from where a war is brewing. We have seen the humble and the poor having the gospel preached to them. The signs of divinity are in the Far East. The work of the Almighty is increasing, with a tremendous surge. 28

After discussing what he saw as the fulfillment of a prophecy made by Parley P. Pratt three-quarters of a century before concerning the subjugation of Japan, Harold launched into a report of his encounters with Latter-day Saint servicemen and women stationed throughout the Orient. When describing the attitude of the military toward them, Harold stated:

They know our boys. They know of the work of the Latter-day Saints, and perhaps their attitude towards our boys is best summed up in what General Richard S. Whitcomb said to us down at Pusan, Korea....

"I have always known the members of your Church to be a substantial people. Here in the Pusan area I have the largest court-martial responsibility of any command in the United States Army, but I never have had one of your faith brought before me for a court martial or disciplinary action, in this command. Wherever I have been, I have never known of a Latter-day Saint ever to be brought up for any disciplinary action."...

One of the supervising chaplains, to take another

example, from Clark Field in the Philippines, said this to me as we walked out of a meeting with the Protestant chaplains on the base: "I have never known any group of men in my military experience who have greater devotion to their country, and to their God, and to the Church—no finer characters than are to be found among the boys of the Latter-day Saints."...

Such is the way I found our boys, with the marks of true greatness upon their brows, keeping "with perfect sweetness the independence of solitude."

Concerning the interest in the Church that was spreading throughout Japan, Elder Lee spoke of an unusual invitation he had received while there. He was requested to speak for thirty minutes to the fifteen primary leaders of a group called "The League of New Japan's Religious Organizations"—which supposedly had more than ten million members—and then submit to questions and a discussion. Harold then described what transpired at the meeting:

For that hour, with Brother Tatsui Sato from the mission office translating my words, they listened. Of these men, none claimed to be Christians, and yet in the discussion that followed I learned that they were in truth more Christian than many of the so-called Christians who neither accept the divinity of the mission of Jesus nor of his reality as the Son of the living God.

They recorded my talk on a tape recorder, and when the half-hour was finished for discussion, they were still asking questions, so that our interview extended into two hours and a half, and that recording they promised later would be presented in the quarterly paper where they proposed to give it publicity. I told them that if they were interested and would send me their names and addresses, I would see that each got a copy of the Book of Mormon for them to study.

A few days later I received a letter in Japanese, which Brother Sato translated and wherein the president in charge gave me the names and addresses. His letter reads: "We have no words to express our thanks for your very instructive address, which you gave us the other day. Although you were very busy and must have been tire on your way to preach the gospel in the Oriental area, yet you shared your very precious time for us, for which we have to be very grateful."

Then he said: "May we take advantage of your words that you would present us the Book of Mormon that we may understand better? We send you the list of names who attended the meeting."

Copies of the Book of Mormon have been sent to these leaders. 29

Harold then spoke of a gathering in Pusan, South Korea, which was somewhat of a surprise party because the Church only had three members in the area. In addition to those three, however, there were more than a hundred Latter-day Saint servicemen and 103 Koreans, most of high school age, and most of whom were not yet members of the Church. These young people presented Harold with a silk scroll, written in both Korean and English, which thanked him for his visit and acknowledged their gratitude for the servicemen who had shared the gospel with them.

Finally, Harold described a little Chinese girl—Yook Sin Yuen (called Nora)—from Hong Kong who, with other members in Hong Kong, had no place to meet and so had not received the sacrament in nearly a year. At an outdoor gathering Harold and others with him administered the sacrament, and then he spoke to the gathering and prayed for them and for the people of Hong Kong. Harold's account continues:

Deseret News. Used with permission

The text on the silk scroll Harold B. Lee received in 1954 reads:

"We sincerely welcome Apostle Harold B. Lee who come to Korea. The mission of his visiting Korea is very important and we are thankful to our Father in Heaven from our heart deeply for the great support you have given us for the people of Korea.

"Here we would like to express our gratitude to the soldiers who stayed in Korea and preached the true gospel to us and also the chance we have had of gathering together with them under the name of our Heavenly Father; therefore we are under a vow to repay their kindness. With thanks with all of our eulogy to you for your distinguished service of the faithfulness which will perform your important mission to come to our Korea, and visiting our Korea in spite of its long distance. We humbly pray in the name of Jesus Christ, Amen.

"From: Korean Group in Pusan of The Church of Jesus Christ of Latter-day Saints."

As our bus pulled out from the hotel the next day to take us to the airport, [Nora] reached up her hand through the window and said to me as a parting word: "Brother Lee, tell President McKay to send the Church back to China." I said to her, as the tears were in my eyes also, "My dear sweet girl, as long as we have a faithful, devoted little girl like you, who, without a shepherd, is remaining true, the Church is in China." 30

He concluded his address by summarizing:

Well, I say, President McKay, as I commenced, I have gone now at your appointment to the Far East and I have seen the miracles of God's divine intervention. We have seen that the gospel has been preached to the poor as an evidence of its divinity. God grant that the time shall not be far distant until the death grip of communism shall be unloosed, and those worthy shall be free to receive the fullness of the gospel of Jesus Christ, for I am convinced that there are hundreds of thousands of souls who are begging for the truth. 31

In 1958, President McKay called Harold and Fern to tour the South African Mission as soon as arrangements could be made. Those arrangements included letters of introduction from Harold's friends in banking, railroading, and the insurance industry, as well as government leaders in Washington, D.C., which secured them favors and opportunities for their journey.

After a one-day visit in Rome, Italy, the Lees departed for Johannesburg. Thereafter, the tour was a steady round of meetings, interviews, chapel dedications—interspersed with long drives between cities. Harold quickly saw the need for the mission headquarters to be moved and for Church literature to be printed in the Afrikaans language. He also discerned the difficulties that racism presented for members of the Church. Sunday, October 12, 1958, may have been the spiritual highlight of the South African portion of the tour. Of that day, Harold wrote:

> I held meetings from 9:00 A.M. until 9:00 P.M. with from 200 to 250 in attendance, some coming from Bloomfintein [*sic*] over 300 miles away. Their new chapel, erected at a cost of $90,000, was dedicated at the afternoon session. The Spirit seemed to direct our remarks, which were said to have been as well suited to the specific needs of those present as though we had known beforehand their problems. After I had finished speaking in the evening session and the meeting was closed, the people remained seated. Their branch president came forward and asked them what they were waiting for and if they wanted to hear more. There was a chorus reply of "Yes." I arose again and bore my testimony and gave them my blessing. It was a most impressive demonstration of a people seemingly overcome by the Spirit. Some came afterwards to confess their sins and to declare their determination to live more perfectly. 32

Still, the real highlight of the entire 35,000-mile journey came when they passed through Egypt and entered the Holy Land—the Lees' first visit. In an attempt to understand the real truth of what had transpired on that sacred ground some two millennia before, Harold recorded that they

> read together the harmony of the four gospel narratives so beautifully authored by President Clark and then, as we would leave our room each time, we prayed that the Lord would deafen our ears to what the guide said about historical places, but would make us keenly sensitive to the spiritual feeling so that we would know by impressions from

the Holy Spirit, rather than by hearing, where the sacred spots were located. Although many changes have taken place in this sacred land since Jesus was there, we felt that in certain places there would still linger a spiritual essence that will last forever. 33

Following their Arab guide they came first to Bethlehem's Church of the Nativity, in the basement of which was the cave purported to be the stable of Christ's birth. "'There seemed to be in this place,'" Harold wrote, "'a kind of spiritual assurance that this was, indeed, a hallowed spot.'" 34 Beyond Jericho, the City of Palms, they had similar feelings as they came to the Jordan where Christ was baptized; their hearts burned again as they beheld the cottage of Mary, Martha, and Lazarus outside the walled city of Jerusalem; and yet again near the eight gnarled, ancient olive trees found in the Garden of Gethsemane. Late in the day they followed the way of the cross, supposedly to the place of crucifixion and the place of the holy sepulcher.

> But all of this, according to tradition, we felt is in the wrong place. We felt none of the spiritual significance which we had felt at other places, for had not the Apostle Paul said, speaking of the crucifixion: "Wherefore Jesus also, that he might sanctify the people with his own blood, suffered without the gate." (Hebrews 13:12.) To us, we felt this meant he suffered to his death upon the cross for the sins of mankind, not within the gates of Jerusalem, but outside the gates, and yet the guides were trying to make us think that his crucifixion took place inside the walls. Again, what we were seeing there did not square with John's description of the place where the crucifixion and burial took place, as John described it in John 19:41–42. 35

Almost as an afterthought, Harold and Fern were taken to the spot known as the Garden Tomb, then owned by the Church of the United Brethren. It was hewn out of a hill outside the gate of the walled city and was only a short distance from where the hall of judgment had stood just inside the city's walls. As Harold wrote:

> The garden was right close by or "in the hill" as John had said, and in it was a sepulchre hewn out of a rock, evidently done by someone who could afford the expense of excellent workmanship. There was something that seemed to impress us as we stood there, that this was the holiest place of all, and we fancied we could have witnessed the dramatic scene which took place there. That tomb has a mouth which could be sealed by a rolling stone in the shape of a huge millstone and there was a channel at its mouth that had been built to guide the stone as it had been rolled across the opening to close the tomb. Although the rolling stone door had been taken away by those seeking sacred relics, the stone channel was still there. Within the tomb there is a room large enough to accommodate a half-dozen people; and across one end is a slab raised about a foot and a half from the floor beautifully carved out to fit a human body, with a place at the foot and the head where one might sit.
>
> In the beautiful garden, the holiest place of all, we looked at the hill nearby and gazed into the empty tomb. The sun was setting and the soft shadows fell around us, shutting out the whole world as it seemed. The peace of those few moments we shall never forget. Yes, at the Garden Tomb, outside the walls, we had the feeling that it, and the Mount of Golgotha, or the skull, seemed right. They were the holiest of all....
>
> As we stood before the empty tomb in Jerusalem we too knew that because of this sacrifice, we too can have our

sins remitted and be made worthy to stand in his holy presence in the days to come. I came away from these experiences never to feel the same again about the mission of the Lord and Savior and to have impressed upon me, as I have never had it impressed before, what it means to be a special witness. I say to you with all the conviction of my soul, I know that Jesus lives. I know that he was the very Son of God and I know that in this Church and in the Gospel of Jesus Christ entrusted to this Church is to be found the way to salvation. 36

As they departed from the airport in Tel Aviv, Fern recorded her own witness:

Here closed our wonderful opportunity to come to this great land. As I have thought about it...I know that our prayers had been answered and the glorious truths of the mission of our Lord and Savior were anchored deep in our hearts. My heart sings out with love and gratitude for him who has done so much for us; and the wonder and the glory of it all was beyond understanding. 37

The final major tour of Harold's second apostolic decade was a tour of South America, which took place in 1959. His assignment was to take Fern, tour the missions, and create two new missions, one in Brazil and the other in Chile. After their call but before their departure, Harold was rushed to LDS Hospital one night in early June when he suffered an internal hemorrhage—a bleeding ulcer had erupted, and at a family dinner he fainted from the loss of blood. Weeks of careful diet and rest restored him sufficiently to make the journey. Near the end of June, Harold's mother passed away of a heart attack. He was in New York when he heard of it, but after arriving home he found that she had been well prepared to go, even having put away the cost of her burial. Some years later

Fern and Harold B. Lee enjoyed traveling together   CA. *late 1950s*
Above: at Chitzen Itza; Below: Andes Mission Tour

he offered this final, loving tribute: "'She was an angel from heaven and she passed through the lights and shadows of life with great fortitude.... And when everyone else gave up, she didn't.'" 38

When Harold finally departed from the Salt Lake airport for this South American tour, leaving a week earlier than Fern so he could attend corporate meetings, President McKay came to bless him and see him off. It gave Harold a deep thrill to think that the prophet would so honor him.

From New York, after Harold had attended his usual business meetings and Fern had joined him, the Lees set sail for South America on the *S.S. Brazil* on August 29, 1959. The trip seemed to do him good. After a week at sea, Harold wrote: "'I'm feeling a return to normal health and vigor and hopefully believe that my physical difficulties are greatly lessened. Fern seems to have enjoyed this voyage.'" 39

In company with President William Grant Bangerter and then with President Asael T. Sorensen, Harold toured the soon-to-be-divided Brazil Mission, meeting constantly with missionaries, members, and investigators. At one point, he wrote:

> We went by "air-taxi" from Claro to Bauru in a small one-engine Stinson plane.... Here we were to see one of the surprises, a black woman president of the branch Relief Society with her husband and children all members, and a young girl with black blood in charge of the Primary. Both, they tell me, are well received by the whites. We enjoyed here the most spiritual missionary meeting of any in our tour so far. The spirit of the Elders seemed characterized by one Elder who said: "We found ourselves by losing ourselves in the red dirt of Maringa." A pair of Elders told of traveling five hours in a hot, dusty bus to a new town and of bearing testimony to each other that entire distance. 40

It was at this meeting, dramatized in the vignette at the beginning of this chapter, that Harold met Brother dos Santos, his small son of mighty faith who was called Joviniano, and Elders Tolman and Jensen, who had prepared the dos Santos family for the miracle the Lord would give them through his chosen servant. Concerning what happened next, Richard R. Tolman, one of the two missionaries involved, has written:

> After the meeting, we introduced the family to Elder Lee and we went into the branch president's office where I anointed Joviniano and Elder Lee sealed the anointing with a powerful blessing. The Spirit's influence was so strong in the room I thought my back bone was going to crawl off my body. Some of the details of the blessing have slipped from my memory, but I do remember some of the more powerful words that Elder Lee pronounced on Joviniano that night. He rebuked the illness that was in his body and commanded strength into the muscles and bones of his legs. I specifically remember the word "rebuke" because, at that time, that was the only word he used whose equivalent in Portuguese I did not know. Nevertheless, the Spirit was very helpful in obtaining an exact translation for the family to understand.
>
> When Elder Lee had finished, tears were seen in the eyes of every person in the room. He gave Joviniano a big hug and placed him in his father's arms.
>
> The next day we visited the family, and the father proudly showed us that Joviniano could now stand shakily on his own two legs for the first time in his life. I telephoned the mission home with the good news and they promised to relay the message to President Sorensen and Elder Lee.
>
> In the city of Porto Alegre, as Elder Lee was about ready to leave Brazil and go to Uruguay, he bore a powerful

Alderacy "Joviniano" dos Santos
after he was healed

CA. 1959

Courtesy of the Lee Family Collection

testimony describing Joviniano's miraculous healing. The effect of his powerful parting testimony quickly spread throughout the Brazilian South Mission and greatly stimulated the work....

In my letter to the mission president in October 1959, I reported that Joviniano, whose legs were once useless limbs hanging from his body, was gaining more strength daily and learning how to use his legs. By December, Joviniano was walking and still making excellent progress. His parents had been baptized and were faithfully keeping the commandments. 41

President Asael T. Sorensen, who was accompanying Harold and Fern at this time, remembers other aspects of that testimony borne in the city of Porto Alegre:

During a final missionary meeting held with Elder and Sister Lee in the city of Porto Alegre in the state of Rio Grande do Sul, Elder Lee was inspired to share his beautiful, inspiring testimony. He mentioned that testimonies were of a sacred nature and should only be shared with those who could appreciate sacred truths. During the entire course of that meeting, the Spirit of the Lord was so strongly felt that Elder Lee quietly stated that the veil that separates us from the spirit world was almost entirely withdrawn....

Sister Lee was one of the warmest, most gracious sisters whom we have ever known, one to whom living the gospel came so naturally. 42

There were other miraculous events recorded during the tour, the reports of which ended up in Harold's "Miracles" file. Also in Porto Alegre a "young Brazilian sister missionary was having her companion, Sister Gatenby, translate Elder Lee's English when suddenly she discovered she was understanding without the translation. This sister later told of a miraculous escape from the grasp of a man who accosted her and her companion in Curitiba.

"At the same meeting a remarkable young missionary leader, Elder Ross Leroy Broadbent, who had been called as the first counselor to the mission president a week earlier, related an inspiring experience of when he was hopelessly lost in Petropolis, unable to speak the native language and with no address for the chapel or the missionaries. After a fervent prayer in which he pleaded with the Lord that he must have help to fill his mission, he heard a voice which told him twice to follow the man on the corner. Obediently he followed the man as directed and was led directly to the chapel without further difficulty." 43

The gift of tongues was manifest in Uruguay, where Harold noted that "the audience was understanding and reacting to what I said before the interpreter had repeated it, even though they knew no English," and again in Paraguay, where "three faithful sisters came up excitedly at the close of the meeting to declare that they had understood what Elder Lee had said before it had been translated, although they knew no English." 44 The the gifts of the Spirit followed Harold and Fern constantly as they traveled among the South and Central American people on their three-month errand for the Lord.

By 1960, at the end of Harold's second decade of apostolic service, he had established himself in the minds of the Saints as a man of God—one who was intimately acquainted with the Lord and who carried his Spirit wherever he went. He had also become well-enough traveled that he knew the world and its peoples, and he understood thoroughly that the righteous, no matter their color, culture, or language, all responded the same when under the influence of the Holy Ghost. Finally, he had reached the point where he "stood next in seniority to his revered friend and much more senior associate Elder Joseph Fielding Smith, whom he was destined to follow into the First Presidency after the death of President David O. McKay. Not only had he risen quickly due to the passing of the older Brethren, but also his talents were being increasingly called on and his leadership abilities increasingly expanded with new and larger responsibilities." 45 Life as apostle was indeed proving to be schooling for a prophet.

GREAT TRIALS OF FAITH

As Harold sat alone in his office in a second-floor corner of the Church Administration Building, he held in his hand a very professional looking report. He was finding difficulty holding back his tears. Once again the Lord had done it! Once again he had whispered his instructions through the still, small voice of the Spirit and had then pulled back in order to allow Harold and the host of others involved to experience the growth he knew each of them needed. And yet, now that things were truly moving forward and results were coming in, the sum of what had happened—what was continuing to happen—seemed far greater, and of much more significance, than any of the separate parts might have indicated. This, Harold understood perfectly, was a witness to both him and the Church that the Lord had indeed been involved and that what had been accomplished had been God's will all along.

Church, priesthood, and organizational correlation. For Harold personally it had been a thirty-year labor, most of that time with a sense of discouragement and even failure hanging over his head. Yet now, as Harold again thumbed through the recent report that had been submitted by Dr. Frank Magid and Associates, his heart felt to rejoice that the Lord had been kind enough to allow him the privilege of playing a small part in bringing this to pass.

How well he could remember the day President J. Reuben Clark, who had befriended him even before his call to the Twelve, had once again called him down to his office. There the great Church leader had shown Harold the projected growth of the Church and then thrown out some of his ideas as to how the General Authorities might handle it. Chief among his proposals had been the idea of assigning men to supervise various areas of the Church under the authority of the Twelve, much as Harold had set up the Church's welfare program to function on a regional basis. This would free the brethren of the Twelve from much of the administrative burden they were then carrying, which Harold would soon learn was enough to tax nigh unto death even the most robust among them. President Clark had also been concerned that auxiliaries, programs, and even lesson manuals had no central supervision but seemed to multiply upon themselves without so much as a hint of proper authority.

For years after that meeting Harold had pondered these things, always remembering the lesson he had learned the morning in 1935 when he had been called by the First Presidency to develop a Churchwide program of providing welfare relief to the Saints. Hours following the call, as he had labored in prayer in a secluded spot in Memory Grove over how to organize such a vast effort, the whisper of the Spirit had reminded him that the organization was already in place—and had been since the days of Joseph Smith. It was the organization of the priesthood the Lord was referring to, and all Harold had to do, therefore, was find the proper way to mobilize it.

It was due to that same lesson that he had known, even as he and President Clark had sat brainstorming that day in the early 1940s, that it must be through the Lord's divinely revealed priesthood organization that solutions to Church growth and correlation would be found and implemented. Yet it had taken so very long to accomplish—

First had come the assignment from the First Presidency, in the late 1940s, to serve on a committee that was to do a study on ways to simplify the programs of the Church and at the same time improve the effectiveness of the General Authorities in their assigned labors. Dutifully, the committee had done their work and presented their findings, only to have them tabled—ostensibly because certain brethren could not bear to part with their favorite programs, or perhaps were loathe to make the difficult changes the committee had recommended.

Harold had felt such a keen disappointment, and yet when President Clark had urged patience, he had dutifully turned the whole matter over to the Lord and done his best to fill his assignments exactly as they were given—never criticizing or complaining.

In 1960—nearly twelve long years later—the First Presidency had made a similar request to the general priesthood committee, of which Harold had then been chairman. Find a way, they had been directed, to organize the priesthood of the Church so that the burdens of administration might be carried by local leaders instead of just the Twelve. In addition, they had also been asked to work out a correlated system of gospel study for the entire priesthood and auxiliary programs of the Church—to the end that every member of the Church, worldwide, would be learning the same eternal truths that God had revealed from the heavens.

The result, Harold had seen immediately and with great clarity, would be to strengthen the family, which must also become the program's focus or theme. President David O. McKay's then-famous quote, "No other success can compensate for failure in the home," had been its harbinger. Henceforward, and the thought of this had thrilled the very fibers of Harold's being, every single program and event in the Church needed to focus on helping families become successful—helping them to create and then strengthen within their own familial bonds peace, joy, refuge, safety, faith, and spiritual strength and power sufficient to unite and seal them eternally.

In short, he had thought with deep emotion, Church members throughout the world should be as happy within their families as he was in his—and the Church should do everything in its power to see that this was so.

After dutifully making their recommendations, many of which hearkened back to suggestions made in the late 1940s but now somewhat or entirely modified to focus on the family, committee members were thrilled when the First Presidency accepted them and then organized a Church correlation committee, appointing Harold as chairman.

Leaning back in his chair, Harold smiled at the memory of all that had followed. In addition to his other assignments—those common to all members of the Twelve—and in spite of the personal losses that had afflicted his own family during the first years of the decade, he had still done his best to employ all his talents and knowledge so that a systematic program for teaching the gospel to children, youth, and adults might be implemented. In other words, so that all members of families within the Church, no matter their age, might learn God's eternal truths together.

In addition, he had also led out in inaugurating and perfecting a system for better communications between Church leaders at all levels of administration. At the heart of his philosophy was the idea—again harking back to that morning in Memory Grove when the Spirit had taught him so pointedly—that all programs of the Church should be placed more fully under the direction of the priesthood. Only in that way, he had begun to understand, could the focus on families remain strong and intact.

Now almost another full decade had passed. Because Elder Joseph Fielding Smith had been called as one of the ailing President McKay's counselors, and at the same time was retained as President of the Quorum of the Twelve, Harold was now serving as Acting President, directing the work of the Twelve as they did the work of the Lord. And now in his hands was evidence, clear and concrete, that the correlation program first envisioned by dear President Clark so many years before—the one the Brethren were constantly in the process of implementing—was finally bearing fruit.

Arch Madsen, who several years previously had been brought to Salt Lake City by President McKay to head up Church broadcasting and who was now head of Bonneville International, had suggested some time before that a comprehensive survey of those who were not members of the Church, taken in certain key areas of the country, might have merit in helping focus the Church's internal and external communications. Arch had already commissioned similar surveys in cities where the Church owned or was considering purchasing radio and television stations and had found them extremely useful in building Bonneville.

Making contact with his friends and associates in New York City and then following their recommendations, Harold and the others of the Twelve and First Presidency had settled on the same outside consulting firm used by Arch and Bonneville—Frank N. Magid Associates, Inc., of Cedar Rapids, Iowa—and had hired them to do a comprehensive survey regarding "outsider" attitudes toward the Church.

The firm's significant findings relative to getting nonchurchgoers to become churchgoers, for instance, were that people would most likely try a church if that church would (a) Help them achieve peace with themselves, (b) Help them achieve peace with God, (c) Be a warm and friendly place to enjoy fellowship, (d) Not force strict acceptance of dogma, (e) Provide practical help for solving everyday problems, and (f) Help solve major problems facing the country.

In an "image association" portion of the survey, which was what Harold was finding most interesting, individuals were asked what they first thought about when the "Mormon" religion was mentioned. According to the document now in his hands, after the obvious—

"Excuse me, Brother Lee, but some of the Brethren are getting anxious to hear what the report has to say."

Harold smiled at his secretary, Frances Cardall. "Thank you, Frances. I'm sure they are." Then his eyes twinkled with his nearly silent chuckle. "Perhaps you are as anxious as they?"

"Well," Frances smiled with characteristic embarrassment, "you've spoken of it so often lately, I have wondered—a little."

"Then I shall tell you—a little." Harold smiled to insure that Frances knew he was teasing. "I was just reviewing the image association portion of the survey—where people were asked to say the first things they thought of when hearing about the Church. After the obvious geographical links with the state of Utah and Salt Lake City, as well as the strictness of our code of living, they thought that Mormons were 'closely united' and 'help one another.'

"Do you see the significance of that, Frances? Those are family-related traits that were inaugurated as the heart of the correlation program back in 1962! That means that we are succeeding! Not only are our families being strengthened within the Church, which is the Lord's way of bringing to pass the exaltation and eternal life of man, but now the world is beginning to see the Lord's work and to recognize the value of it."

"That's wonderful, Brother Lee."

Again Harold smiled. "Yes, it is. What is the purpose of the Church, Frances? The Lord told us in the 115TH section of the Doctrine and Covenants. It has been repeated in every dispensation of the gospel in a similar way. He said: 'Thus shall my church be called in the last days, even The Church of Jesus Christ of Latter-day Saints. Verily I say unto you all: Arise and shine forth, that thy light may be a standard for the nations; and that the gathering together upon the land of Zion, and upon her stakes, may be for a defense, and for a refuge from the storm, and from wrath when it shall be poured out without mixture upon the whole earth.'

"Again, Frances, where is the first line of defense in this church? Is it the Primary? Is it the Sunday School? That is not the way our Heavenly Father has revealed it. Read the sixty-eighth section of the Doctrine and Covenants, verses twenty-five through thirty-two. You will find that the Lord placed the family squarely on the forefront of the battlefield against the powers which threaten down these defenses. The family is and must remain the first line of defense."

Rising to his feet, Harold tapped the survey results with his finger. "Dr. Magid has shown that the world is already beginning to recognize it, Frances, and will flock to the Church in droves because of it. Now if only we as Latter-day Saints can keep it in mind. If we don't—if there should ever come a time where we should be so absorbed, or our programs should be so inclusive as to take all the time of the child by our various Church organizations, it would be a tragic thing, I am sure, in our Heavenly Father's eyes.

"It seems clear to me that the Church has no choice—and never has had—but to do more to assist the family in carrying out its divine mission, not only because that is the order of heaven, but also because that is the most practical contribution we can make to our youth—to help improve the quality of life in Latter-day Saint homes. As important as our many programs and organizational efforts are, these should not supplant the family but should support it always."

Again Harold's eyes twinkled. "Now, Frances, you mustn't keep me talking this way, not when the Brethren are waiting—"[1]

Ten years after the survey mentioned above, Frank N. Magid Associates did a follow-up survey. Though by then Harold had passed away, the findings were even more unequivocal—the Church's focus on strong families was becoming renowned. Under the title "Comparative Evaluations," the report states:

Without question, the strong, close family relationships among LDS Church members is its strongest selling point. It is with this criterion that the Church is most associated— and that is significant since it also is considered the most important of the five criteria tested. Scores given the Mormon Church, in general, increase with socioeconomic standing, as well as with knowledge of the Church. Although the Mormons are best rated on this criterion, they are not the only religion to score well. Baptists, Catholics, and Jews also get high grades on this trait, although none of them do quite as well as the Mormons. 2

"This emphasis on strengthening the family, which came into prominence in the early 1960s before today's extreme challenges were obvious, is one of the most powerful evidences that modern revelation flows from true prophets to prepare the Saints of God for the adversary's attacks. Certainly none too soon were the Saints warned to get their houses in order before the true concept of family life was attacked anew and became one of the most bitter battlegrounds between the forces of good and evil. The correlation pioneers were prophetic in their warnings and the Church gained a lasting trademark of family strength, internally and in the world, through the reorganizations of the 1960s led by Elder Harold B. Lee." 3

Harold's third decade of apostolic service, however, began with grief and greater burdens. In 1960 he was appointed to the board of Zions First National Bank and then to the executive committee of that board. At the same time President J. Reuben Clark was experiencing serious health problems and had almost ceased functioning as a member of the First Presidency. In October, Harold traveled to Grantsville to visit him and reported:

Marion Romney and I went to see President Clark, ...who is still in a very depressed state and has apparently ruled himself out of much future activity. He seems obsessed by the idea that a man in his 90TH year has nothing to which he can look forward. 4

Twelve days later, they visited President Clark again, this time taking Henry D. Moyle, who was now Second Counselor to President McKay, with them. Harold wrote:

> We found him waiting to talk about the three of us being speakers at his funeral, ...the handling of his personal library; the possibility of disposing of his Grantsville ranch to some stake as a welfare project; and for Marion Romney to move up on the obtaining of someone to write his biography after his passing. 5

Because of the frail health of both President Clark and President McKay, Elders Joseph Fielding Smith and Hugh B. Brown were both added as counselors in the First Presidency, with Gordon B. Hinckley being called to the Twelve. Only days after most of these actions were taken, on October 6, 1961, President Clark passed quietly away—"a welcome release for this scholarly and statesman-like leader, whose First Presidency service spread through three presidential administrations of the Church." 6

Harold was one of the speakers at the funeral, after which many commented "about the more personal references he made in his farewell eulogy to the most influential man in his life, and that he had remembered President Clark's instructions to 'not make my vices my virtues.'" 7

During this same period Fern's deteriorating health necessitated the sale of the Lee home on Conner Street and a move to a one-level home at 1436 Penrose Drive in Salt Lake City.

> Following the exhausting trip through South America, she had slowly gone downhill, unable to regain her strength. After an operation in January 1961, she fell at home, tearing

some of the stitches. She was then returned to the hospital. By this time, it was apparent that it would be necessary for the Lees to move to a home on one level where Fern would not have steps to climb.... They moved...on October 20, 1961. "Fern said she was so happy and couldn't sleep," wrote Elder Lee on that day, "so I am happy too." 8

It was also at this time (1960) that President McKay felt impressed to push forward the program of correlating and coordinating the work of the Church by introducing system and control into the Church's curriculum and other areas. Harold, as chairman of the general priesthood committee, was to take charge. By 1961 ward teaching had become part of the priesthood correlation program, and fourteen stakes had been chosen to implement correlation proposals in a pilot program. Two weeks before the October 1961 general conference, Harold was called in to meet with President McKay. Harold wrote that President McKay

> said he awoke at 6:30 A.M. with a clear impression as to the proper theme for the general priesthood meeting and that he was impressed that the newly approved correlation program should be the theme. He asked me and Richard L. Evans to speak on this subject. 9

Pleased with the way the correlation program was formally launched during the conference by President McKay, Harold quickly moved to meet with Marion G. Romney, Richard L. Evans, and Gordon B. Hinckley of the Twelve, who were "'to head up the three divisions of the correlation program.'" A week later, Harold convened the first meeting of what was called "the All Church Coordinating Council, with all the General Authorities present, except the First Presidency, and 'with all heads of all church [headquarters] units in attendance.' Thereafter, Elder Lee met periodically with this council to help everyone understand his role..., to encourage its members to carry the message into the field, and to promote unity and cooperation between the priesthood and the auxiliaries." 10

Between 1963 and 1966, the membership of the Church, through stake and general conference addresses, as well as training meetings, were given "a thorough education with respect to priesthood dominance and the new focus of correlation centering on the importance of the home.... With this foundation established, Elder Lee could look for a more basic organizational change which would take the Church into its future of unprecedented growth." 11

While recovering from stomach surgery in 1967, Harold began thinking through the "many problems confronting a growing Church numbering 2.5 million members, most of them living in 434 stakes. Elder Lee focused on the seventy already constituted regions of the Church. He wrote his musings in his journal:

> If we could have in each region three "Church-service-time" assistants to the Twelve, answerable to the Twelve, to conduct the regional meetings twice a year, and between times work with individual stakes needing their attention in all phases of priesthood activities, ...then the Church could meet the growth now taking place. 12

On May 16, still pondering his idea, Harold "spent some time at his office dictating a memorandum relative to...naming 'regional coordinators' in the seventy regions of the Church. He began to envision the auxiliaries coming to the regional meetings...to hold training sessions with their stake and ward auxiliary leaders.... The plan was jelling in his mind." 13

When all was said and done, the position of Regional Representatives of the Twelve had been created. The Brethren "were careful to define the scope of the authority of a Regional Representative. He was not to be an officer in the priesthood line but was to serve merely in a staff capacity, teaching and training local leaders in matters as directed by the Twelve. Regional Representatives were to serve without compensation for a period of years. Concurrent with this development [was] the need for a training committee...to help structure training seminars for the Regional Representatives and instructional programs to be taken into the field as part of stake or regional conferences." 14

By July 1967, steps were being taken to identify, call, and train these men. Meanwhile, Harold was "working behind the scenes with Elder Thomas S. Monson [on] plans for the training committee. On August 9, they and other members of the correlation executive committee met with the First Presidency in President McKay's Hotel Utah apartment, where the plans for training the Regional Representatives were approved. Also, 'the names of proposed regional representatives were approved, with few exceptions.'" 15

At length everything was ready for this historic action—installing a new level of Church leadership. Harold's journal records the momentous day, Thursday, September 28, 1967.

> We began the day with an hour's devotional in the Salt Lake Temple with the General Authorities and the Regional Representatives of the Twelve. The meeting was held under the direction of the First Presidency.... With the exception of President McKay and Elder Antoine Ivins, all were in attendance.... I was particularly blessed in a closing instruction on the subject, "How to Use the Scriptures in Our Teaching." In the evening, all the General Authorities, Regional Representatives of the Twelve, and their wives, with all our correlation workers, attended a dinner in the Lafayette Ballroom of the Hotel Utah. 16

Two days later Harold presented the new regionalized program to "an estimated audience of 100,000 priesthood holders who were gathered in the Tabernacle on Temple Square and in 475 different chapels throughout the world." 17

From that date forward the seminars for Regional Representatives were held for two days preceding general conferences. "Beginning with the first seminar in October 1967 a tradition was established which lasted many years: as chairman of the Correlation Committee and encouraged by President McKay, Elder Lee set the stage and the spirit with a major address at the beginning of each seminar.

"As Elder Lee ripened in leadership and spoke for the First Presidency, and finally as President of the Church, he presented the confidential 'State of the Church' addresses as the keynote speaker at each seminar. Because of the exclusive audience and the absence of pressures brought on by reporters, television cameras, and time limitations—which characterize the general sessions of conference in the Tabernacle—these sermons have emerged as being among the most significant addresses to the priesthood leaders attending general conferences since 1967." 18

Such a major triumph, however, didn't come to Harold without a price. Earlier in the decade, Harold had entered into what would prove to be the most difficult period of his life. "God has always exacted the highest price of personal sacrifice from those whom he would trust to become his prophets, the spokesmen-leaders over his children here on earth. They must go through the fiery furnace and have their mettle proven beyond question and doubt." 19 So was it to be with Harold.

At the beginning of 1962, just barely settled into her newly redecorated home, Sister Fern T. Lee's deteriorating condition manifested itself. On the first Saturday of 1962, she blacked out three times during the night; Elder Lee cancelled his stake conference trip to San Bernardino, California, to stay with her.

A similar episode occurred in April, 1962, while Elder Lee was in New York City; she was hospitalized after becoming unconscious twice during the night and suffering a slight concussion from a fall. After ten days she had improved, but the neurosurgeon consultant attending her warned that more such attacks might be expected because of her long history of high blood pressure. 20

Through the spring and summer Fern seemed to improve and was able to attend several community and family functions and be with Harold on one or two assignments. She also hosted a dinner for the family on the patio of her new home on July 4TH, though her fainting spells continued intermittently.

In September she was diagnosed, in addition to her hypertension, with periodic brain clots. On September 14, when Harold called home from the Logan Temple where he had gone to teach newly called missionaries, he learned that Fern had been seriously ill the entire day. He immediately called her doctor and returned home.

About 3:00 A.M. she called for me to take her to the bathroom. She blacked out, with her head becoming cold and clammy, as also her feet and hands. For thirty minutes her sister Emily and I worked over her with all the faith and prayer we could muster. Her body gradually became warm again. For a time we wondered if we would bring her back. She went to sleep until about 6:00 A.M. As she awakened the entire nausea returned. I called Dr. James F. Orme, her doctor, and he advised that we take her immediately to the hospital....

After the first day her condition improved markedly. The neurosurgeon told Helen and me that he was convinced her nausea was still caused by minor arterial "accidents" in her brain, which might be classed as mild strokes. This reasoning argued the necessity of keeping her pressure to a minimum to prevent reoccurrences. She seems to be worrying about my cancelling of trips to the East, as evidence of a more serious condition than we had told her. President McKay has advised that I attend my Equitable and Union Pacific meetings, which I probably will do if Fern remains the same or improves. I will make plans to further her sense of security. I have had a strong feeling that I should not go East this week, but probably next week. 21

By the following Saturday Fern seemed to be doing sufficiently better that Dr. Orme encouraged Harold to keep an appointment for a stake conference at the Lake Mead Stake in Nevada. Fern agreed with this, and they discussed plans for her homecoming the following week.

That night, however, Fern "suffered a massive cerebral hemorrhage. Her spinal fluid indicated that her condition was near fatal.... Helen's husband, Brent, notified Elder Lee in Nevada by a phone call at 12:30 A.M..... Elder Lee was forced to charter a small, two-engine plane which flew him to the Salt Lake Airport, arriving at 4:00 A.M.

"[He] then began a long vigil at the bedside of his beloved wife, praying mightily for the preservation of her life. With profound grief, he watched his dear companion slipping, responding less and less to the [machinery] ...sustaining [her] life. Finally he was urged to go home to bathe and rest. At home, reflecting on having watched her frail unconscious body suffer for thirty hours, he realized what he must do. Only then could he kneel down and ask the Lord to take her quickly if she couldn't be returned to a normal life. After he was resigned to placing her in the hands of a loving God, the end came quickly." 22

At 9:00 A.M., while Harold was at Helen's home eating breakfast, Maurine called to say that their mother was failing rapidly. "Arriving in the hospital room Elder Lee felt [Fern's] presence so strongly that he began quietly talking to her as though she could

Fern Tanner Lee

CA. *late 1950s*

hear what he was saying. With his fingers lovingly stroking her forehead, the minutes ticked on while he whispered to her...ten, fifteen, thirty...until the nurse attending her suddenly stepped out of the room to summon the doctor. The doctor came, checked her in that final moment, and said gently, 'She's gone, Brother Lee.'

"Harold B. Lee straightened up, left her bedside with a departing kiss, and said to his family waiting close by, 'Mother always said, after each funeral sermon she heard me deliver, that I would have to speak at her funeral someday because I said all the words that were important to her.' He continued, 'But of course we both knew I could never do that, so I've just been reminding her of those precious truths which I thought she would like to hear as she embarks on this great new experience.'

"She had passed away peacefully, and no doubt, contentedly, upon hearing her dear husband recite as only he could the message of hope which will link them eternally as loving companions." 23

It was midmorning, Monday, September 24, 1962.

The funeral, held three days later, was preceded by a public viewing at the mortuary and a private viewing in the home. Harold wrote: "I had the feeling that Fern would want to say her farewell in her beautiful home which she loved so much. So, after a public viewing where about 1,000 or more persons came to the mortuary, we had her casket brought and placed before the living room mantel in our home at 1436 Penrose Drive at 10:00 A.M. the next morning." 24

In his own home and surrounded by his loving but sorrowing family, Harold once again became the teacher, putting aside his own grief as he appealed particularly to his grandchildren, tenderly showing them how beautiful and sweet death could be, especially to one so nearly perfect as their beloved "Nana." The General Authorities then came to the home to pay their final respects, after which the cortege left for the stake center and Fern's beautiful and moving funeral. Presidents McKay and Moyle were two of the speakers, a double mixed quartet from the

Harold B. Lee   CA. 1963

Deseret News. Used with permission

Tabernacle Choir performed part of the music, and in every way the service was a fitting tribute to a woman who had lived so faithfully and sacrificed so much in behalf of the Lord's earthly kingdom.

Still, "at day's end, when all had gone, and Elder Lee was left alone, the full impact of his loss struck home. No conviction of a reunion in the afterlife, nor glowing memories of past joys, could erase the sense of present loss and deprivation. Aware of this, Elder Lee's sister, Verda, and her husband, Charles Ross, now stepped forward, offering to move into the home, there to assume the responsibility of maintaining it while providing some semblance of family life for him. Avidly accepting this unexpected offer, Elder Lee, to his death, could never adequately express his gratitude for this loving gesture. With the Rosses in the home and with his daughters and their families nearby, he had all the support one could hope for to adjust to life without Fern." 25

One who has not experienced the loss of a beloved spouse, even though he might be a prophet, can never fully understand the intense and lingering pain engendered by the experience. Thinking to help, however, President McKay arranged for Harold to attend conferences in Europe with his good friend Walter Stover. Unfortunately, the time of the journey coincided with Fern's birthday and their wedding anniversary, and the memories generated that day led to spells of nervous tension and depression, oftentimes accompanied by tears. In Berlin Harold could not even attend one of the meetings because of his state.

Back home, despite the best efforts of himself and his family, Christmas seemed cold, lonely, and meaningless. A short time later he had to leave a testimonial dinner in honor of President McKay because he could not endure being there due to his agitated nervous system, and for a time he avoided attending Sunday School in his own ward for the same reason.

These feelings dominated Elder Lee's waking hours and troubled his dreams until mid-January 1963, when help came from an unexpected source. Following an Equitable meeting in New York, board member John A. Sibley, Atlanta banker, took him aside to share his experience in losing his own wife. "This is the most severe test you will ever be confronted with in your life," said his friend. "If you can meet and surmount this test, there will be nothing else in life you cannot meet and surmount." This thought seemed to infuse him with a new vitality and sense of purpose. It also seemed to bring into focus counsel given by Fern before she died and events of the past two weeks. When death seemed imminent for her, Fern, ever sensitive to his needs, had urged Harold to remarry when she passed on, and not to delay unduly. She also shared this advice with Helen and Maurine. For three months after Fern's death, Elder Lee, caught up in mourning, had given no apparent thought to his wife's counsel. But during the Christmas season in 1962, conscious of the loneliness of single life and the potential hazards of remaining unmarried, he began to take Fern's advice to heart. 26

Carefully and methodically, Harold sat down and itemized the things he would hope to find in a new companion. Because of the demands of his calling, he felt she should be near his own age. He also wanted her to have been familiar with both Fern and his daughters and to have been admired by his wife. Finally, it seemed best to him that she never have been sealed to another. When all this was evaluated, the one who

fit these criteria perfectly was Freda Joan Jensen, a well-known educator, who for years had been the supervisor of primary education in the Jordan School District. She was well known to the Lees as she had served on the general boards of both the Primary and the YWMIA and, being about their age, had been involved in social and other activities with that age group. She had never married, although Elder Lee learned later she had been engaged to be married to a widower who died unexpectedly two weeks before the planned nuptials. Given these circumstances, there remained the delicate task of how to open up a dialogue with her, to determine her feelings and whether the personal chemistry between them was such as to give hope of a happy and successful marriage. Elder Lee's task was simplified when Sister Jensen was among those who called at the Lee home during the holidays to pay their respects. Following up on that fortuitous contact, he chose a means of furthering their acquaintance that was ideal for two professional teachers. He gave her a book. It was a copy of President J. Reuben Clark's most recent book to which Elder Lee had written the foreword. Calling in advance, he went to her home on January 2, 1963, to deliver it in person. From the beginning of their relationship, both seemed to know intuitively that they were destined to be man and wife. There was the circumstance of Joan's (the name she preferred Elder Lee to use instead of Freda, which was used by most others) aborted marriage. There was the special blessing she had received years before in Alberta, Canada, from temple President Edward James Wood, who told her that in the future she would occupy a place of high distinction, such that she could then hardly imagine. As for Elder Lee, his prophetic sense whispered that this was the woman whom the Lord had raised up to stand by his side in matrimony and to help assuage the grief caused by Fern's death. 27

As an eighteen-year-old on the farm in Clifton, Harold had

Freda Joan Jensen

N.D.

Courtesy of the Lee Family Collection

received his patriarchal blessing from Patriarch James Reid McNeil. In it he was promised "'wives and children who would be caught up in the clouds of heaven to meet thy Redeemer.'"[28] Thus he knew that in this life he had been foreordained to have more than one female companion. This gave him added impetus to continue.

Using the downtime following a hernia operation to draw his family into his plans, Harold recorded:

> This was a rare opportunity for intimate and satisfying talks about events ahead for us as a family and our lovely Joan, without detracting from our wonderful mother and my darling, Fern.[29]

Following the temple meeting on June 6, 1963, Harold told President McKay of his plans to marry Joan—now only eleven days away. The President was pleased and asked Harold if he and Sister McKay might meet her. At this meeting President McKay offered to perform the sealing, after which he confided to his wife that he thought "Joan [was] a wonderful girl.'" Sister McKay added, reporting this observation later, "'and when he says that it means something!'"[30]

> Elder Lee shared his marriage plans with only two other intimate friends of the Council of the Twelve. His journal reveals this conversation: "After the Sunday concluding session of June MIA conference I told Marion Romney of my plans to be married Monday. He was very emotional. Henry Moyle came and asked if he could be at the marriage. I asked if he would like to be a witness. With emotion he replied, "Would you permit me to?" Marion Romney asked also. I told them if President McKay would perform our marriage ceremony and they two would be witnesses it would be perfect.[31]

Harold and Joan were married in the Salt Lake Temple on June 17, 1963. A wedding breakfast followed at the Hotel Utah. Later in the

Joan and Harold B. Lee at home when BYU filmed
"Strengthening the Home"—a video which was sent
throughout the Church—warning members of the
crumbling of the American home

CA. 1971

day they boarded a plane for New York, where they "checked into the 'palatial' bridal suite of the Waldorf Astoria. They remained in the city four days. Except for a meeting with the Equitable board and checking on preliminary plans for the Church's World Fair pavilion, Elder Lee spent the time with Joan, acquainting her with the city that had almost become his second home.... 'My days with Joan were glorious,' he wrote of this abbreviated honeymoon. 'Each night we sat up talking, sometimes until 1–2 A.M., talking about things we had little opportunity before to say.'"

When the couple left New York they flew to Chicago, where "the private [railroad] car of Union Pacific's president was made available to them. 'This was travel deluxe,' Elder Lee wrote of the trip from Chicago to Salt Lake City. Still later, they took the private car on a trip to California. With them were Verda and Charlie Ross and Lou and Geraldine Callister, 'for a little diversion and as an expression of our gratitude for all they have done.'"[32]

Thus, at age sixty-six, Joan Jensen Lee was fully launched on her career as the wife of the man who was destined to become the president of The Church of Jesus Christ of Latter-day Saints. She never ceased to marvel at the extraordinary turn of events that had brought this about, nor at the spiritual sensitivity of President E. J. Wood who had predicted it, even though in veiled terms. And both she and Elder Lee were struck by the way in which Joan, over the years, had slowly and faithfully acquired the talents, the qualities of character, and the spirituality that equipped her to fill this niche. Later, she would become a role model for many Latter-day Saint women who, deprived of the opportunity to marry worthy men in their youth, were encouraged to continue to grow and mature as individuals, to develop professional and other skills, and to live happy, productive lives, not with any idea of marrying

Harold and Joan Lee enjoyed
visiting with Saints throughout
the world

CA. early 1970s

Courtesy of the Lee Family Collection

a great man like Elder Lee later in life, but with the idea of making the most of the circumstances and opportunities that each life affords. 33

Joan was to be Harold's wife and companion for ten and a half years, and in that time she would cross almost every part of the globe in meeting with the Saints. She spoke frequently and well, inspiring missionaries, members, leaders, and especially children, with whom she knew intuitively how to communicate. "She was the widow of the President of the Church for another eight years before her passing, which she welcomed, on July 1, 1981, one day before her eighty-fourth birthday." 34

Unfortunately, the grim specter of death was to strike Harold again, not very long after Joan had become a part of his life. On Friday, August 27, 1965, while he was with Elder Paul H. Dunn on assignment in Hawaii, an early morning call shattered him with the news that his daughter Maurine was in critical condition in a Provo hospital, where doctors were fighting for her life but giving the family no hope. Harold immediately obtained reservations for a flight home, but only minutes later his son-in-law Ernie Wilkins called to tell him that his daughter was gone—at age thirty-nine. "This bright, vivacious, friendly woman, whom her father called 'Sunshine,' was carrying her fifth child when she died.... 'My heart is broken as I contemplate the passing of my darling "Sunshine,"' wrote he, 'and the great need of Ernie and her little family.' After the sadness of the funeral, he wrote disconsolately, 'Somehow, I seem unable to shake off this latest, shattering blow. Only God can help me.'" 35

He did, but it took time. Four years later, speaking at a stake conference at BYU, Harold reflected on the experience in this manner:

Suddenly, and without warning, that little mother was snatched away in a moment. The pleadings of Grandfather

Helen Lee Goates and Maurine Lee Wilkins
in the last photo taken before Maurine's death

CA. 1965

over in the Hawaiian Islands and the piteous cries for the mercies of the Almighty to spare her were unavailing. And in the hospital, surrounded by doctors with all the medical skill that they could summon, she slipped away. The children were called, and around the lonely table in the family room they sat with bowed heads sobbing their hearts out. The grandfather was summoned to come and that night flew home, and all the family were at the plane to meet him, hoping that surely he could do something to lift the burden. And with arms surrounding that little family the grandfather said: "I do not know how you can be so brave. Grandfather is crying his heart out and you stand here with your arms around each other, seemingly with no tears." And one of them said: "Grandfather, we have no more tears to shed. We have cried our tears away all day long."

That drama was enacted right here in your community. I was the recipient of that phone call; I was the grandfather who pleaded at five o'clock in the morning, "Please, God, don't let her die." But it was as though our Heavenly Father was saying, "I have other plans," and all the faith that could be mustered was unavailing. 36

Yet Harold's faith, and the faith of his grieving family, brought to pass great spiritual healing. Helen, who spent two weeks with Maurine's family after their mother's death, slept the first night with twelve-year-old Marlee, to comfort her. During the night she awakened Helen to tell her of a most vivid dream.

"I dreamed we were sitting in the family room with Mother—you and me and Jane [her cousin]. Mother was sewing a button on Jay's shirt. [Jay was her younger brother.] We were all talking while Mother sewed. Jay came in and said he was sad because Mother was gone, and I said, 'No she's not gone—see, she's right here—can't you see her?'

Jay couldn't understand what I was saying, and I asked you and Jane if you could see her, and you just smiled. None of you could see her, but I could—I knew she was there. Isn't that funny, Aunt Helen?"

Aunt Helen, conditioned by the wise teachings received in her childhood home, replied: "No, Martsy dear, that's not just a funny dream. I think it's Heavenly Father's way of letting you know that even though your mommy has been taken from you, she can still be with you when you need her. You won't always be able to see her as you did in your dream, but she'll be close by and you'll feel her presence. Remember your dream, Martsy, when you're sad and lonesome for her, and it will help to make you feel better." Reassured, Marlee went back to sleep. [37]

Still, his grief was extremely difficult for Harold to bear. "Elder Gordon B. Hinckley of the Council of the Twelve, who had been Elder Lee's close friend for many years, said, 'These searing experiences, difficult to bear, served to increase his sensitivity to the burdens of others. Those who have sustained similar losses have found in him an understanding friend and one whose own tested faith has become a source of strength to them.'" [30]

Some time thereafter, as he honored Latter-day Saints who had lost their lives in the Vietnam conflict, Harold comforted those who grieved by declaring:

Having gone through some similar experiences in losing loved ones in death, I speak from personal experience when I say to you who mourn, do not try to live too many days ahead. The all-important thing is not that tragedies and sorrows come into our lives, but what we do with them. Death of a loved one is the most severe test that you will ever face, and if you can rise above your griefs and if you will trust in God, then you will be able to surmount any other difficulty with which you may be faced.... So to you who have lost loved ones, ...we say to you that faith can lift you beyond the sordid trials of the day and point you to the glorious tomorrow that can be yours. 39

In spite of the adversities of the decade, Harold's life was typically filled with many joys—some of them most exquisite and sweet. "With ten grandchildren, four of Maurine's (Alan, Marlee, Larry, and Jay Wilkins) and six of Helen's (David, Jane, Hal, Drew, Jonathon, and Timothy), Elder Lee felt rich indeed. The aspirations he had for them were succinctly stated in a diary entry he made after seeing a group of them together at Aspen Grove during a family vacation in July 1965. 'As the older ones reach their maturity...we are prayerfully hoping that we can [help them to be] clean, get their schooling, and fill missions, and marry in the temple.' "40

In 1967, Harold's dreams and aspirations for his posterity began to be fulfilled when his two eldest grandsons were called to serve missions. David Goates

was called to serve in England, and when his grandfather was there during November of that year, they spent a day together in Leeds. The next day, when Elder Lee and the mission president drove to Sunderland to hold missionary meetings, Elder David Goates was at the wheel of the mission car. No doubt, the grandparent was neither irritated nor annoyed when the mission president told him that David was the "most outstanding of his missionaries," and that he was "thinking of him as an assistant."

Three months before Elder Lee saw David in England, he attended Alan's missionary farewell in Provo. Ironically, it was on August 27, the second anniversary of Maurine's death. On this account, Alan was very tender in his feelings, and as he sat on the stand beside Elder Lee, he whispered to him: "Oh, Grandfather, Mother would have wanted so much to be here. I have prayed constantly that the Lord would permit her to come."

The third grandson to enter the mission field was Elder Lee's namesake, Harold Lee Goates, who was called to the South Africa Mission in March 1968. Elder Lee accompanied Hal Goates to the temple when he received his endowment on March 19, 1968, commenting that, "Perhaps heaven was very close; a proud grandmother and Auntie Marr." The grandfather was no less proud of this grandson, and his other grandchildren, than was Fern, although on attending David's homecoming, he was quick to explain that he was "righteously" proud. On December 19, 1969, when he performed David's temple marriage to Patsy Hewlett, he referred to it as "a historic occasion for our family." 41

Meanwhile, aging was taking its toll on Harold as well, and Elder Lee found himself struggling with fairly constant health problems. Besides his constant headaches and stomach problems, he underwent surgery for a hernia in 1963 and contracted a serious virus infection while on a trip to the east coast a year later that developed into pneumonia. In 1966, during another thorough physical, he learned that his blood count was only fifty-six percent of normal—and received a series of transfusions that helped stabilize him. The same problem developed again in 1967—resulting in the same treatment plus iron shots in the hope that he could be strengthened for his upcoming tour of the Florida Mission.

After an exhaustive pace in Florida, he and Joan flew north for further assignments. There Harold became seriously ill again, received a priesthood blessing from the mission president and two of his missionaries, and made it through his Sabbath day labors.

On Monday morning, however, even after a full ten hours of sleep, and despite the fact that he had business meetings lined up for the next few days, Harold had the overwhelming feeling that he needed to return home immediately. Quickly Joan made reservations, and it was during this flight that the incident dramatized in chapter one of this volume took place.

Four days later, on April 12, 1967, Harold underwent a three-and-a-half-hour operation during which more than half of his stomach was removed because of a large perforated ulcer that in most other cases proved to be cancerous. In Harold, however, no cancer was found. Sobered, he wrote in his journal:

> One can only suppose that the Almighty has it in his hand to give or to take and he alone keeps the timetable. To the thoroughness and the skill of the doctors I owe much, but I'm not unmindful of the spiritual power which has been in evidence in the events leading up to the operation as well as circumstances resulting therefrom. When I was released to come home I found I weighed but 150 pounds, a loss of 15 pounds. 42

It was obvious, despite his already numerous accomplishments and contributions, and despite his mounting and almost continual health problems, that the Lord had further work for Harold to accomplish.

HEARING THE VOICE OF THE LORD

The reporter sat across the desk from Elder Harold B. Lee, now the senior member of the Quorum of the Twelve Apostles, uncertain how to proceed. Oh, he knew what he wanted to ask, all right—the same question being asked by half the membership of the Church. The problem was, he didn't quite know how to put it. Elder Lee was a powerful man—a brilliant thinker—and he had a reputation for brutal frankness when aroused or upset that could give a man a "bad day" for weeks!

Of course, the reporter reminded himself, he was no nit-picking Gentile, himself. He was a member of the Church like Elder Lee—a good member! He held a fairly significant calling in his ward; he had a current temple recommend; he and his family faithfully attended their meetings at home and even when they were traveling—which as a feature reporter he did quite a bit of; and in his considered opinion he enjoyed a rock-solid testimony of the gospel. He had served a mission and been a leader; he and his wife had been married in the temple and were in the midst of raising righteous children; they held Family Home Evening about fifty weeks out of the year; he knew the scriptures pretty darn well; and not once, so far as he could recollect, had a gospel doctrine teacher ever managed to stump him. Not that he meant to be prideful, he told himself, but this was his Church as much as it was Elder Lee's or any other General Authority's, and he had an absolute right to be concerned about its future!

Outside the January wind was whipping new snow past the window, and for an instant the reporter shivered. It was going to be a cold day for President McKay's funeral—there was no doubt about that! Cold, and very, very sad. Like most of the younger members of the Church, he could hardly remember when President McKay hadn't been the prophet. His parents talked of Presidents George Albert Smith and Heber J. Grant, but they were only names to him—men he had read of but couldn't really remember. Why, he felt a greater closeness to Joseph Smith and Brigham Young. At least they'd been young when they served, filled with vigor and keenly alert. Like Elder Lee would turn out to be, he thought—maybe even within the next few days, if the Brethren did what was best for the Church.

What was Elder Lee? Seventy, maybe? Old, yes; but not that old! Not like Joseph Fielding Smith, who was somewhere in his mid nineties! Worse, he was a doddering old man, who one day seemed to have his faculties about him and the next day didn't! In that condition, how in the world could he direct the affairs of a complex and rapidly expanding worldwide Church?

The trouble was, the reporter reminded himself, it had become the custom in the Church, at the death of a prophet, to appoint the next senior member as the new prophet and president. Which meant that Joseph Fielding Smith would follow David O. McKay. Or maybe it was policy—he didn't know. What he did know was that it wasn't scriptural, at least not that he'd been able to find in his recent perusal of the Standard Works. And if it wasn't scriptural, then why for goodness sake couldn't the Brethren skip Joseph Fielding and turn the reins of the Church over to a younger man who still had a little vitality and energy about him— like Elder Lee? Why—

"Was there anything else, Brother?" Elder Lee was glancing at his watch, making little effort to hide his impatience with the whole process of being interviewed—something the reporter had heard he was renowned for. Elder Lee was all business, very shrewd—

"I have just one more question, Elder Lee." Pausing, the reporter drew a deep breath to steady himself. "Is it correct what I have heard—that they're going to make Joseph Fielding Smith the next President of the Church?"

For a fleeting instant Elder Lee's eyes seemed to narrow behind his thick glasses, and the reporter sensed that his question hadn't been the best to have asked the apostle—at least at that moment. But doggone it, the question was a legitimate one, and besides, Elder Lee's eyes now looked perfectly normal. He was even smiling a little, which the reporter took as a good sign—a very good sign!

"What I mean," he pressed, now quite encouraged, "is—well, how can a man of Joseph Fielding Smith's age, when his body is old and worn down, still direct this Church?"

"I know exactly what you mean," Elder Lee responded softly as his fingers drummed the top of his desk. He didn't say anything more, at least not for a moment or so, and again the reporter was heartened. Harold B. Lee was struggling for an answer—so his question had obviously hit home! Which meant that maybe there really was hope—especially for thinking, rational members of the Church such as himself—

"My good brother," Elder Lee finally responded, "do you know what it takes to be a prophet of the Lord?"

Surprised that he was being answered with a question, the reporter decided now was not the best time to display his knowledge. "Well," he replied humbly, "I guess I really don't know—not exactly."

Elder Lee, his slight smile unchanged, was not about to let him off the hook. "Well," he pressed, "what do you think it would take?"

"I...uh.... Well, I suppose he'd have to know all about genealogy, the missionary program of the Church, and all the missionaries and what they're doing and how to supervise them. He would also need to know about the Primary and the Relief Society and the building and construction programs." Feeling humbly proud of his knowledge, the reporter continued, naming numerous other major and minor functions of the Church—some of which he was certain few outside the General Authorities had any knowledge of whatsoever. But he'd been doing his homework like a good reporter—

"No, that's all wrong!" Elder Lee's denunciation was so pointed that it set the reporter back, almost unnerving him. But it didn't, not quite, and his mind was already forming a rebuttal when the apostle deftly took away from him any chance to make it.

"Shall I tell you what it takes to be a prophet? There's only one capacity; just one. And that is to be able to hear the voice of the Lord. That's all. He's got all the rest of us to do the work. He just has to do one function. Do you suppose that this great living apostle, who has been sustained as a prophet for six decades, longer than any other man presently on earth, might be able to do that?"

Feeling completely chagrined, the reporter had no idea whether Elder Lee wanted an answer. But he wasn't about to open his mouth and make an ever bigger fool of himself, not unless he was forced into—

"Do you suppose that Joseph Fielding Smith, who was a home teaching companion of President Wilford Woodruff, might know something about that?"

"I...uh...I suppose he might," the reporter responded lamely, now in full retreat.

"You suppose?" Elder Lee's smile now grew more wide and open, completely sincere, and abruptly all the edge vanished from his voice. "So do I, my good brother; so do I."

For a moment there was silence, and then Elder Lee the senior apostle disappeared and Harold Lee the gifted teacher of righteousness appeared sitting behind the old desk. "You know, Brother, a man cannot lift another until he is standing on higher ground. You must be sure, if you would educate or rescue a man, that you yourself are setting the example of what you would have him be. You cannot light a fire in another soul unless it is burning in your own."

Elder Lee's smile was tender now, just as the reporter remembered the ever-patient smile of his now deceased father being when he read one of his son's news stories that had not been up to par. And that was what this was all about, he knew—his article, his feature story on the choosing of the next prophet. Elder Lee was schooling him, rescuing him from his own prideful ignorance—

"Brother," Elder Lee said as he rose to his feet, signaling the end of the interview, "you will know you're beginning to be converted when your heart begins to tell you things you do not know."

Stepping around the desk, Elder Lee took the reporter's hand in his with a firm grip, at the same time putting his other arm around the reporter's waist and squeezing him lightly, letting him know he was loved, and that all was well.

"You know," he said as he steered the reporter toward the door, "I am grateful that you brethren of the priesthood are so well trained and so capable of representing us in the news media, for there is a great danger that confronts us. According to reports that have reached us, there seem to be those among us who are as wolves among the flock, trying to lead away some who are weak and unwary. Thank you, brother, for being willing and able to report the truth."[1]

As ninety-six-year-old President David O. McKay's health began to fail, there was much speculation—both in the Church and outside of it—concerning the wisdom and advisability of elevating the next in line of apostolic authority, Joseph Fielding Smith, to the position of president upon President McKay's death. Joseph Fielding

Smith was, after all, ninety-three years old himself, and his health seemed just as frail as President McKay's. So people speculated, some of their speculations became public, and these caused pain even in the highest circles of Church leadership. Following President McKay's death on January 18, 1970, such speculation escalated rapidly.

"On the day prior to President McKay's funeral, President and Sister Joseph Fielding Smith came to Elder Lee's office and seemed most nervous about the rumors which were abounding that an effort might be made to bypass the traditional appointment of the senior Apostle to be the next President, due to his age and poor health. The Smiths indicated that if Joseph Fielding Smith were sustained as President, he wanted Elder Lee to be 'by his side,' which Elder Lee interpreted to mean that he wanted him to serve as a counselor in the First Presidency....

"These speculations before the decision induced in Elder Lee an overwhelming sense of obligation and responsibility. He wrote, 'I could not assume such burdens without the Lord's help.'"[2]

Because of the worldwide nature of the Church and its scope and level of commitment, the Brethren convened a meeting in the upper room of the temple early on the morning following the funeral. "'There was an air of expectancy and some tension,'" Harold wrote, "'as each spoke, beginning with the junior member of the Twelve.'"[3] When it was his turn, Harold, who had carefully prepared for the moment, read a letter written by President Wilford Woodruff to Elder Heber J. Grant, "in which he answered the question as to whether an Apostle other than the President of the Twelve could become the President of the Church."[4] In part, the letter read:

"When the President of the Church dies, who then is the Presiding Authority of the Church? It is the Quorum of the Twelve Apostles (ordained and organized by the revelations of God and none else). Then while these Twelve Apostles preside over the Church, who is the President of the Church? It is the President of the Twelve Apostles. And he is virtually as much the President of the Church while presiding over twelve men as he is when organized as the Presidency of the Church, and presiding over two men."

After commenting that the principle taught by President Woodruff had been carried on for 140 years—in fact since the organization of the Church—Harold continued with President Woodruff's letter.

"As far as I am concerned it would require...a revelation from the same God who had organized the Church and guided it by inspiration in the channel in which it has traveled for 57 years, before I could give my vote or influence to depart from the paths followed by the Apostles, since the organization of the Church and followed by inspiration of Almighty God, for the past 57 years by the Apostles, as recorded in the history of the Church." 5

Following his reading of the letter, Harold "moved that Joseph Fielding Smith be named as the president of the Church. Elder Spencer W. Kimball seconded the motion, which was carried unanimously. With all the apostles present joining, and with Elder Lee acting as voice, Joseph Fielding Smith was then ordained and set apart as the president—the prophet, seer, and revelator—and the trustee-in-trust of The Church of Jesus Christ of Latter-day Saints. President Smith then named Harold B. Lee and N. Eldon Tanner as his first and second counselors, respectively, who, being approved by the council, were set apart. During the same meeting, Elder Lee was sustained and set apart as the president of the Quorum of the Twelve Apostles and Elder Spencer W. Kimball was sustained and set apart as the acting president of the quorum." 6

President Joseph Fielding Smith (center)
with counselors Harold B. Lee (left)
and N. Eldon Tanner (right)

N.D.

Deseret News. Used with permission

Following the ordinations and setting apart of the various brethren, Harold wrote: "'This procedure thereby nullifies any political lobbying which, if we didn't follow precedent, could be a very dangerous threat to the unity of the Church.'"7

At the first meeting of the new First Presidency, official responsibilities for each of the three members were determined. Because of his stewardship over all keys pertaining to sealings, it was decided that President Smith would oversee temple and other related matters, with Harold assisting him.

> President Lee's chief responsibilities were to be in education, budgeting, finance (shared with President Tanner), management systems (computer technology), and communications (KSL radio and TV, Bonneville International Corporation and Deseret News). Also, he was to have executive responsibilities in certain Church-owned or controlled corporations: Zions Securities Corporation, ZCMI, Utah Idaho Sugar Company, Hotel Utah, Beneficial Life, Deseret Book Company, and Deseret Management Corporation, a holding company. In addition, Elder Lee would be the first contact in the First Presidency for the Primary and Relief Society auxiliaries, Church personnel, and Church correlation. These responsibilities were in addition to those in corporations not controlled by the Church: Union Pacific, Equitable Life, and Zions First National Bank. 8

And so the work went forward under ninety-three-year-old President Smith, and Elder Lee with it, despite the wisdom of the critics.

Shortly before President McKay's passing, the Church's position on priesthood came under attack. At Stanford University a Brigham Young University athletic team was attacked both verbally and physically, and a few months later, after Harold had become a member of the First Presidency, there was a near riot at Colorado State in Fort Collins. This was

triggered by a group of militant black students from CSU who used this means of protesting the Mormon Church's policy on priesthood. These militants were permitted to offer an invocation before the game, which was little more than a broad indictment of the Church. There also was an overt show of protest during the warm-ups when a group of blacks massed beneath the BYU basket, shouting threats at the players. At halftime vulgar insults were made against the BYU Cougarettes and the players, eggs were thrown onto the playing floor, and an iron object and a lighted torch were thrown toward the floor. Finally, fights broke out in the arena. Order was restored only when the city police were called in.

A few days after this incident in Fort Collins, a militant activist named Jerry Rubin, who was then under indictment for rioting in Chicago, spoke on the campus of the University of Utah in Salt Lake City. During his incendiary remarks, the speaker bitterly berated the Latter-day Saints, warning, "We will either integrate the Mormon Church, or we will destroy it." These incidents were symptomatic of broad-based attacks being made on the Church around the country by its enemies and detractors. Adding to the turmoil this created was the upheaval caused by America's involvement in the Vietnam War. At the time, a member of the Church, a Vietnam War veteran, had been speaking in Church meetings, "arousing people to fever pitch," according to President Lee, "with scare stories about impending doom." 9

It was under these conditions that the Brethren determined to set in place extensive security measures—not only to protect themselves and the Church's property, but also its numerous employees and volunteer workers. Under the direction of the Presiding Bishopric, individuals who had been trained in security measures were hired, windows on the ground floor of the Church Administration Building were replaced with riot-proof glass, television cameras and monitors were installed, a trained male receptionist was positioned in the foyer of the Administration Building to screen out those who did not have a legitimate reason for being there, extensive communications systems including hand-held radios were given to all security personnel, and every eventuality was considered.

These preparations, as well as attacks against the Church, seemed to culminate as the April 1970 general conference drew near. Prior to conference there was a wonderful spirit in the meeting of the General Authorities in the Salt Lake Temple. Presiding Bishop Victor L. Brown briefed those present on the security measures that had been taken to protect the Saints, but none became overly concerned by the possibility that the civil unrest and racial tensions raging across the country could do damage to the Church.

As conference opened on April 4TH, however, it did so amidst frightening threats of bombings on Temple Square. On Thursday night the Tabernacle Choir rehearsal had been threatened with a bombing, and on Friday evening the Utah Symphony had to be evacuated from the Tabernacle because of more threats. Thus, as Harold conducted the Saturday morning session, many were worried and fearful of what might occur. All went well, however, through both Saturday sessions as well as the evening priesthood session.

On Sunday morning Harold was again conducting—this session broadcast nationwide—but again nothing happened. "The far-reaching and potentially disastrous climax came as feared in the Sunday afternoon conference session, when another bomb threat occurred as Elder A. Theodore Tuttle was at the pulpit preaching on the theme 'If ye are prepared, ye shall not fear.' A telephoned message was delivered [by note] to President Lee on the stand of the Tabernacle stating that a bomb would go off during that session. According to Salt Lake City Public Safety Commissioner James Barker, President Lee emphatically said to the policeman delivering the note in the Tabernacle: 'There is no bomb in here; relax.' The session continued uninterrupted.

"The responsibility for that instantaneous decision and the assurance of that conviction are mind-boggling. It is one of the most significant illustrations of the seer-like qualities of President Lee. It was his gift to be guided by an intuitive inspiration, which quality his associates of the General Authorities understood and deeply admired in him." 10

Harold's seership made itself manifest in another way during this time of crisis. It was clear to him that the real solution to the threatened attacks wasn't security, though being prepared for violent eventualities was the course of wisdom. The real solution, he felt, was to forestall, or minimize, opposition to the Church arising from a misunderstanding of its teachings and objectives.

> In a word, he sought to put the Church on the offensive in the arena of public opinion. He felt that for too long the Church had merely reacted to news events, or had silently watched emerging groundswells of anti-Mormon sentiment, without any effort to stop or to mitigate them. In this effort, one of the most significant of his long and distinguished career, President Lee brought into play all of the skills and know-how he had accumulated over the years as a Church leader at the local and general levels, as a teacher, as a politician, as a strategist in developing and executing plans for Church welfare and correlation, and as a high official in charting the course of major corporations. 11

While in New York City for his monthly business meetings, Harold called together a group of men from both Church leaders and the business world he felt were particularly suited to bring his idea to pass. In his journal he recorded: "'We had a two and a half hour meeting in a committee room at the Waldorf.... The purpose of the meeting was to seek counsel as to how the church could get the offensive position in public relations which, because of the negro priesthood issue, are at a low ebb.'" 12

As it turned out, this was the beginning "of the Church's department of public communications. Out of this also grew the idea of a department of internal communications, which was organized to simplify, expedite, and economize...the process of preparing and distributing Church instructional and other materials. This meeting also sheds important light on some of the special leadership qualities of Harold B. Lee. In the first place, he was never a one-man show. Rather, he served as a catalyst to bring together many people of talent and ability and to mold them into a team in which each played his essential role. In this process, he was meticulous in gathering the facts and in obtaining advice from the people most qualified to give it. All this was aimed toward the solution of a specific problem or the fulfillment of a vision he held. Finally, the objective, as refined by the team, was pursued with single-minded purpose, sometimes awesome in its intensity." 13

Of these men, Lee Bickmore, CEO of the National Biscuit Company, [Nabisco] emerged as a key player in Harold's vision. It all took time, but within a year and a half from that first meeting, a committee of LDS industrial leaders, headed by Bickmore, was recommending that Church communications be divided into two departments—internal, for functions within the Church Office Building; and external, for the Church's public relations challenges with the public. After screening numerous qualified individuals, J. Thomas Fyans was recommended by the committee as the top executive in internal communications. Six months later they recommended Wendell J. Ashton to be the director of external communications. Immediately after these departments were created, in June 1972, "Elder Mark E. Peterson was named an adviser to the External Communications Department and Elder Gordon B. Hinckley was released from the Internal Communications leadership to also aid in the new public relations work.

> Meanwhile, Brother Ashton moved vigorously to launch the new program. President Lee found him full of ideas and plans. For example, he proposed that a dinner be planned for Lord Thomson of British broadcasting and publishing fame, that a national release be prepared on the appointment of Lee Bickmore as a special consultant to the First Presidency, that an announcement of the new mission representatives appointments be made to obtain greater publicity, and that a release be made announcing the forthcoming Mexico City regional conference. After observing this burst of energy and the helpful ideas from Wendell J. Ashton, President Lee wrote in his journal, "It is delightful to see how quickly he is moving into his new responsibilities."
>
> Thus the correction of one of the Church's most glaring weaknesses that had worried President Lee as he joined in the new First Presidency in January 1970 was finally brought to fruition two and one-half years later, with the hope that the Church could reverse its negative public image and become better known for its worthy accomplishments. [14]

Brother Bickmore's influence was felt in other areas as well. In response to Harold's long-held concerns about several aspects of Church organization, Brother Bickmore recommended that the Church hire a consulting firm in the East with which he was very familiar—Cresap, McCormick, and Paget, Inc.—to begin a comprehensive study of Church operations to establish more objective administration guidelines. With President Smith's and President Tanner's approval, Harold saw to it that the firm was hired.

> President Lee used an interesting approach in making this assignment. He gave the nonmember consultants copies of the Doctrine and Covenants with sections marked pertaining to Church priesthood government operation and told them to read how the Lord had directed the Prophet Joseph to set up the kingdom of God. He then asked the consultants to translate this information into the best management organizational theory for the business world. In this approach President Lee capitalized on his exposure to big corporate management. His fertile and ever-searching mind permitted him to use his background in industry to challenge old concepts and introduce the best of his new learning experiences from all reliable sources. 15

Soon the studies were beginning to show results. Ren Hoopes, an industrial engineer from the Safeway Stores organization, presented a thorough analysis of the Church's distribution problems and suggested solutions for the Church's system. Shortly thereafter "Mr. Fredericks, one of the senior account executives of Cresap, McCormick, and Paget, Inc., made his first report on the internal operations of the Church, pointing out specifically that the Twelve Apostles were doing 'staff' work assignments, rather than centering their efforts in broader policy-making functions. President Lee wrote of his impressions regarding this report:

> This we have been aware of before. These studies will now be placed in the hands of Lee Bickmore and his committee to study further, with the assignment to come back with recommendations. Hopefully these studies will point us to

a clearer look at our problems and the most effective solutions. The transition, I foresee, may be "painful," but necessary, if we are to keep pace with the mounting problems of rapid expansion of the Church throughout the world. 16

Harold spent Thanksgiving of 1971 putting together an outline of proposals on how to implement the recommendations the Church had received, his goal being to strengthen the missions of the Church and restructure the work of the Twelve. "Application of these delegation principles began to take place in early 1972 as members of the Council of the Twelve Apostles were taken from daily supervision over departments and other managerial advocacy roles so that they could fulfill their primary roles as special witnesses of Jesus Christ and of watching over the affairs of the Church generally. Accordingly, Elder Howard W. Hunter was released as the Church historian and Elder Alvin R. Dyer was installed as the managing director of the Historical Department, with Dr. Leonard J. Arrington as Church historian and Earl Olson as archivist. The new managing director then began reporting through two of the Twelve, Spencer W. Kimball and Howard W. Hunter." 17

Quickly, other departments, including the Genealogical Society, were streamlined to relieve the Council of Twelve leaders of day-to-day management responsibilities, thus establishing a new pattern of Church government. "On May 31, 1972, the First Presidency held a two-hour meeting with the Twelve. In this special session, President Lee sought to impress on the Twelve their newly focused responsibilities in planning, policy-making, and exercising strict control of the funds being budgeted by the departments over which they were assigned as advisers, but not managers. The Presidency stressed that as much work as possible should be turned back to volunteers and regularly appointed priesthood and auxiliary leaders, rather than hiring specialists to do it.

"This major restructuring effort of the highest echelons of Church government continued to serve well the quickly growing kingdom and make possible the administrative efficiency required as the Church expanded its worldwide borders."18

Other changes instituted at this time included the creation of the corps of officers to be known as Regional Representatives; the formation of a Churchwide teacher training program; a consolidation of Church magazines into just three—the *Friend*, the *New Era*, and the *Ensign*; the discontinuation of paid advertising in all Church publications; the creation of health service missions under Dr. James Mason for deprived areas of the world; a thorough restructuring of the Church Educational System under the new Commissioner of Education, Neal A. Maxwell; the restructuring of the Sunday Schools under new General Superintendent Dr. Russell M. Nelson; and the creation of the department of physical facilities under Presiding Bishop John H. Vandenberg, which "combined the functions of the old building, real estate and maintenance divisions."19

Lest it be thought that Harold's years as First Counselor in the First Presidency consisted of nothing more than the administrative actions described above, a typical day's description from his journal should be instructive.

Besides meeting with President Smith and the Expenditures Committee, I was kept fully occupied with many problems. A complaint came relative to the proposed demolition of the mission home in Hong Kong; the decision to go forward with plans for the new 18TH Ward and the demolition of the old historical building on that site; complaints about the proposed water fountain on the plaza of the new Church Office Building; the lack of security at the temple. Then word came that President By Woodbury, famous mission president, had been told by his doctor that he didn't have long to live....

[The next day included] a special meeting to consider some matters needing attention, principally to approve nine members of the Executive Committee for the new General Sunday School Board. We also made plans for the solemn assembly at the St. George Temple on November 13, 1971, and the opening of the Ogden and Provo temples. 20

And on another day, a Saturday, he wrote:

The continual round of meetings and interviews left me no time to tend to my personal affairs, much less to give some thought to my preparation for the forthcoming conference sessions. I came to the office and spent the entire day so that I could be undisturbed in trying to get the needed spiritual direction for a conference address. 21

Since his first tours of missions and countries outside the United States, Harold had worried that far too many of the Saints would never meet or even see the prophet or have the privilege of experiencing a general conference. This worry increased with the growth of the Church, until, as a member of the First Presidency, he recommended to the Brethren that they begin holding what came to be called area conferences in distant nations—in effect taking general conference to the people. The first of these was scheduled for Great Britain; the site was to be Manchester, near Preston, where the early apostles had first initiated missionary work in England nearly a century and a half before.

When it was made public that such a conference was scheduled for Great Britain in the summer of 1971, an English media frenzy ensued. Among others, including the *London Times*, the BBC sent a television team of four men and a young woman reporter to Salt Lake City for two weeks to do a documentary about the Church. With all their equipment they sat in Harold's office "and explored for one and one-half hours his thinking on his family background, positions most enjoyed in his Church service, the nature of revelation in the Church, the place of blacks in Mormon doctrine, the relationship between Church and state, how the Church retains its contact with Church members, the secret of Mormon longevity, and other similar topics.

"Later Esther Ramtzen [the woman reporter] came back to see President Lee for a brief personal visit, and he gave her a copy of his book *Youth and the Church*. She informed him that her team would attend the Manchester conference. Elder Richard L. Evans was present for the entire interview and pronounced it 'magnificent.'" 22

As the date for the conference approached, it was decided for security reasons that while President Tanner remained at home, Presidents Smith and Lee would go to England by separate routes and on separate days. Harold and Joan stopped in Midland, Michigan, on their way so that Harold could dedicate a stake center for a stake he had created in 1968. In the process of changing planes back in Detroit, Harold somehow lost his briefcase, in which were his area conference papers, his sermons, and his and Joan's passports.

Distraught, he spent an hour frantically searching the various terminals, retracing his steps in a vain attempt to locate the lost case. Finally, he went out to board the shuttle back to the American Airlines terminal, thinking he had possibly left the briefcase on the bus. As he stepped toward the bus he happened to glance to the side, "and there was my briefcase," he wrote, safe and unmolested. "'Why I hadn't seen it before, I will never know; and why it was safeguarded for nearly an hour, I will never know. Only the good Lord could explain. It was a miracle.'" 23

Staying in the Piccadilly Hotel in Manchester:

President Lee was closeted with the prophet...reviewing

the plans for the conference, scheduled to begin officially on Friday [August] twenty-seventh. That evening, he went to the Manchester stake center where he addressed a group of young people. After returning to the hotel, he and President Smith decided to call the General Authorities together for a special meeting to prepare for the conference. It was held in a conference room in the Piccadilly Hotel. It turned out to be the first ever official meeting of the Council of the First Presidency and Quorum of the Twelve held outside the United States. Present were two members of the First Presidency, Joseph Fielding Smith and Harold B. Lee, and seven members of the Twelve.... Joining the brethren of the council were other General Authorities.... Elder Thomas S. Monson, whose arrival late in the evening provided the required number for an official council meeting, had flown in from Europe during bad weather, which had threatened the plane's ability to arrive on time. 24

This unusual meeting, which culminated in the bearing of testimonies, set a high spiritual tone for the conference, which began at 2:00 P.M. the next day. Two sessions were held simultaneously—youth and adult. Harold conducted the adult session, as he did every other session of the conference except the youth and women's sessions. Following the opening hymn in the adult session, which was Parley P. Pratt's "The Morning Breaks, The Shadows Flee," the words to which had been printed on the cover of the first edition of the *Millennial Star* in Manchester in 1840, President Joseph Fielding Smith declared the following:

> We are coming of age as a church and as a people. We have attained the stature and strength that are enabling us to fulfill the commission given us by the Lord through the Prophet Joseph Smith that we should carry the glad tidings

of the restoration to every nation and to all people. And not only shall we preach the gospel in every nation before the second coming of the Son of Man, but we shall make converts and establish congregations of saints among them. 25

In the Sunday morning session, Harold counseled those in attendance to "heed the words of the living prophet, to guard against the intrusion of Satanic influences in their lives, and to conduct themselves so as always to have the Spirit of God to be with them. He then affirmed that the answers to life's complex problems could be found through adherence to the gospel and cited basic principles and programs of the Church that contributed to individual and group happiness and security—tithing, fast offerings, Church welfare, missionary work, family prayer, and family home evening. At the conclusion of this comprehensive and compelling discourse, President Lee bore a fervent testimony." 26

> As a little boy, ... I had my first intimate touch with divinity. [He then retold the story of having heard the voice warning him not to go near the broken-down buildings and sheds across the field.] I looked in every direction to see where the speaker was. I wondered if it was my father, but he couldn't see me. There was no one in sight. I realized that someone was warning me of an unseen danger—whether a nest of rattlesnakes or whether the rotting timbers would fall on me and crush me, I don't know. But from that time on, I accepted without question the fact that there were processes not known to man by which we can hear voices from the unseen world, by which we can have brought to us the visions of eternity....
>
> President Lee then spoke of the difficult events that accompanied his being called as an apostle and their aftermath:

After a long night of searching...and days of spiritual preparation that followed, I came to know as a witness more powerful than sight, until I could testify with a surety that defied all doubt, that I knew with every fiber of my soul that Jesus is the Christ, the Son of the living God, that he lived, he died, he was resurrected, and today he presides in the heavens, directing the affairs of this church, which bears His name because it preaches His doctrine. I bear that testimony humbly and leave you my witness and my blessing here this morning, in the name of the Lord Jesus Christ. Amen. 27

It is no wonder President Joseph Fielding Smith had said of Harold, as he made his concluding remarks at October conference a few weeks later, "'May I express before you the profound appreciation I have for the faith, devotion and service of the two great men who stand beside me.... President Harold B. Lee is a spiritual giant with faith like that of Enoch. He has the spirit of revelation and magnifies his calling as a prophet, seer and revelator.'" 28

Among Harold's more choice experiences during his tenure as counselor in the First Presidency were the dedications of the Provo and Ogden Temples, his unique experiences with Elder Spencer W. Kimball, and a vision of his departed wife and daughter. That transcendent event occurred the day he spoke at the funeral of a Sister Pearl Lambert. He recorded:

There was a remarkable spirit at the funeral and I was uplifted thereby. As I was seated on the stand, I seemed to see a congregation facing me which included Fern in a black dress. Over her shoulder was someone whom I surmised might have been Maurine. 29

"While time probably didn't permit further comment on such an unusual experience, [Harold's] family members were aware of how he had prayed mightily for such reassurance after these two loved ones had passed away. None came then for him, but this experience is one of the only two instances where his beloved family members were permitted to be with and comfort him."[30]

Many spiritual experiences were enjoyed during the dedications of the two temples mentioned above. As an example of events that transpired in Ogden, President Lee's oldest grandchild, David Goates, reported that "'when the First Presidency stood at the pulpit during the last session, he saw a special light surrounding them.'"[31]

During his main address at the dedication of the Provo Temple, Harold

related the spiritual experience he had had at the dedication of the Los Angeles Temple when the prayer of President David O. McKay corresponded almost exactly with a vivid dream he had had some time before. In the prayer and in the dream, the prophet admonished his listeners, an admonition President Lee felt was directed pointedly to him, about "the meaning of the love of God, as it relates to the love of our fellow men and of His service." The spirit that attended these dedicatory services at the Provo Temple was quite remarkable. One of the General Authorities later told President Lee that he clearly saw President David O. McKay in vision in the company of several men whom he could not identify. The wife of another General Authority reported that during the services, her mother appeared to her in vision, clear and distinct. "I was watching the strange look on her face," wrote President Lee of the incident, "as she probably witnessed this vision." And still another General Authority reported that during his sermon, there was opened to his mind a vision of young people seated in the Marriott Center and that thereafter he directed his remarks particularly to them. As for President Lee, he was uplifted spiritually by the dedication to a high degree. It provided an important impetus for the heavier duties that would come to him in a few months. 32

For most of his tenure as a member of the Twelve, Elder Spencer W. Kimball had dealt with health problems that seemed calculated to stop him from performing his ordained work. Cancer of the throat made it almost impossible for him to speak, and a serious heart ailment brought on such weakness that he could hardly function. Because he sat next to Harold among the Twelve, the two men developed a deep closeness, and this bond brought Harold into joint consultations with Elder Kimball's wife and doctors, and brought Elder Kimball to Harold on several occasions seeking advice and priesthood blessings. On each of these occasions Harold encouraged Elder Kimball to take care of himself, to rest, and to continue with his labors as best he could.

In 1972, Harold was invited to meet with Elder Kimball, Camilla, and his doctors relative to his heart condition.

> His choice was to go on without an operation, with progressive weakness and loss of effectiveness (he gave himself just two months to live, and Dr. Wilkinson said death would come in the not-too-distant future), or to undergo open-heart bypass surgery to correct a valve leakage in his heart pump and to submit to a second procedure calling for bypass surgery to correct an obstruction in the main arterial supply line to the cardiac muscle, which would increase the blood supply to his heart.
>
> Elder Kimball and his presiding authorities heard the medical report of this high-risk surgery. He wearily stated that he was an old man and perhaps a new, more vigorous replacement should be sought to do the work he could no longer do. President Lee and President Tanner were

Deseret News. Used with permission

Harold B. Lee and Spencer W. Kimball enjoyed
a close friendship which began early in their
church service together as apostles

CA. 1973

surprised that Elder Kimball should question whether they thought his continued service was important enough to seek an extension of his life.

Aroused by Elder Kimball's plaintive doubts, President Lee, speaking for the First Presidency, rose to his feet, pounded his fist to the desk, and said, according to Dr. [Russell M.] Nelson's written summary of that crucial moment: "Spencer, you have been called! You are not to die! You are to do everything that you need to do in order to care for yourself and continue to live."

This positive declaration seemed to settle the issue President Kimball said he would submit to surgery. Sister Kimball wept at the thought and Dr. Nelson sunk under the weight of the newly transferred burden which passed to him. The momentous decision, which was to shape the history of the Church, was not made by the physicians, Dr. Nelson reported, but was based solely on the desire of an Apostle of the Lord to follow the inspired direction of the First Presidency. 33

Harold's involvement didn't end there. In the temple the First Presidency gave both Elder and Sister Kimball blessings, Harold being voice. Then, on the eve of the surgery, Harold also gave a blessing to Dr. Nelson, telling him that the operation would be performed without error. The next day Dr. Nelson sent word that the surgical team had completed the entire procedure "without loss of a blood vessel or a broken stitch," and Dr. Nelson stated that "he felt like a baseball pitcher who had just thrown a perfect game." 34 Harold's remarkable promise to Dr. Nelson had been completely fulfilled.

Eight days later Harold gave his future successor in the line of prophets stretching forward from Joseph Smith another blessing, and several weeks after that he and Joan made a special journey to

California so they could again encourage Elder Kimball and Camilla. After that last visit Elder Kimball's depression lifted entirely, his healing began in earnest, and he was ready to move forward in the work the Lord had given him to do.

As for himself, Harold continued to struggle. His migraine headaches didn't let up, and the pain from them continually plagued his efforts to serve. He wrote, for instance: " 'Following the temple meeting today I became ill with an intensely severe headache and nausea. I was unable to come to the office, as I had promised, to set apart and ordain my Dr. Hal Borne a bishop, for which I was very sorry.' " 35

He also continued to experience difficulty in preparing his talks for the various sessions of general conference. For instance, prior to the April 1972 conference, he wrote:

> During the past two days or more, and really for the week in particular, I have spent many "lonesome hours," but hopefully not alone spiritually, pondering what the Lord would have me say at the forthcoming general conference. My decision was to undertake the subject heading "Time of Decision," the caution in controversies, political and otherwise, and to offer five guidelines suggesting how all might be guided to wise decisions in their personal and public life. I feel content after my diligent search.

The five profound certainties that Harold listed in his talk, "by which one could detect and know the path to safety in the search for truth," were "(1) Follow the Light of Christ within us. (2) Follow the positive teachings of the gospel of Jesus Christ. (3) Do your business by the voice of the people. (4) Seek for statesmanlike men. And (5) Judge by the light of gospel truths." This advice is as profound today as it was when it was given thirty years ago. 36

Ever since their marriage, Joan had wanted Harold to show her Clifton and the area where he was born and reared. In 1971, while vacationing in Wellsville, he acquiesced to her desires and toured through the area, telling her all his favorite stories and experiences. He then recorded in his journal:

> The old saying: "You can never come back home again," came back forcibly as I saw the sad deterioration of the old homes where the pioneer families had with pride kept their lands in a respectable condition. These people have now passed on, and those who have come along to inherit or purchase from the former owners have built newer homes, but have left the old homes to fall to pieces and present a shocking spectacle of a dying generation. I was comforted somewhat when I found that our old home had been torn down and a fine new home had replaced it. 37

After returning to Salt Lake City, at Joan's and his children's urging, Harold sat down and recorded on tape some of the events of his boyhood and youth. "The following Sunday, with his entire family gathered at his daughter Helen's home for a monthly fireside, President Lee played the tape for his grandchildren. It became a cherished possession, an authentic recitation of his most inspiring childhood stories, told in his own voice." 38

With this personal task completed, though he did not know it, Harold was now ready for the Lord's next dramatic and soul-wrenching assignment.

PREPARED FOR THE
LORD'S MANTLE

"Why, Helen, is everything all right?"

Helen Lee Goates smiled at her father. "Of course it is, Daddy. I just thought that Aunt Joan might like the rest of her birthday cake."

Harold smiled in return. "How very thoughtful. It was such a delightful afternoon. Joan says it's one of the nicest birthday celebrations she's ever had."

"I'm pleased that she enjoyed it." Carefully Helen looked at her father. During the birthday celebration she'd had little time to spend alone with him, or even to look at him closely, for that matter. But now that they were standing facing each other, and she had a moment to think about it, she could see that he looked terribly weary. "Are...you feeling okay?" she ventured.

"Yes, dear, I feel well enough. Won't you come in and sit down? There was so little time this afternoon—"

"Oh, Daddy dear, you look far too tired. I'll just leave these things and run on. You don't need to visit tonight; you look like you're all visited out."

Harold shook his head. "No, you wait a minute. Joan is in changing her dress, but I know she'll want to see you."

"Well," Helen smiled, knowing that she could never argue with her father, "maybe for a minute—"

And so they stood together in the kitchen, father and daughter, visiting about this and that while Helen worried about him and he worried about all the things in the Church that she couldn't even begin to imagine. She had tried to get him to slow down a little; oh, how she had tried. But no, he had told her that after giving the matter serious thought, he had discerned three options. First, to slow down, which he did not feel he could do while still honoring his calling and his Lord, who had set the example by giving everything, even to his very life. Second, he could not slow down, but then moan and complain about his ailments and make everyone suffer for the sacrifice he was making. Or third, not slow down but simply go forward calmly, doing his best while quietly enduring whatever came next. The third choice, he had explained to her, had been the one he had made. Yet now—

"How are my grandchildren doing in Provo?" he suddenly asked. "Is there anything about them you might have heard that I need to know—"

Before Helen could answer, the telephone rang, and Harold looked toward the bedroom where Joan was answering the call. For a few seconds there was silence, and in the interim Helen glanced at the clock. It was 9.30 P.M., time she was getting home to Brent while her father and Aunt Joan—

"Harold," Joan called as she stepped into the hallway, "this is President Smith's son Douglas on the phone. He seems very agitated."

Quickly Harold took the phone and held it to his ear, said hello, and waited. Helen, who was watching her father, knew that she would never forget the stricken look on his face. He kept repeating: "Oh, no. No. Oh, no." Finally he covered the phone receiver and looked as though all the cares in the world had suddenly settled upon him. Then, very gravely, he said to his wife and daughter, "President Smith is gone."

"What?" Helen gasped. "But—"

"Oh, my dear Harold," Joan whispered as she took hold of a chair to steady herself, seeming to grasp in the instant the import of that message.

Meanwhile Harold finished his conversation with Douglas, though he was visibly shaken by the news. Still, he was able to give instructions to Douglas about whom should be notified and again offer condolences before finally hanging up. Whereupon he slumped against the door frame close by and put his head in his arms. Then he just kept shaking his head, over and over—

"Daddy," Helen soothed as she and Joan both went to him in an attempt to hold and support him. "Daddy dear, I guess the day has finally come that you must have thought through the years you would never be prepared for."

"Oh, Helen, I'm afraid I'm not, I'm afraid I'm not."

"But you are, darling," Joan remonstrated. "If anyone on this earth is prepared, then surely it is you!"

As Harold and Joan spent those few intimate moments together, Helen stepped back. Never had she seen her father look so weak and so completely at a loss. All through the years of her life—with the exception of the time of her mother's passing—he had been like the Rock of Gibralter to the family, to each and every one of them. In every way he had been the epitome of strength and goodness. But now—well, all Helen could think of was that he appeared totally and completely devastated.

Miraculously, then, or at least it seemed miraculous to Helen, Harold straightened up, squared his shoulders, and began to take charge.

"Now, dearie," he said to Joan as he gently took her by the arm, "you must go change your dress again while I make some phone calls, and then we must quickly go to Bruce's home."

Helen was amazed. Her father's moment of weakness was gone. It seemed as though he had reached back into his thirty-one years of apostolic preparation and found there the resources at his command to meet the challenge of this inevitable moment. She was no longer needed there, and Helen knew it.

Tenderly she bid her father and Aunt Joan good-bye and returned home to find her husband, Brent, working at his desk. Quickly she conveyed the news; then she took her husband by the hand and pulled him to his feet.

"Let's hurry and gather the children together. We must pray for Dad. I'm sure he needs the strength of our prayers—he looked so tired and so ill. You could read the pressure of the situation on his face. Let's all gather now in family prayer for him."

For the Goates family it was a choice experience to unite their faith under such grave circumstances. As they knelt around their large bed, Brent prayed and then called on Helen to pray. Then he asked each of the children to add whatever they wanted to the prayers of their parents. It was a sweet, lovely experience as they poured out their hearts to their Heavenly Father in behalf of their grandfather.

Even at that point, however, none of them were allowing their minds to jump ahead to what might occur after the Council of the Twelve met to select a new president. Their only concern at the moment was that their father and grandfather needed the Lord to give him strength to face the extreme pressures and circumstances of the next week, including the funeral service and all else which would follow. They wanted to give him their united faith and help, and whatever came after that, they would leave in the hands of God. 1

On Sunday evening, July 2, 1972, President Joseph Fielding Smith passed away at the home of his daughter Amelia and her husband, Elder Bruce R. McConkie. He had been seated in his favorite chair reading the scriptures when Amelia left the room for a moment or so. When she returned, her father, and the tenth president of The

Church of Jesus Christ of Latter-day Saints, was slumped over in his chair—gone. Had he lived seventeen more days, President Smith would have been ninety-six years old.

President Tanner picked up Harold, and the two former counselors spent some time visiting with the Smith family, comforting with them and praying with them. Immediately upon their arrival at the McConkie home, however, Harold had gone directly to the couch on which the body of his dear friend rested. For some time he held the lifeless hand in his own, reluctant to part with his longtime associate in Church leadership.

On their way home Harold and President Tanner determined to convene a meeting of the Twelve in the Administration Building council room the next morning—a Monday. All fourteen of the Brethren attended, including Elder Kimball, who had an additional ailment he was suffering from—Bell's palsy, which had partially paralyzed his face and was causing him great discomfort.

"President Lee, who presided at this meeting as the president of the Twelve, was calm and subdued, reflecting the burden he carried as the *de facto* head of the Church. The inference drawn from his appearance was that he had slept little, if at all, the previous night as he wrestled with the intricate problems he now faced.

"The agenda of the meeting was brief, but important: The Brethren were reminded of the procedure governing events connected with the death of a prophet when the minutes of a similar meeting held following the death of President David O. McKay were read; a committee was appointed to meet with the Smith family in making the funeral arrangements; it was agreed the Brethren would meet in the upper room of the temple the following Friday to consider the reorganization of the First Presidency; approval was given to issue all checks necessary to carry on the work pending the reorganization; and President Lee, acting as the president of the Twelve, was authorized to sign all correspondence and documents during the interim period, which documents

ordinarily would have been signed by the First Presidency." 2

That evening all Harold's family gathered in the Lee home. Harold greeted them warmly, but soon an "uncomfortable pall hung over the group. All were reluctant to speak of the events that would shortly come to pass. President Lee asked Jane to play her violin. At the conclusion of the performance he expressed his pleasure and asked for a second number to be played. Jane explained that she had brought no other music with her, so she agreed to play some hymns while the rest of the family sang. Jane asked her grandfather to choose the hymns he wanted to sing. He immediately requested two, 'Love at Home' and 'I Need Thee Every Hour.' Then President Lee said he would like to finish with 'How Firm a Foundation,' reciting these words from the third verse, which at that moment were particularly significant to him:

> Fear not, I am with thee, O be not dismayed,
> For I am thy God and will still give thee aid;
> I'll strengthen thee, help thee, and cause thee to stand,
> Upheld by my righteous, omnipotent hand.

Son-in-law L. Brent Goates' account continues:

> Recognizing that all of his grandchildren would have in their minds many questions about that which would shortly unfold in the history of the Church as it related to their grandfather, President Lee then explained the events in the coming week. He told them about making the arrangements with President Smith's family for the funeral and about their requesting him to be one of the speakers. Then he told them that the day after the funeral all the members of the Council of the Twelve and the counselors to President Smith would meet by appointment in the council room of the First Presidency and Council of the Twelve in the Salt Lake Temple. He explained that it was the order

of the Church that following the death of its President, the keys of leadership are immediately transferred to the Council of the Twelve, and that as the President of that quorum, he would have the responsibility to take the lead in governing the Church until such a time as that body would direct that the First Presidency would be reorganized.

President Lee carefully explained, in words that even the little children would understand, that three options were open to the Council of the Twelve: (1) the First Presidency could be reorganized and, if that were done, the senior member of the Council, himself, would likely be chosen as the new President of the Church, if precedent were followed; (2) they could take no action and allow the Quorum of the Twelve to govern the Church as was happening at that moment; or (3) by revelation they could choose any member of the Twelve, if so directed by the Lord, to preside over a new First Presidency.

The children asked many questions and a good discussion followed the words of President Lee, who was always the teacher to his family when the teaching moment arose. A phone call interrupted the discussion and soon President Lee announced that he must leave. Before the family meeting was adjourned, however, Brent Goates asked: "Before you go, Dad, would you just tell us what you want us to do as your family to help you the most, not only during this week as you move through these historic and emotional experiences, but in the years ahead? What is it that we can do to support you most as your family?"

Hesitating only a moment, President Lee responded with this challenge: "Be true to the faith—just live the gospel as I've taught you to do, as you know it to be right. That is all I want my family to do for me. Be undeviating in the path of righteousness. That's all I could ask of my loved ones, you who are dearest to me. There is nothing you could do that could help me more or make this grandfather happier than that."

His message was clear. None of the family members looking back on this experience could have any doubt as to his expectations. He was acting in the role of a true patriarch, emulating the Heavenly Father of us all in repeating the simplest yet most important message of the ages in a clarion call to keep the commandments. Family members still remember him most for the gospel truths he taught and the powerful direction he provided throughout their lives, but especially for that family home evening where all their hearts were united and intimately entwined through his leadership. 3

Throughout the day of their memorable family home evening, Harold had been experiencing severe pains in his side. Joan finally insisted that she be allowed to call his doctor, did so, and the doctor's return call was the one that interrupted the family gathering described above. After Dr. James Orme examined him on July 4, Harold was immediately admitted to the hospital for further testing—which discovered blood clots on his lungs.

That day and night Harold remained in the hospital receiving treatments to thin his blood, Elder Lee thinking all the while of whom he would choose as his counselors in the new First Presidency. When he was released from the hospital the next day he first spent an hour in the temple, and prayed constantly the rest of the time, seeking the Lord's confirmation of the impressions he had been having. He wrote:

I knew who I had in mind,... but I wanted the confirmation of the Lord. I spent an hour or more in the temple and [prayed] throughout the night. When the morning came [Thursday the sixth], there was no doubt that N. Eldon

Tanner was to be named as the first counselor.... I also was certain that Marion G. Romney should be named the other counselor; and that was likewise spiritually confirmed to my satisfaction. 4

On Thursday, July 6, 1972, Harold conducted President Smith's funeral in the Tabernacle on Temple Square. No one suspected that Elder Lee had only recently been in the hospital, and the few who knew told no one. As for Harold, it simply didn't matter. The Lord had given him a work to do, and it was time he was about it. Of the deceased prophet, he said that day:

> As we have been associated, particularly in the last two years as the counselors of President Smith, we have marveled at the clarity of his mind, the health of his body, the fact that he could speak well, and could walk without difficulty when most men at his age could have done neither....
>
> This we have witnessed time and again, as we were engaged in discussing very serious matters—decisions that should only be made by the President of the Church. It was then that we saw this sparkling wisdom come to light as he recounted, undoubtedly beyond his own present understanding, things that he called up from the depths of his soul. 5

Harold then did what he was already known for, and for which he was about to become famous. He expressed before the assembled throng his innermost feelings and thoughts as he closed his eulogy for President Smith:

> Since the shock of his passing came, and realizing now that the Twelve would have the responsibility to take up the labors and determine what path to take in order to reorganize the Presidency of the Church, and serving as I do as the senior member of the Council, I have been concerned.

I have wanted to know what the Lord's will would be. I wanted to do nothing except I knew it was of the Lord. I have sought most earnestly to know, to be guided, so that this Church could go on and be worthy of those who have sacrificed, who have given their lives that this Church might grow.

I have received a special witness these last few days. I had a comfort from one who wrote, "Men who are called to these leading positions in the Church were foreordained to that mission before they came to this earth." If I didn't believe that, I wouldn't dare stand in the place where I am today; believing that, I have no fear, anxiety, and concern, because I know the Lord is at the helm in guiding the work of the Church.

If the Lord knew me before I came here, as my friend reminded me, and he knows me now and has accepted of me, the Lord being my strength, we will attempt to follow in the footsteps of this beloved leader of ours. Brother Tanner and I have loved this man these last two and one-half years. It hasn't been pretended. He begat love. Because he loved us, we have stood by him, as he stood by and trusted us. We have mourned his passing with you, his dear family; and we want to express to you our feeling that now he has gone, you may not feel that you are alone. You still belong to us. We want you to know that the arms of our love are about each and every one of you here in this great family of President Smith. 6

After the funeral Harold again went to the temple, feeling acutely "the need for additional spiritual strength as he faced perhaps the most momentous day of his life. He went alone to the temple for this purpose where he spent several hours praying, planning, and reminiscing. The record he left of this illuminating interlude opens a revealing window into the heart and soul of Harold B. Lee.

> As I viewed the paintings of the presidents of the church
> ...from the Prophet Joseph Smith to the present, I had
> brought to me the overwhelming responsibility that will
> rest upon me to follow where these great leaders have led.
> I also sat for a moment where I was joined in marriage to
> my darling Fern by President George F. Richards and again
> in the sealing room where my lovely Joan was sealed to me
> by President David O. McKay. I poured out my soul in
> gratitude for these two of the greatest women who have
> ever walked the earth who have been brought to me
> through circumstances which attest to the divine guidance
> of the almighty who knew my need. 7

As seemed to be becoming typical, there was much speculation
about who might be the next President of the Church. A veteran
national newsman, knowing that Harold would never speak of
such things, approached Brent Goates for information relative to
a press release he hoped to have prepared by the time of the
announcement. His questions: " 'What type of leadership may be
expected when Harold B. Lee becomes the President of the
Church? What are his dominant leadership characteristics?' "8

Taken aback by the penetrating questions, Brent thought of
how well he knew his father-in-law both as a person and as a leader.
Yet therein lay the problem. Though "the analysis required was not
difficult,...the communication of those conclusions to the unbeliev-
ing readers was extremely complicated. Brent's answer by necessity
eliminated the prime characteristic of the next President of the
Church. How could he explain that Harold B. Lee's primary virtue
was his spirituality, his intimacy with the God who directed his
thoughts and footsteps, his totally uncommon ability to obtain
flashes of inspiration and illuminating light in answer to his ponder-
ings and prayers? He was a revelator and seer and he possessed the

miraculous powers of his office and calling in unusual abundance. But how could this be explained, and if explained, comprehended by those not understanding continuous revelation to the leaders of the Church?

"The spiritual depths of President Lee's leadership simply had to go unspoken, Brent concluded. And so the interview emphasized other salient qualities of President Lee, which also were impressive. His amazing organizational ability was cited, as attested by the development of the welfare plan of the Church, and recently proven anew through the correlation reorganization of all phases of the Church. His ability to instill confidence in Church members, develop discipleship among the leaders, and thrill the young people with a sense of their importance were among other characteristics mentioned. Yes, greatness could be expected of this man of God in many aspects of leadership, but the greatest quality of all, his spirituality, would not find its way into print on the pages of *The New York Times* or any other public media." 9

On Friday morning at 8:00 A.M., the Brethren convened in the sacred room of the Salt Lake Temple to consider the reorganization of the First Presidency. After Elder Hugh B. Brown offered an opening prayer and Elder LeGrand Richards offered the prayer at the altar, each of the Twelve, starting with the newest member, stood to express his feelings about how they should proceed. When it finally became time for Elder Kimball to speak, he made a motion that Harold B. Lee become the President of the Church, which motion was seconded and unanimously approved. Harold then took his seat as the prophet.

> With all of the Twelve participating, Spencer W. Kimball was voice in ordaining Harold B. Lee and setting him apart as the eleventh President of The Church of Jesus Christ of Latter-day Saints, as prophet, seer, and revelator, and as Trustee-in-Trust of all Church properties. Then President

Lee set apart and blessed President Tanner as first counselor and Marion G. Romney as second counselor in the
new First Presidency, and also Spencer W. Kimball as
President of the Quorum of the Twelve Apostles. 10

As was mentioned earlier, Elder Kimball was suffering that day
from Bell's palsy, which caused his face to sag noticeably. Elder
Kimball felt embarrassed by his weakened condition and poor
physical appearance and even apologized to Harold for it. After the
blessing in which he was set apart as President of the Twelve, however, there was a marked change in Elder Kimball's appearance. It
was an indication, according to President Lee, that his friend had
received a special spiritual blessing. And it was further indication
to everyone else involved as to just what sort of president Harold
B. Lee was going to be.

President Harold B. Lee (center)
with counselors N. Eldon Tanner (left)
and Marion G. Romney (right)

CA. 1972

Deseret News. Jay Hesslop

16

A Deep, Universal Love

"Hey, Elder, isn't this great?

Steven Pogue, still not used to being called "elder," paid no attention to the young missionary seated beside him. Instead, his attention was drawn to the room in which they were seated; the assembly room on the upper floor of the Salt Lake Temple. He was still feeling amazed that there was such a room, and he hadn't yet begun to think about how remarkable it was that he and the others were actually there.

"Hi," the missionary intruded again, thrusting forth his hand, "I'm Elder Gardner, Elder Paul T. Gardner, from Lehi, Utah. And you are?"

"Steve Pogue," he replied quietly, at the same time returning the handshake. "From San Jose, California. Quite a room, isn't it?"

"I'll say!" Elder Gardner whispered. "What I meant by great is that its the prophet who is going to speak to us. That's what's so great!"

"The prophet?" Elder Pogue's mind was still elsewhere. "You mean President...uh...President—"

"President Lee," the enthusiastic missionary finished for him. "Harold B. Lee! The man who signed your mission call. Good grief, Elder. Where have you been?"

Good question, Elder Pogue thought as his mind darted backward. Where had he been? Or more importantly, where was he going? And why? He didn't mean to England, of course. Or because he had been called by the prophet. He meant with his life! And for the first time since he could remember, he now knew! And felt good about knowing—

Yes, it had been President Lee who had signed his call to the England East Mission back in October—a fact that had impressed him mightily. A personal letter from the Lord's prophet, he had felt certain, had to be an indication from the Lord to him, Steven R. Pogue, that he was doing the right thing by going on a mission.

As a matter of fact, up until then he hadn't been all that committed, drifting in and out of the Church almost as convenience dictated. Finally, though, he had decided that a mission might be a good way of showing the Lord that this time he meant what he was saying—that he really did intend to stay active this time.

So now, as of December 1, 1973, he and more than two hundred other missionaries were being trained in the mission home in Salt Lake City. Those who were going to English speaking missions spent only five days there—but what a glorious five days they had been! The General Authorities had come daily to give them guidance and counsel for the work that lay ahead, and all of them had been spiritually nurtured in a way he had never imagined, let alone experienced.

But this last day before their departure, Elder Pogue was thinking, was the grandest, most spiritual day of all! They had been attended an endowment session in the temple, after which they had been brought up to this incredible assembly room for a question-and-answer session with the prophet—President Lee. His hour would be followed by another endowment session, with most of them paying more attention, Elder Pogue thought, because they would no doubt know a lot more than they had prior to this meeting.

Any question any of them might have, he thought as he continued to gaze around. All of them had been invited to participate, and President Lee would do his best to answer as many of their questions as he could. At least that's what they had been told, and for his part Elder Pogue believed it. After all, the man was a prophet, just like Moses had been. In the young missionary's mind he could see him already, assuming a prophetic stance, hand on forehead, giving forth revelations from the Lord in answer to each missionary's earnest query.

What a rare opportunity to gather with the Lord's chosen servant in the holy temple, Elder Pogue thought, and just so he could address the concerns of a bunch of young missionaries! It was amazing that the prophet had such time, especially in light of the fact that he was also required to govern the affairs of the whole Church. As Elder Pogue considered that, once again he felt the witness that his work as a missionary must truly be important—

"They say he's been doing this practically every week since he was an apostle," his neighbor suddenly whispered.

"How old is he now?" Elder Pogue questioned.

"He's seventy-four; not very old when you consider that President McKay was ninety-six when he died, and President Smith was ninety-five. President Lee could easily be the prophet for the next twenty years!"

"No doubt," Elder Pogue mumbled, impressed that the missionary, Elder whatever-his-name-was, knew so much. "And he's been coming here and answering questions every week for how long?"

"Well, he was ordained an apostle when he was forty or forty-one, I'm not exactly sure. And the lady downstairs told a bunch of us that he started these classes not very long after he was ordained. So, something more than thirty years, I'd guess. That's dedication, wouldn't you say?"

Soberly, Elder Pogue nodded. He couldn't even imagine thirty years. Neither could he imagine—

"What'd you say your name was?" he asked.

"Elder Gardner. I'm from Lehi, down in Utah Valley. And you're—"

Suddenly President Lee entered the room, and as one the assembly of missionaries rose to their feet in respectful silence. As the not-so-elderly man made his way to the stand Elder Pogue studied him. He had never in his life been near a prophet, and he was intrigued. President Lee's hair was thinning and wavy, very dark but with quite a bit of gray in it. His face was unlined; he wore dark-rimmed glasses. He looked to be about five feet eight or nine inches tall, and he probably weighed about a hundred and fifty pounds, though his suit made that a guess and nothing more. All in all, though, he was pretty normal looking, and for an instant Elder Pogue felt disappointment. Then he reminded himself of the revelations President Lee was about to receive in order to answer the more dark and mysterious questions being asked, and he was again excited.

As President Lee stepped to the podium, the missionaries sat back down, their eyes as one upon him. Carefully, he explained that if they had questions pertaining to the gospel, the temple, the endowment, or missionary work, they were to stand and speak up, and then sit back down while he did his best to answer. With no more preamble than that, he commenced by calling for the first question, which was immediately asked by an elder on the other side of the room. A short but complete answer followed; another question was asked, this time by a sister, and as President Lee answered it Elder Pogue found himself thinking with surprise that the prophet was not acting like a Moses at all, but seemed more like a familiar, kindly teacher.

Even more surprising to the young missionary, instead of spouting forth new revelations, almost before each questioner had finished asking his or her question, President Lee was turning to a pertinent passage in the scriptures before him. He used no index, but quickly leafed through the sacred works as though he had written them himself. Each question that was asked he answered strictly from the holy writ, reading passages that Elder Pogue could see were as familiar to him as his own name.

In a friendly, fatherly way, the prophet opened up to the missionaries' understandings numerous scriptures that Elder Pogue had never even heard of before. And he found himself marveling greatly. Never did President Lee reply, "Hmm, that's a new one on me. I'll have to check with the Lord." Not once! He simply skimmed through the pages of his scriptures and then read to them what the Lord had already said about the issue in question—a very long time before.

In that manner the prophet answered questions about the special clothing worn during the endowment ceremony and about the sacred covenants the missionaries had each made. He took care to emphasize the symbolic nature of the ceremony, the need to show integrity in honoring their covenants, and the elevating effect doing this would have on their lives. He sought, also, to eliminate any false or fanciful ideas the young missionaries had about the endowment or the temple. He adroitly turned away questions about reported appearances of the Savior in the temple by saying that because it was the house of the Lord, it would not be unusual for him to visit there, nor should one be surprised to find him in virtually any part of it. And all that time President Lee was using his scriptures, reading first one verse and then another from an entirely different place, quite literally allowing the Lord to answer the questions instead of himself.

Suddenly Elder Pogue's mind was opened to what was happening, and an astounding realization swept over him. The Lord, he could now see, was not going to give new revelations on a subject when he had already revealed his mind on it—especially when his will on the matter was available in the scriptures. That was not his way. And while President Lee no doubt received many revelations, which is what prophets were called to do, he certainly didn't need any revelations that day to answer the missionaries' questions. Instead, he needed only to be familiar with the revelations the Lord had already given.

In other words, the prophet had done his homework, and like the amazingly knowledgeable Elder Paul Gardner had said, he had obviously been doing it for a great many years before any of these young missionaries had even been born.

Dropping his gaze for a moment, the stunned elder found himself considering his own life. He had never been particularly diligent in gospel study; he had not even enjoyed Sunday School or seminary, for that matter. Too boring, he'd always said. Oh, he'd pretty much always believed. But his attitude had always been that if he knew the scriptures were true, then what was the point of knowing what was in them?

Now, though, in almost an instant, that attitude had changed, for he had now been at the feet of one who had spent a great portion of his life learning what was in them—and his knowledge was awesome! More than that, it was powerful, but in a spiritual sort of way that...that...well, it made him feel good all over; it made him want to sit there forever just being taught out of President Lee's scriptures—

"Oh, no," Elder Gardner suddenly breathed as a sister in front of them began to express herself, and scant seconds later Elder Gardner's hand was gripping Steve Pogue's arm and his mind was back. "That sister's weird, Elder Pogue! She's in my district, and every time she opens her mouth—"

"President Lee," the sister was saying, "the 89TH Section of the Doctrine and Covenants says that if you are obedient to the Word of Wisdom you shall run and not be weary, walk and not faint. I don't know how we can teach that to a person who is paraplegic, has lost his limbs, or is in a wheelchair."

With one hand President Lee snapped shut his scriptures, almost making both young missionaries jump. Looking carefully around the room instead of just at the sister who was standing, he declared, "That's the trouble with Latter-day Saints today. They put question marks at the end of revelations where the Lord put periods!"

As the sister wilted back into her seat, an elderly missionary arose. Speaking in behalf of the entire group, he said that they knew President Lee to be a prophet of God and that they sustained him as President of the Church.

To Elder Pogue's amazement, President Lee was visibly touched by the man's words. He then spoke of some of his difficulties since the passing of President Joseph Fielding Smith and explained how impossible it was for him to fulfill his calling without the sustaining vote of the Church. Thanking the assembled missionaries he then opened his scriptures once more, and using the Lord's words as if they were his own, he bore a powerful testimony of the divinity of the work that he—and each of them—had been called to perform.

"Amen," both Elder Pogue and Elder Gardner breathed fervently and tearfully as God's living prophet concluded his witness and stepped from the stand. And then and there Elder Steven J. Pogue, called to carry God's word to the good people of England, determined that he was going to learn the scriptures so that he, too, could carry the word to others as spiritually and powerfully as had his beloved president, Harold B. Lee! 1

One of Harold's qualities that both surprised and endeared him to others was what might be termed his positive openness. Never negative but always optimistic, he was forthright and straightforward under every condition except when confidentiality was required, and these qualities could not have been better illustrated than during the press conference held immediately following his ordination. There, fifty or more media representatives had gathered to ask him questions. When asked what his first message would be, to Church members or to the world, his reply was scriptural: "keep the commandments of God, for therein lies...safety." 2 When asked about the frightening conditions in the world at the time, he pointed out that the Prophet Joseph Smith had prophesied 140 years earlier that peace would be taken from the earth and Satan would have power over his own dominion. He then said:

> After 140 years, is there anyone here who doubts that that time is here? But the Lord said he would reign among his people, and the most powerful weapon that can ever be forged against the wickedness of the world is the powerful teachings of the principles of the gospel of Jesus Christ. That's what he gave them to us for, to combat fear and untruth and wickedness in the world. 3

When asked his opinion regarding the greatest challenge facing himself and the Church, Harold replied that the task of leading more than three million members of the Church was " 'ominous.' " He also said that the greatest challenge facing the Church was to keep pace with the growth in the membership:

> We approach this task knowing that the Church is grow- ing, which is our greatest challenge today. To keep pace with the growth and to see that the members everywhere are properly shepherded, taught, and led becomes now our greatest responsibility. Through the graces of the Almighty we have been directed to lay some cornerstones, and we hope to build on that foundation in the years ahead. We approach the future like the prophets of old...like Nephi, when he said: "I, Nephi, went forth not knowing before- hand the things which I should do." We will lean on the spiritual guidance of the Lord.

As the members of the Church, particularly those who had not been familiar with him, were to discover, Harold meant every word of this. Moreover, it quickly became obvious that the Lord was leading this new prophet and president, and he wanted people to know it as clearly as did he. In introducing his counselors, N. Eldon Tanner and Marion G. Romney, he declared:

> May I say that it is my responsibility to name counselors. We have some of the great men of the earth who form the membership of the General Authorities of the Church. Any one of them is just as qualified as any of us, or others; but to know which ones were to receive the sanction of the Lord required some soul-searching, and to that task I devoted myself. I have had the witness as to the men who should be called to be my counselors. They've been called not by the will of men or the choice of men. They've been called by the direction and guidance of the Spirit of the Lord, and they are the men who are acceptable to the Lord. We know that. We have received a witness of it. 5

To another international reporter a few days later, in response to the question about why the Church was growing when so many others were in decline, Harold was delighted to respond. In summarizing his answer later, he wrote:

> This gave me the opportunity to impress the fact that the great strength of the Church is the individual testimony of each member, communicated by faithful missionaries and received after soul-searching by those who are honest seekers for truth. The report of this lengthy interview is to appear in an issue of the *Times*, which also syndicates to a large number of newspapers throughout the country. 6

Seventy-three when he was called, which to that time was the average age of all new Church presidents, Harold was nevertheless the youngest Church president in forty years. However, though there was every expectation that his tenure would be lengthy, it was in fact to last just 538 days—the shortest tenure of any president in the history of the Church up to that time. Harold's presidency was also unique for its international flavor, "since President Lee was born and reared in the United States; President Tanner, although born in the United States, lived most of his life in Canada; and President Romney was born and reared in Mexico."[7]

Before he could begin serving as prophet, however, there was something that Harold still lacked—the very real mantle of power, or pure love of Christ, that a loving God bestows on his authorized servants, be they prophet, bishop, or called to serve in any capacity. Of that transcendent moment, which occurred the morning after his ordination, Harold said:

> As my wife and I kneeled in humble prayer,…suddenly it seemed as though my mind and heart went out to all three million members throughout the world. I seemed to love every one of them, regardless of their nationality or their color, whether rich or poor or educated or not. I suddenly felt as though they all belonged to me, as though they were all my own brothers and sisters. [8]

Uncomfortable with the adoration the Saints immediately began showing him because his divinely given love for them was so obvious and sincere, one of Harold's first actions was to direct that all three members of the First Presidency and their wives should ride in the Days of '47 Parade, instead of just the President, as had been the custom. But this did not stop the expressions of love and reverence, which rapidly increased in intensity. No matter where Harold went, the fruits of the Spirit followed, people were affected and blessed by them and his remarkable love, and this he could not avoid. His first talk as President of the Church, an impromptu one for young employees of the Jackson Lake Lodge and its environs where he was vacationing, had an overwhelming effect on the congregation. "'There was a remarkable spirit which prompted many tears,'" he wrote of the event. "The reason seemed to derive from the spiritual intensity and sensitivity of the man and from the spiritual focus he gave to everything he did. His elevation to the prophetic office magnified this reaction." 9

One young man at the lodge who had attended, a nonmember named Steve Rogers, requested baptism immediately following the service. When Harold was notified of this circumstance by the man who had taken charge, he wrote back:

> I was interested in the story of the conversion of this young man. I was not surprised because the Spirit that was in our meeting at the lodge was the kind that could have brought joy to the hearts of all who were there. I felt it and I suppose this young man did likewise. 10

Another example is similarly illustrative. One evening when he was obviously ill, Harold spoke to a group of Latter-day Saint student leaders from across the country. One of the adults in charge, E. LaMar Buckner, recorded what transpired. After being introduced by Elder Marion D. Hanks, Elder Lee

> walked slowly to the pulpit and softly began to speak. One was almost required to strain and to lean forward to hear him. With each sentence, however, there was evidence of resurgent strength as this "special witness to Jesus Christ" bore testimony of [his] remarkable experiences....
>
> [He said] that since his call to the General Authorities...he had witnessed 30 of his companions being called home. He especially emphasized the...occasions when the Prophets of the Lord were called home. He then

reported how impressed he was when he saw President George Albert Smith speak at the funeral of his predecessor, President Heber J. Grant, and how the mantle of the Lord fell upon him and transformed the Apostle to become the Prophet.

He told about his lonely experience in conducting a funeral service honoring his fellow apostle Charles A. Callis in Florida, and how just as the brethren were in their temple robes praying for him in the Salt Lake Temple, at that very moment in Florida he felt a rush and strength of the Holy Spirit....

He related an experience of where a man's injured arm was healed while shaking hands with Elder Lee. That man later joined the Church. He added, this was not by Elder Lee's doing but by the power of the Lord....

With each passing minute he [became] stronger and stronger, drawing us all closer to the Lord. At the close, he bore his testimony that God lives and told how as a special witness of Jesus this truth had been revealed to him. Everyone knew, too, that he knew.... It seemed that waves of the Spirit of the Lord were passing over the audience.

After [Elder] Lee's sermon, the benediction was given by a young man, a converted atheist. In his unique prayer he pledged and committed to God the determination of all the youth there to sustain and support those principles that had been taught....

When he returned to his seat the meeting was formally over but not a soul stirred. The sound of silence was deafening. The silence lasted perhaps ten minutes, although to me it felt much longer. Even when Elder Hanks went to the pulpit he said nothing, thus allowing the overpowering spirit to continue through the chapel. I could see tears in the eyes of [Elder Lee]...and in the eyes of students in the congregation....

When several of [the] individuals who had been on the stand [stood up to leave], the remainder of the audience rose to their feet but remained standing silently while [Elder] Lee...left.

As [he] left, Brother Marvin Higbee, who had so beautifully sung "I Walked Today Where Jesus Walked," began to sing "The Spirit of God Like a Fire Is Burning." The congregation joined him, but it soon faded out for even this sacred song was viewed as an encroachment upon the pervasive spirit.

It was to me a manifestation unequalled to anything I had before seen. [Elder] Lee had borne testimony as I had seldom heard....

The spirit there was felt by all and it was one of the greatest witnesses that I had ever seen of the work of the Holy Ghost....

As we left the chapel we were surprised to see [Elder] Lee...standing in the foyer shaking hands with each and every one of those in the chapel as they filed by, still not speaking but openly weeping. The strength of...Harold B. Lee was still being transmitted to us. 11

Despite such transcendent experiences, "even as the pure love of the Savior did not protect him from the agony of the cross, neither did President Lee's feelings of universal love provide immunity from the hatred and threats of vicious men. Two days after the Mexico City area conference ended, an anonymous call was received at Church headquarters warning that two men, members of an apostate cult in Mexico, were in town to assassinate President Lee. Soon after, it was learned that a week before, the leader of this apostate cult had been murdered by one of the assassins reported to be in Salt Lake City, seeking the life of the prophet. Immediately on learning this, security personnel were assigned to stay constantly with President Lee until the danger had abated. The next day, the Salt Lake City police were called in to help protect him. Such was the uncertainty the threat created that on the first Sunday after returning home from Mexico, President Lee did not attend meetings in his own ward but stayed home. Meanwhile, automatic, electric locks were installed on the door leading to his office and security procedures were tightened up all around Church headquarters." 12

Though the threats ultimately came to nothing, the heightened security and escorts when he walked or in companion cars when he traveled was one more burden to President Lee—one more deplorable way in which this humble man seemed to "stick out."

As mentioned, Harold's first area conference as President of the Church was held in Mexico City in August, 1972. This conference brought to the fore a whole series of historical firsts. Never had such a large gathering of Saints met under one roof—more than sixteen thousand. It was also the largest gathering of Spanish-speaking Saints and the largest gathering of Latter-day Saint descendants of Lehi. A new method of translation was introduced, a system of direct, simultaneous transmission such as was then being used in the United Nations. Those who attended the conference also "had the privilege...to be the first to sustain President Lee and his counselors in the new First Presidency. (They had been set apart just two months earlier on July 7.) It was also the first time a separate Aaronic Priesthood session was held in connection with an area conference. 13

People traveled from as far away as Tijuana—a fifty-three hour bus ride—and from Panama, Honduras, and Costa Rica. One of these faithful members declared: "'To be able to sit and listen to [President Lee's] words and to know and feel in your heart that you are listening to a prophet of God is one of the most beautiful experiences in my life.'" 14

The prophet did not disappoint. "In his keynote address, President Lee briefly traced the growth of the church in Mexico, noting that the membership there then stood at 115,000. He attributed this vigorous growth to the influence of the Holy Ghost brooding over the land and to the diligence of the missionaries and members. He counselled that investigators be admonished to study and to pray since true conversion comes to an individual only through the power of God. He also blessed the parents with a new resolution to keep their houses in order, to be faithful to their companions, and to promote the teaching of young people. 'Teach so many good things to them,' he admonished, 'that they can't find time to be bad.'... In this spirit, the prophet extended his love and blessings to the audience, invoking the spirit of the Lord to abide with them always." 15

President Lee's words evoked a remarkable depth of feeling among the assembled Saints, and "herein lies the explanation of the true greatness of Harold B. Lee. What he did or accomplished during his remarkable career does not define or explain that greatness. It is rather what he was or what he became that does so. That he spearheaded the welfare program, nurtured and shepherded the correlation program, and was the moving force behind the restructuring of the headquarters organizations, are extraordinary achievements, not to be disparaged. But they pale in comparison to the quality of genuine, universal love that at last found lodgement in the mind and heart of this prophet. And, unlike the many things he accomplished during his life that required the exercise of his own initiative, diligence, and discipline, this premier attribute came to him as a gift from God, without a conscious act of will or self-determination on his part. This quality of love was evident in every aspect of his short tenure as the president of the Church. Those who associated with him, or who heard him speak, were conscious of it and felt its influence." 16

That summer President Lee and his wife, accompanied by

Deseret News. Used with permission

President Harold B. and Joan Lee
traveling with Marjorie and Gordon B. Hinckley

CA. 1972

Elder Gordon B. Hinckley and his wife, also traveled to Europe. In London they met with Lord Thomson of Fleet, a wealthy and influential newspaper owner, and they visited the London Temple where the prophet "gave the sealing powers to seven brethren." After both Harold and Elder Hinckley spoke that evening in the Hyde Park Chapel, Elder Hinckley wrote: "'President Lee appears extremely tired and even sick. He says he is all right, but I am concerned. He has been the victim of too much "police security" at home, in addition to the very heavy demands of his office.'"17

Following the next two days' activities, which were even more strenuous, the party flew to Athens, Greece, where they held a meeting with Latter-day Saints at a military base, made attempts to obtain official recognition for the Church (they failed), and climbed the famed Acropolis to gaze at the Parthenon on Mars Hill where Paul had preached his famous sermon on the "unknown God." Early the next morning, after another night of severe pain in his lower back, Harold spoke in the same spot. In part, he taught:

> Here then was the opening of the work among the Grecian people. As Paul began to expound the doctrine, he gave us a key as to how we all could know that Jesus was the Christ. He said to the Corinthians, "No man speaking by the Spirit of God calleth Jesus accursed: and no man can say [the Prophet Joseph Smith said that should have been translated 'and no man can know'] that Jesus is the Lord, but by the Holy Ghost." So we who have been baptized and received the gift of the Holy Ghost, we too can know by the witness of the Spirit that he is the Christ, to know which is to gain eternal life....
>
> As we come to positions of trust and responsibility centuries later, bearing the same message, teaching the same gospel, worshipping the same God, faced with the same opposition, we must not hesitate or slacken our zeal

to project the work of the Lord. The work of the Lord never was presented with ease. It had to be brought forth out of blood and sweat and tears and sacrifice. So it may require that in our day, too, more than we know. As I read back over the history of the Presidents of the Church in our dispensation, I have become aware that all of these men went through periods of trial and testing before they came to their position in the Church. So, today, may this kind of a meeting make each one of us have a feeling of dedication. 18

Following President Lee's magnificent testimony, Elder Hinckley offered the closing prayer. "It was so eloquent and sweeping yet so humble that President Lee summarized with a powerful statement: 'We shall let that prayer become a prayer of rededication of this land.'" 19

From Greece the travelers flew to Israel. There they visited with government leaders and discussed their desire to build a visitors center and monument to the dedicatory prayer of Elder Orson Hyde, offered on the Mount of Olives in the 1840s. Because Joan had never been to the Holy Land, the group toured many of the most significant sites, ending in the evening at the Garden Tomb, "where about thirty Saints who live in Israel gathered to be with the prophet. The light from a bright, September moon filtered through the olive trees, spreading a soft glow over the Garden Tomb area in Jerusalem. Ordinarily at this hour the spot would have been deserted, but on this [night, September 30, 1972], a special meeting was about to take place....

"President Harold B. Lee, the prophet of God, who only recently had been ordained to that calling, was now presiding at a meeting in those holy surroundings. Hymns were sung and prayers were spoken. Organizing a Jerusalem branch of the Church was an idea which came unpremeditated as inspiration of the moment.

Illustration by Robert T. Barrett

[Under President Lee's direction] David B. Galbraith was sustained as the president of the first branch of the Church of Jesus Christ to be organized in the Holy Land in nearly two thousand years. A children's chorus sang 'I Am a Child of God.' Then, Elder Gordon B. Hinckley spoke movingly, recounting from the book of John some of the events of the death, burial, and resurrection of the Savior. President Lee's sermon was then delivered. Elder Hinckley recorded these statements in his journal:

> President Lee said that when he and his wife Fern came to the Garden Tomb in 1958 there was a feeling about this place that was different from all other places. He read the scripture: "In the place where he was crucified there was a garden." "That is," President Lee went on, "in the hill where he was crucified there was a garden." He had concluded that Golgotha was right up on the top of the hill above here and that this was indeed the very garden where Joseph of Arimathaea brought the body of the crucified Lord.
>
> He told the group assembled, "Though you are few in number, you are laying the foundation of something that will be great." He indicated that in the visits we had made to various officials during the day, there had been a respect of us greater than we could have hoped for.
>
> We sang "Now Let Us Rejoice," after which Brother Brandly offered a prayer. We set apart Brother Galbraith and Brother Tvedtnes and then we sang "God Be with You till We Meet Again." No one present will ever forget this occasion. 20

What occurred over the next few hours will also be remembered. "The fast and long pace of the day had fatigued President Lee, whose body was weakened by his lung disease. Back at the hotel President Lee wrote of his concern over his physical condition and pain: 'These are exhausting days. My physical strength is at a seriously low ebb. I know something is seriously wrong. There is a severe pain in my lower back and a weariness that was emphasized by a constant effort to expel mucus. Joan insisted that I have Brother Hinckley and President Cannon administer to me.'

"Just as the Hinckleys, next door in the hotel, were about to retire, Sister Lee knocked on their door and asked if Elder Hinckley would give President Lee a blessing. President Cannon [president of the Swiss Mission, which had responsibility for Israel,] anointed him and Elder Hinckley sealed the anointing. Concerning the blessing Elder Hinckley wrote: 'I felt the power of the Spirit of the Lord as I spoke the blessing. I felt confident that the Lord would heal his servant.'

"The journal account of President Lee reveals the fulfillment of the blessing:

> The next morning, after a severe coughing spell, I expelled two clots which seemed to be blood—one, about the size of a dime, was like dried blood, and the other one was red, as a fresh clot. Immediately my shortness of breath ceased, the weariness was diminished, and the back pains began to subside, and twenty-four hours later they were entirely gone.
>
> I now realize I was skirting on the brink of eternity and a miracle, in this land of even greater miracles, was extended by a merciful God who obviously was prolonging my ministry for a longer time, to give to him in whose service I am all the strength of my heart, mind, and soul, to indicate in some measure my gratitude for his never-failing consideration to me and my loved ones. 21

And so Harold's ministry continued, the Lord sustaining him as he ministered through word and deed to Saints and others the world over. Finally, at a solemn assembly during the October 1972 general conference, he was sustained by the Saints as prophet, seer, and revelator, and President of The Church of Jesus Christ of Latter-day Saints. In the first of his four major addresses delivered during the conference, he declared:

> Today at the greatest moment of my life, I find myself without words to express my deep and innermost feelings. What I say, therefore, must be actuated by the Spirit of the Lord, that you, my beloved Saints of the Most High God, may feel the depths of my soul-searching on this momentous and historic occasion....
>
> Again, in the mighty demonstration of this solemn assembly, I am moved with emotions beyond expression as I have felt the true love and bonds of brotherhood. There has been here an overwhelming spiritual endowment, attesting, no doubt, that in all likelihood we are in the presence of personages, seen and unseen, who are in attendance. Who knows but that even our Lord and Master would be near us on such an occasion as this, for we, and the world, must never forget that this is his church, and under his almighty direction we are to serve! Indeed, I would remind you what he declared in a similar conference of the Saints in Fayette, New York, and undoubtedly would remind us again today. The Lord said: "Behold, verily, verily, I say unto you that mine eyes are upon you. I am in your midst and ye cannot see me. (Doctrine & Covenants 38:7.)"[22]

In that and his subsequent addresses, Harold painted "a striking picture of an introspective man who was fully conscious of the magnitude of his new role and of the qualifying steps necessary to attain it, yet who seemed mildly surprised it had happened to him. They also defined the chief criterion by which he felt the success or failure of his ministry should be judged and included a comprehensive

President Harold B. Lee was a
speaker beloved for his youthful
vitality and candor

CA. 1972

review of the essential doctrines and aims of the Church.

"The deep introspections in which he had indulged were suggested in his keynote address, delivered immediately after he and the others had been sustained. He recounted how, the previous July when he was ordained, he had gone to the upper room of the temple to meditate and to pray. There he had gazed reflectively at the portraits of those who had preceded him, whose lives and characteristics he then briefly outlined for the audience. After referring to President Joseph Fielding Smith, he said, 'As "the finger of God touched him and he slept," he seemed in that brief moment to be passing to me, as it were, a sceptre of righteousness as though to say to me, "Go thou and do likewise."' Then followed the prophet's own criterion by which to judge whether he had measured up to this mandate:

> Now, I stood alone with my thoughts.... Somehow the impressions that came to me were, simply, that the only true record that will ever be made of my service in my new calling will be the record that I may have written in the hearts and lives of those with whom I have served and labored, within and without the church....

"He then shared with the audience insights into his feelings as he undertook his new duties. He prefaced this by quoting from a sermon of Orson Hyde, which described the 'tribulations and trials' through which a prophet must pass to prove himself worthy of the office. He also quoted from the statement of the Prophet Joseph Smith in which he likened himself to a rough stone being polished by the buffeting experiences of his life. President Lee then added:

> These thoughts now running through my mind begin to give greater meaning to some of the experiences in my own life, things that have happened which have

been difficult for me to understand. At times it seemed as though I too was like a rough stone rolling down from a high mountainside, being buffeted and polished, I suppose, by experiences that I too might overcome and become a polished shaft in the quiver of the Almighty. Maybe it was necessary that I too must learn obedience by the things I might have suffered—to give me experiences that were for my good, to see if I could pass some of the various tests of mortality. 23

In the general priesthood meeting, he candidly admitted:

Never had I thought of myself as one day becoming the President of the Church. As a boy in my rural community, I used to hear the Brethren talk about a "pillar" in the Church. I wondered what in the world it meant. It must be something great to be pillar in the Church. Well, now, maybe I am beginning to realize something about what that means....

I bear you my solemn witness that [modern revelation] is true, that the Lord is in his heavens; he is closer to us than you have any idea. You ask when the Lord gave the last revelation to this Church? The Lord is giving revelations day by day, and you will witness and look back on this period and see some of the mighty revelations the Lord has given in your day and time. To that I bear you my witness. 24

Harold's remarks at the conclusion of the conference were just as unusual, just as poignant. His final words to his beloved Saints were:

My love goes out to my own family, to my associates, to all within the sound of my voice, even the sinners; I would wish that we would reach out to them and those who are inactive, and bring them into the fold before it is too late.

God be with you. I have the same feeling as perhaps the Master had when he bid good-bye to the Nephites. He said he perceived that they were weak, but if they would go to their homes and ponder what he said, he would come again and instruct them on other occasions. So, likewise, you cannot absorb all that you have heard and that we have talked about, but go to your homes now and remember what you can, and get the spirit of what has been done and said, and when you come again, or we come to you, we will try to help you further with your problems. 25

As his own evaluation of the conference, Harold wrote:

I gave the closing remarks of the conference and opened my heart to all my people and gave them my blessing as they were to now leave for their homes. Never has there been...a greater spiritual experience when it seemed as though the Lord was indeed in our conference. There began an avalanche of letters, not only from our faithful leaders and members, but from those not in the Church. One of the choicest was a letter from my dear old friend, John A. Sibley, a great Southerner and a former director of the Equitable Life Assurance Society of the U.S.A. with whom I worked. 26

Harold had conducted every session, making "little editorial comments and admonitions between the speakers," and he had opened his heart to the Saints, as even the international television audience was allowed to look for the first time into the heart of a prophet. "The Saints loved it and loved him for it. During the interlude before the morning session on Sunday, the last day of the conference, the Saints began to sing spontaneously, 'We Thank Thee, O God, for a Prophet,' as they caught the first glimpse of their President. It was an expression of love for him who had been so magnificent in his leadership of the conference, lifting the congregation to the highest spiritual peaks and yet remaining ever so humble." 27

Through the fall and winter Harold continued with his same almost frantic pace, dealing with the FBI as they became involved in the threats made against him; organizing and conducting the weekly temple meetings with the Twelve as well as the next area conference, which was to be held in Munich, Germany; holding press conferences; giving counsel and priesthood blessings; dealing with continued respiratory problems that baffled the doctors; spending all the time he could with his family; teaching the new missionaries on a weekly basis; building up his "Miracles" file; and setting his hand to bring into priesthood correlation yet another long-standing and somewhat ineffective program—at least in terms of the Church's single members.

> This contemplated the merging of the activities of the young people under the Presiding Bishopric and the creation of an organization to supervise the activities of the single adults over the age of eighteen.... [T]he activity program for the single adults was designated as the Melchizedek Priesthood MIA. 28

"As President Lee explained at the June conference in 1973, when this new program was formally presented to the Church, it did not represent a change in substance or in doctrine, but was only a change in form made necessary by special circumstances. The whole thrust of this program was to use the full facilities of the Church to reach 'the one,' that is, the one who had special needs." 29

> The death of his wife Fern had made President Lee acutely aware of the lonely and often neglected status of

[the single adults]. After her death and prior to his remarriage, he felt awkward and alone, even in the presence of married couples with whom he had been acquainted all his adult life. His later relationships with Joan and her unmarried friends gave him special insights into the thinking and the needs of these members who had never married or were divorced. As he reflected on this group and their special status, President Lee realized that every member of the Church who grows to maturity will, at some time, and for varying periods of time, be a single adult.... Although bishops, home teachers, Relief Society sisters, and priesthood quorums have shepherding responsibilities for the single adults, President Lee knew, because of the Church's strong emphasis on marriage and family life, and other factors, that, as a practical matter, the needs of the single adults were being largely neglected. So, as these factors provided impetus for change, President Lee gave long, prayerful thought to the steps to be taken to help solve these problems. When the changes had been effected, he said they were as far-reaching and significant as any organizational changes made in his lifetime. 30

Harold also continued his traveling and his teaching, never allowing a teaching moment to escape unused. For instance, Elder Wendell J. Ashton recalls: "In the summer of 1973, I accompanied President Harold B. Lee and his wife, Joan, to the Hill Cumorah Pageant. While there, he conducted a special meeting of members of the Church who gathered in the Sacred Grove. I recall President Lee explaining to the congregation there in that sylvan setting that Joseph Smith could not behold the Father and the Son with his natural eyes. He explained that the boy, Joseph, was transformed in that First Vision in a way that he could, indeed, behold the manifestation." 31

Elder Victor L. Brown recalled an incident that occurred after Harold had given him a priesthood blessing in regards to cancer that had been detected in his body. The blessing was wonderful, and Elder Brown made the comment that it seemed there was no further need for his surgery. "President Lee's response," Elder Brown continued, "was to me one of the great spiritual teachings of my life. He indicated that it was my responsibility to obtain first whatever medical attention was necessary, after which the Lord would bless me. He said there was no question but that I should do whatever my physician recommended." 32

At a conference in the New Jersey Stake Center in April, 1973, a young woman who identified herself to President Lee only as A.M.L., waited vainly in line to shake his hand before the meeting. Failing in that, she listened to the prophet speak, feeling the Spirit become very strong within her. The account she sent him continues:

When it was announced that President Lee would shake hands with people, I knew I had to get to him. As we sang the last song, I began to cry and could hardly sing.

After the closing prayer, people poured forward to see him. When he said he would have to leave, I knew that would be as close as I would get to him. Still, I felt such a strong urge to get to him somehow. I watched to see which way he would leave the building, but lost him in the crowd.

I went outside and looked around for him. I saw where the people were clustered and moved toward the parking lot. His car was completely surrounded. As I waited, I spoke briefly with some missionaries from my ward, then someone asked me to move so the car with President Lee could back out. I stood about three feet away from the car as it passed by. Disheartened, I thought that would be the closest I would get to him.

My car was parked down the road from the stake center, and as I began to walk to it, I watched as the car with President Lee drew up near my car. I quickly crossed the street, expecting his car to pull away at any moment. I finally passed his car and went to mine.

I stood there and thought to myself, "Should I go stand by his car?" A myriad of scriptures crossed my mind. No, I decided, it would be unfair to bother him. Then a force turned my body around and gave me the strength and courage to approach his car.

As I walked up to his window, President Lee rolled it down partway.

"Would you shake my hand for my son?" I asked him. "He couldn't come today because his foot is in a cast." My four-year-old son had a great admiration for the prophet because his name is Lee and that has a special significance to him. Lee had hurt his foot playing and the doctor had put a cast on and warned my son to stay off the foot for the next two weeks. Lee wanted to get up and play and so had ruined the cast after only two days. The doctor and I were both afraid that his foot wouldn't heal properly. That morning my son complained of pain in his casted foot so he had stayed home.

President Lee took my hand and shook it, then continued to hold it. "I bless your son," he said, "that his foot will heal properly and correctly with no deformities." His voice was very soft and kind, gentle and compassionate....

Back in my car, I put my head down and cried, thanking the Lord that such an unworthy servant as I had this special experience and blessing for my son....

At home my four-year-old son told me his foot didn't hurt anymore. I told him what [had] happened and he smiled. "President Lee gave me a blessing from you," he said. "Now we can take my cast off."

The next day I called the doctor and made an appointment. The doctor looked at Lee's foot. "The cast needs to come off," he said. When the cast was off, he pressed on the area where the fracture was. "Does that hurt?"

"No," said Lee. The doctor looked disbelieving. "Well, it looks like it's healed. The foot will probably swell and you'll feel a lump, but don't worry. Just call me if your son has any trouble." But nothing of the kind happened, nor did Lee have any trouble with his foot after that." 33

And so the 538 days of Harold's prophetic ministry slipped inexorably away. Certainly he gave no indication of suspecting that his time was so short. Neither did those very few who knew of his serious health problems. Instead he simply tried, every day, to do more, to do it faster, and to do it better. During March, 1973, he learned that Elder Gordon B. Hinckley was to attend a youth conference in Johannesburg, South Africa. This gave him the idea of meeting Elder Hinckley afterward and going to Brazil where they could explore the possibility of locating a site for a stake-center-sized temple. Though the two never made it to South America together, this was the initial appearance of the small-temple concept that is so revolutionizing and blessing the world of the twenty-first century.

It was also in March that Harold underwent further extensive treatment to cure a chronic lung infection. He had suffered from a lingering cough and the presence of more dark-colored mucus, and now underwent an intensive physical therapy program that kept him away from the office for some time. Yet, he wrote: "'With the aid of my faithful Arthur Haycock, my son-in-law Brent, and plus Joan's untiring help, I have managed to keep

Harold B. Lee

*CA. **early** 1970s*

Deseret News. Used with permission

meeting my responsibilities.'" 34

April's general conference was a repeat of the previous October's spiritual feast, only somehow heightened in every possible way. After bearing his concluding testimony, Harold wrote that "'it seemed to have lifted me spiritually beyond my natural self and made me know that that which I felt was heaven sent.'" 35

Meanwhile another "idea" had been germinating in his fertile mind. Two weeks after conference he met with Neal A. Maxwell, Church Commissioner of Education, to discuss the advisability of a "single voice" in the preparation and production of teaching and training materials for the entire Church. Harold wrote: "'This seems to be, in light of experience, much needed to avoid the overlapping and confusion now in existence.'" 36 Ultimately this idea developed into the powerful Correlation Department of the Church.

Among Harold's favorite assignments during his short tenure—he assigned them to himself—were youth conferences. As President of the Church he spoke to youth wherever he went, but he addressed large youth groups in Pocatello, Idaho; Long Beach, California; Mesa, Arizona; Billings, Montana; the University of Utah Institute of Religion; and the Brigham Young University Marriott Center, where he received the Exemplary Manhood Award and was honored by an attendance of more than 23,000. In Long Beach,

> President Lee spoke of sanctification, which produces the right to "see Him, for He will unveil His face unto you," and said that the laws and ordinances of the Lord are the way by which we are purified and made holy. Continuing this thought he added: "Keeping every law that the Lord has given us is one step closer to receiving the right to enter one day into the presence of the Lord. The most important of all the commandments of God is that one

that you're having the most difficulty keeping today."

The sermon was an intensive scriptural study. President Lee believed that the youth of the Church were hungering for the gospel truths. He taught them how to find Christ and gave them his powerful witness that here was the sure ground on which they could build happiness. His final admonition was: "You keep your eye on him whom the Lord calls, and I say to you now, knowing that I stand in that position, that you don't need to worry about the President of the Church ever leading people astray, because the Lord would remove him out of his place before he'd allow the President to lead his children astray." 37

The October conference, which was to be Harold's last, seemed to build toward a spiritual crescendo. The weather remained unusually warm, and many of the listeners heard the talks from the grounds of the temple and Tabernacle. Once again Harold conducted every session, and once again he brought joy to the congregations as he "editorialized" thoughtfully after each of the chosen speakers.

His own topics were both wide ranging and thought provoking and clarified many of the things the Lord wanted of his people. In his opening address, President Lee indicated that he had been thinking of self-respect.

> [W]hen one...has departed from the path which would have given him peace, [he] is like the troubled sea, casting up mire and dirt [Isaiah 57:19–21]. ...[I]t seems to me that it all results from the failure of the individual to have self-respect....
>
> Who are you? You are all the sons and daughters of God. Your spirits were created and lived as organized intelligences before the world was. You have been blessed to have a physical body because of your obedience to

certain commandments in that premortal state. You are now born into a family to which you have come, into the nations through which you have come, as a reward for the kind of lives you lived before you came here and at a time in the world's history, as the Apostle Paul taught the men of Athens and as the Lord revealed to Moses, determined by the faithfulness of each of those who lived before this world was created. 38

To the men and boys attending the priesthood session, he declared:

One of the painful things that I have as a responsibility is to have to work through the flood of recommendations for cancellations of sealings of those who have been married in the temple. It is frightening, brethren, and much of it stems from one of the greatest of all sins, next to murder, the sin of adultery, that is running rampant throughout the Church. Brethren, we must ourselves resolve anew that we are going to keep the law of chastity; and if we have made mistakes, let's begin now to rectify these mistakes. Let's walk toward the light; and for goodness sake, brethren, don't prostitute the wonderful opportunity you have as men, as those who may link hands with the Creator in the procreation of human souls, by engaging in an unlawful relationship that will only go down to disgrace and break the hearts of your wives and your children. Brethren, we plead with you to keep yourselves morally clean and to walk the path of truth and righteousness, and thereby gain the plaudits of a Heavenly Father, whose sons you are. 39

In Harold's closing remarks, which were not only to bring an end to the conference but an end to his prophetic and warning voice emanating from the Tabernacle—which it had now done in his lifetime more than sixty times—he became almost intimate. At last he hinted—but it was only a hint—at how desperately difficult it was becoming for him to carry the burden of his office—the burden of his beloved people. To each of them, over whom his heavenly capacitated heart both ached and yearned, he declared:

> And so, in the closing moments of this conference, I have been moved as I think I have never been moved before in all my life. If it were not for the assurance that I have that the Lord is near to us, guiding, directing, the burden would be almost beyond my strength, but because I know that he is there, and that he can be appealed to, and if we have ears to hear attuned to him, we will never be left alone.
>
> I am grateful for strong men like President Tanner and President Romney and the Twelve and all the General Authorities, who are united more so than I have ever experienced before during my lifetime. The General Authorities are united and working together and are speaking with one voice to the world.
>
> Follow the Brethren, listen to the Brethren. I bear you my witness as one whom the Lord has brought to this place, as Brother Gordon Hinckley has said. I thank the Lord that I may have passed some of the tests, but maybe there will have to be more before I shall have been polished to do all that the Lord would have me do.
>
> Sometimes when the veil has been very thin, I have thought that if the struggle had been still greater that maybe then there would have been no veil. I stand by, not asking for anything more than the Lord wants to give me, but I know that he is up there and he is guiding and directing....
>
> Peace be with you, not the peace that comes from the legislation in the halls of congress, but the peace that comes in the way that the Master said, by overcoming all the things of the world. That God may help us so

to understand and may you know that I know with a certainty that defies all doubt that this is his work, that he is guiding us and directing us today, as he has done in every dispensation of the gospel, and I say that with all the humility of my soul, in the name of the Lord, Jesus Christ. Amen. 40

17

A TRUE SEER

"Harold B. Lee? You want me to tell you about President Harold B. Lee?" President Marion G. Romney, now President of the Quorum of the Twelve, sat behind his desk smiling—but only barely.

Soberly I nodded, President Romney's smile making me feel a little like he had me just where he wanted. For a moment I wondered what I was doing there. What sort of crazy effrontery had driven me to come to the office of this great man, to take up his precious time just to talk about another? I didn't know, except that I'd heard they had been close. Besides, ever since—

"Well, how about if I tell you that President Lee was my best friend?" The smile was still there, only perhaps a little softer. "Will that do you?"

"I...uh.... Well, I was hoping for something more—perhaps a little detail."

"What sort of detail?"

Now I was really feeling uncomfortable. "I don't know, at least not exactly. I...I just never had the opportunity to know him, at least not until—"

"Ah!" Now President Romney's smile brightened considerably. "You wish to get to know him! Well, son, I don't blame you! That's just how I felt when I first met him. Almost instantly I wanted to know him better. The operator of a neighboring grocery store introduced me to his brother-in-law, who turned out to be Harold B. Lee. Harold was dressed in striped coveralls. His left hand was on his breast, and he reached out his right to shake my hand. Captivated by his magnetic presence, I felt I had found a friend. Now I can say that I have never had a closer relationship with any man than I did with Harold. After we met, he invited me to his home to meet his Fern, and I invited him to my home to meet my Ida. I felt a little self-conscious because I had made some of our furniture—Ida and I were quite poor, you see—and I thought he might be above that sort of thing. Even then he appeared very dignified and mature, quite handsome with his trim figure and thick wavy hair. I needn't have worried, though, for it turned out he was a country boy like me and was used to making do.

"Yes, sir, Harold B. Lee was a unique man. I was well acquainted with him, and I have been well acquainted with many great men during my last forty years with the General Authorities. Very few men enjoyed a friendship like I had with President J. Reuben Clark and Harold. We were as close as men could be!"

"I'm discovering that President Lee was an exceptional President of the Church."

President Romney nodded. "True enough, though it went far beyond that, for he was no ordinary man. His influence in Church councils was effective from the beginning. It continued to increase until the day of his passing. All the programs of the Church operative during the nearly thirty-three years he served as one of the General Authorities bear the mark of his prophetic genius.

"Another thing; he loved the youth with a divine compassion. He sorrowed over the rebellious and unrepentant and rejoiced over the returning prodigal.

"Yes, Harold was one of the most powerful men in modern Israel. He was not only a prophet but also a great seer and revelator.

I have never been associated with a man who drew more heavily on the powers of heaven. The source of his strength was in his knowledge that he himself lived in the shadow of the Almighty. To him, his Heavenly Father was a senior partner, daily giving him guidance. Few indeed have had contacts with heaven as direct and regular as did he. He knew that the gospel of Jesus Christ is eternal truth."

President Romney now leaned forward, his smile gone and his eyes ablaze with intensity. "I'll tell you something else, young man. In one aspect of his life and his character he was different from any other man that I've ever been with. I felt with him like I'd imagine the Prophet Joseph Smith was, with respect to the inspiration that came to him. Joseph Smith spoke by the power of the Spirit out of a personal knowledge and association with the Father and the Son. Brother Lee, in my judgment, was more like the Prophet Joseph Smith in this respect than was any other man I've ever associated with. He seemed to get the inspiration of the Lord spontaneously.

"He didn't approach his decisions and counsel like a lawyer and argue or reason things out. President J. Reuben Clark was painstakingly slow in making a decision. He would study it out and, using his great mind, would come to his conclusion. In contrast, Harold just seemed to me to speak directly from inspiration and could jump, as it were, from peak to peak as he went along in his teachings and his interpretations of the gospel and in his answering of questions."

President Romney paused again, leaning back in his chair, and for all the world I hoped he wasn't finished. As it turned out, he wasn't—not quite.

"I remember reading once," he said thoughtfully, "that the Prophet Joseph Smith wrote that he and Oliver Cowdery and W. W. Phelps were laboring one afternoon in Kirtland. If memory serves me, it was October 1, 1835. They were working on the Egyptian alphabet, and—and this is a quote, for I memorized it—

'during the research, the principles of astronomy as understood by Father Abraham and the ancients unfolded to our understanding.'

"But that's the way Brother Lee used to get inspiration, as I associated with him and heard him time and time again. He just spoke as the inspiration of the Lord enlightened his mind, without the reasoning and arguments that so many of us go through as we labor.

"Humility before God and fearlessness before men were the essence of his character. His ministry has been characterized by an uncommon originality and daring. He was neither circumscribed nor restricted by the learning of the world nor by the wisdom of men. We who sat with him daily were frequently amazed at the breadth of his vision and the depth of his understanding.

"And that, my young friend, is the point! He obtained his knowledge immediately from God by revelation. He was a seer!"

President Romney paused again, his eyes behind his thick glasses gazing into the distance. I knew he was remembering, but I had no idea what until a sudden tear started down his weathered cheek.

"I miss him," he said softly, confirming my thought. "It seems to me to be impossible that Harold is gone." Abruptly, then, he brightened and rose to his feet, signaling that the interview was over. "I'm surely looking forward to the time when I will see Brother Lee again and associate with him. It'll be a happy reunion, I'm sure."

Coming around the desk he took me by the hand and squeezed it, though it was obvious his mind was still on his—on our—departed friend. "Yes, young man," he concluded as he led me toward his door, "I look forward to that day. I'll be glad to join him and go on with our intimate association." [1]

Though Harold had no idea the October 1973 general conference would be his last, there is no doubt he felt good about what had transpired. Ever appreciative of the impressions and/or suggestions of others, and always willing to improve if he could see the way, he spoke of the afterglow of the conference as being most impressive. As he wrote in his journal:

> From everywhere, and including the Council of the Twelve, the unanimous expression came that there was something unusual in this conference. The Brethren were inspired to define the problems confronting us today, and then suggested the application of gospel teachings to supply the solution. There seemed to have been something in my closing remarks which came spontaneously that seemed to many to be prophetic of the times, and to outline the need for our people to "stand in holy places and be not moved" as the Master has counseled, when the signs of his second coming were drawing near. 2

And Harold was right. His closing sermon "assumes special significance because it was the last one delivered to the entire Church by this prophet, because most of it was delivered extemporaneously as President Lee was moved to speak, and because of the powerful, confirming spirit that accompanied its delivery." 3 It is little wonder the Saints had been so moved.

The week following conference the General Authorities and their wives joined in a traditional post-conference dinner and social. As part of the entertainment, a seven-year-old boy whose name was Michael Van Harris acted as a messenger to various members of the group. Finally he handed Harold a note asking that he leave his blessing on those attending and then led the prophet to the podium. There Harold picked the child up in his arms and said to the group:

> This is about the greatest honor that I've ever had, to be led by Michael's hand. The Savior said, "and a little child

shall lead them and…he that would be the greatest among you must be the servant of all." Michael says I am supposed to give you our blessing. I asked him what that meant, and he said, "I guess it means to pray."

Harold complimented Michael and his parents, then put him back onto the floor and instructed him to stand by his side. Then he explained:

> We've just come, Michael, from a great conference—our Heavenly Father's conference. We've felt a great spirit that our Heavenly Father wanted to pour out upon his Saints and we were there, and as we bowed our heads in prayer, and lifted our eyes to heaven, we knew he was up there. You know he is up there, don't you? You've talked to him, haven't you Michael? You know that he answers prayers. So now, you and I, you silently and I will speak a prayer tonight…; you close your eyes and just whisper to yourself your prayer, and I'll pray out loud.
>
> "Heavenly Father…we present ourselves in this glorious company where have been assembled some of the most choice Saints in all the world. We have felt the joys of thy attending influence, our Father. We've known what it has meant to hear Thy voice, through thy servants. We've heard thy words, as thou hast spoken into our minds, and impressed upon our hearts, and the Saints have felt that, Father, for this is a day when thy people need so much, realizing as we do, that we have the keys for the salvation of all mankind. In a day of great troubles, when waters are heaving over their banks, great earthquakes occur, wars and rumors of war, bloodshed, horrors, oh, if it please thee, our Father, that in the tops of the mountains thou hast builded a throne to which thou could come, even a Holy Temple, that we've tried to keep clean and worthy.

We remember the lament that thy Son did make. It saddens our hearts when He said, 'the foxes have holes, the birds have nests, but the Son of Man has no place to lay his head.' Holy Father, we trust that that may never come in our time, where there shall not be a place where thou canst come and where thou canst lay thy head. We'll try our best to keep these sacred places for thine abode. Keep us under thy watchful eye, our Father. As never before, we need thee.

So, tonight with united hearts, we thank thee our Father, for the privilege of being in thy service. We know what it means to humble ourselves realizing that in order for us to win thy favor, we must, like thy Son, be willing to kneel at the feet of those who need their feet bathed in cooling water and lifted up above the sordid trials and miseries of today. Give us the grace, Father, to be that humble, and follow the pattern that was laid down by Thy Son.

With these humble words of prayer, led to this point by this dear, sweet pure child, take us home in safety. Let our homes be filled with thy love, and to thee we will ascribe the honor the praise and glory, forevermore." 4

While the sweet picture this paints of a humble, loving prophet is sufficient to endear him to anyone, it is not the end of the story. In some marvelous way Harold and little Michael developed an instant kinship with each other. Harold invited him to come to see him in his office, and once the child and his parents were there, the boy was invited to sit in Harold's chair. As the Harris family prepared to leave, Harold "put his arms around Michael's parents and said:

I have never been so impressed with a child's spirit in my life. He has a very special mission to perform. If you will guide him in the paths of righteousness, you will stand back and marvel at the things that this boy will accomplish. 5

For his part, after exchanging photographs and letters with the prophet, Michael said to his mother, "'President Lee is my very best friend, and Mom, President Lee really loves me.'" 6

When Harold passed away two and a half months later, little Michael mourned "as though one of his immediate family had died. His parents comforted him with the thought that if he would always choose to do right, as President Lee would want him to do, he could see him and be with him again.

In the spring of 1976, two and one-half years later, a sudden unprecedented foreboding came on nine-year-old Michael and his family. Their thoughts turned to death and dying, for no apparent reason. Within two weeks Michael became ill and was treated at the hospital to clear his lungs from congestion. The congestive attack occurred again when his father was at work, and his mother, Jane Urry Harris, hurriedly prepared to make another emergency trip to the hospital. After arranging for the other children, Sister Harris came out of the house to find Michael sitting on the step of the porch with a beautiful, peaceful look on his face. He had an almost transparent, ethereal appearance and was not struggling or fighting for breath as before. When his mother called for him to come, he stood up immediately, then fell backwards, unconscious. From this attack he was not to recover, and he died a few days later....

Elder Boyd K. Packer, who had selected Michael from among many other young boys for his role as messenger...wrote to Michael's parents that, in his opinion, Michael's death was not untimely and that he felt that President Lee had played a part in his passing, because they had such an unusual relationship.

Sister Harris later spoke of this heart-wrenching experience and offered this testimony: "I also believe, with every fiber of my being, that President Lee did come to again take Michael by the hand and lead him, for I will never forget the look on Michael's face before he became unconscious. It was the same look of peace and love that he had the day we spent with Michael's 'very best friend,' President Harold B. Lee." 7

Through the remainder of 1973, Harold seemed to move from one sublime moment to another, everywhere feeling his divinely given mantle of love reciprocated by the Saints.

In Rexburg on October 26, Harold spoke at a devotional assembly at Ricks College. Enlarging on one of his themes from general conference, Harold discussed the ills prevalent in the United States (America was in the midst of the Watergate scandal, and Richard Nixon would shortly step down from office) and then explained to the students what they should do about it and why he felt so upbeat about America's future.

> We are living in a time of great crisis. The country is torn with scandal and with criticism, with faultfinding and condemnation. It is an easy thing to climb on the bandwagon and join the hotheads in condemnation, little realizing that when they do, they are not just tearing down a man, they are tearing down a nation, and they are striking at the underpinnings of one of the greatest of all nations of all the world—a nation that was founded upon an inspired declaration we call the Constitution of the United States. The Lord said it was written by men whom he raised up for that very purpose, and that Constitution stands today as a model to all nations to pattern their lives....
>
> This is the cradle of humanity, where life on this earth began in the Garden of Eden. This is the place where the

New Jerusalem is. This is the place which the Lord said is favored above all other nations in the world. This is the place where the Savior will come to his temple....

Men may fail in this country. Earthquakes may come, seas may heave themselves beyond their bounds, there may be great drought and disaster and hardship, as we may call it, but this nation, founded as it was on a foundation of principles laid down by men whom God raised up, will never fail!...

While it is true there are dangers and difficulties that lie ahead of us, we must not assume that we are going to lie down and watch the country go to ruin. We should not be heard to predict ills and calamities for the nation. On the contrary, we should be providing optimistic support of the nation....

It is the negative, pessimistic comments about the nation that do as much harm as anything to the country today.... We should not be so concerned about finding out what is wrong with America, but we should be finding what is right about America and should be speaking optimistically and enthusiastically about America....

Yes, men may fail, but this nation won't fail. I have faith in America, and you and I must have faith in America if we understand the teachings of the gospel of Jesus Christ. 8

To this day, Harold's classic comments remain one of America's most profound statements on patriotism.

One other event will serve to illustrate the depth and direction of Harold's thinking at this time. As recorded by his son-in-law, L. Brent Goates: "On the first Sunday of November 1973, President Lee spent the early morning hours, as was his practice, at the Salt Lake Temple considering problems on which he alone, as President of the Church, could decide. With these matters weighing heavily on his mind, along with a personal problem on which he had consulted with one of his family members, he came to rejoin Sister Lee at their Federal Heights Ward fast and testimony meeting. He arrived late, quietly sat down, and received the sacrament. Just prior to the close of the meeting, President Lee's familiar voice came from the back of the chapel, asking permission of bishopric counselor E. Douglas Sorensen to delay closing the meeting, for he 'thought the Lord had been so mindful of me in a special way, a few days before, that he would think me an ingrate if I failed to express myself.' According to ward member, Sister Elaine A. Cannon, who recorded his statements in her journal, he spoke these unforgettable words as he remained standing at the rear of the chapel:

> Brothers and Sisters, beloved friends and neighbors, members of my ward family, and those in my own little flock over whom I have stewardship: I'm sorry to disturb you, but I know that it would be disturbing to my Father in Heaven if I don't say something to you at this time.
> By way of testimony I want you to know that I know that God lives, that Jesus is the Christ and our Redeemer, and he is at the head of this Church; I am not. I know that he operates in all the affairs of this church and I say this by way of testimony that you may know that I know he lives....
>
> I say this to you by way of a serious warning, that I also know that the adversary lives and operates in the affairs of man. And he is determined to cause a downfall of men. If he can't get to us, he will try to get to those closest to us, for he is in a mighty battle with the work of the Savior. And I must tell you these words of warning. So keep close to the Lord. Don't be discouraged. The Lord will take care of his

President Harold B. Lee

CA. 1973

own. If you are prepared, you need not fear, if you are on the Lord's side.

"This was a powerful, most unusual testimony, not alone because it came from the prophet of God to his own neighbors, friends, and relatives who had often heard him bear witness to the reality of the Savior Jesus Christ, but also because he had never before borne such a fervent witness to the reality of Satan. It was his last message to the members of his ward." 9

Over the next few weeks, Harold and Joan attended several events that, while exhausting him, show once again his remarkable capacity to love. "On December 5, he and Sister Lee joined several hundred Deseret Industries workers for a Christmas celebration and to dedicate a new DI building in Murray, a suburb south of Salt Lake City. The prophet believed this organization was the best example of applied welfare principles of any agency within the system. Most of the workers were handicapped or aged and unable to compete in the commercial market. Here they worked to the limit of their capacity, performing important service for which they were adequately compensated in cash or commodities. Grateful to be useful and independent, they showed genuine happiness, an attitude that gave a special spark to the evening. President Lee felt uplifted, sensing among these people a spirit in full harmony with the Christmas theme." 10

A few days later he and Joan "were breakfast guests of the Cannon Stake high priests and their wives. There were fifteen hundred present. S. Perry Lee, the prophet's brother, presided over this stake, which included many of the Church units that were once in the Pioneer Stake. It was like a homecoming for the prophet. 'It was a most satisfying experience,' wrote he, 'to recall the years gone by when I was the stake president.'" 11

Two days after that he returned to the temple and one of his all-time favorite assignments—instructing the new missionaries

During his ministry, Harold B. Lee always made time to meet with young missionaries

N.D.

Courtesy of the Lee Family Collection

prior to their departure for their fields of labor. No doubt he was challenged, as always, to answer their searching questions. Official records state that there were 255 elders and sisters in attendance—one of whom was Elder Steven R. Pogue. His uplifting account of his experience at that meeting, sent to the family of President Harold B. Lee, formed the basis of the historical vignette that opened the preceding chapter of this volume. Brother Pogue concluded his account by saying:

> As I look back now, I cannot recall any of the questions the missionaries asked President Lee in the temple that day, nor any of his answers. What I gained from that session was a powerful example and a zeal for knowing the mind and the will of the Lord. Though tempered by time, that enthusiasm for learning and the memory of that example have never been diminished…I shall always hold in fond remembrance the lesson [President Lee] taught me and the fact that he had enough interest in the missionaries to be there to teach it. Though we were never acquainted, nor even so much as shook hands, he changed my life for the better. 12

As Christmas approached, Harold and Joan were terrifically busy attending functions where they were either expected or hoped for. The schedule exhausted both of them, though for Harold it was particularly debilitating. One afternoon a grandson, Alan Lee Wilkins, was visiting and was startled by what he discovered.

> I became aware of the tremendous schedule and the manner in which Grandfather drove himself. As we visited, we remarked that Grandfather looked tired and asked if he couldn't take some time to rest.
>
> He had Grandmother Joan bring out his schedule calendar, and she showed us that they had two and three

appointments, starting at six o'clock every evening during every day of the week through that whole month and into the next month.

I was amazed—a man of his age keeping that kind of a schedule. He put in a full day at the office and then had this kind of a schedule to go home to, plus his travels throughout the Church and the demands that brought. He told us of staying awake most of several evenings during area conference trips. He said to us: "Now you see what my schedule is like. I can't rest. I know the Lord will sustain me as long as he wants me to be here, but I can't rest." 13

On December 12, Harold and Joan attended a dinner they shared with the employees of the Beehive Clothing Mills and their companions. The next evening the prophet hosted a gathering of Church employees in the Tabernacle—where he delivered his last major address. To them, he said:

> I wish I could be a thousand times more understanding, to deal a thousand times more kindly, and with a thousand times more wisdom and foresight.... And I only want to be what you, the faithful members of the church, would wish me to be. 14

The last party the Lees attended was held on December 18 in the LaFayette Ballroom of the Hotel Utah. It was hosted by Douglas H. Smith, the president of Beneficial Life Insurance Company. In his brief comments, Harold said: "'I would not have come out tonight for anyone else except you. I am so weary that I would have stayed home, but I felt strongly compelled to be here in support of you and Beneficial Life.'" 15

After referring to the violence in the Middle East and to the efforts being made by the United States to negotiate a settlement, Harold surprisingly asked the guests to join him in a prayer for peace. The impact of what followed was described by Douglas H. Smith, who later became a member of the Seventy:

> The feeling of direct communication of the prophet and the Father in this emotional appeal was intensely felt by all. There was no question that he, as a prophet of the Lord, was talking with the Father in Heaven, and was sharing this most intimate experience with each of us.
>
> After he finished, there was total silence. Most of us were extremely hesitant to open our eyes, because we knew he was talking with the Lord. His deep, compassionate love for all of the children of the Lord—Arab, Jew, and Gentile–was appealingly expressed. 16

Elder Ezra Taft Benson, as he left the ballroom, asked if President Lee's message had been recorded. Learning that it hadn't, Elder Benson expressed keen disappointment, adding, "'In all my experience I have never been more deeply touched' by a prayer." 17 Harold's brief remarks and profound prayer were a fitting benediction not only to the evening's festivities, but to his apostolic career. He never spoke in public again.

Like most others, Harold and Joan spent the last few days before Christmas in the joys of preparation. There were gifts to purchase for family, friends, and associates; envelopes in which to put a little cash for each of the grandchildren; and of course grocery shopping in preparation for the celebration of Christ's birth. And often Harold was in his office, taking care of business and making plans for the next area conference, which was to be held in Stockholm, Sweden, in the summer of 1974. Certainly there was nothing in his demeanor that indicated he thought the end was near. "He was looking forward to the duties ahead." 18

Christmas morning the Lees spent together in quiet celebration and then prepared to spend the rest of the day at Helen and Brent's home. There was a delay, however, when a young family appeared unannounced at the Lee's door, seeking the prophet's advice. The mother, whose three small sons accompanied her and her husband, had recently been diagnosed with a rapidly moving form of terminal cancer. Since the doctors had given them no hope, they were there to ask the prophet if he thought they should return to their home in California or remain in Utah with their extended families, whom they had been visiting.

In replying, Harold said: "'There is a time of testing ahead. When you are a "golden nugget" you must prepare for a fire. Go back home and live each day, and when the Lord wants us he'll take us, and it will be all right.'" 19

Thanking him profusely, the "little family returned to California, comforted by the prophet. In departure, they took the last photograph of President and Sister Lee. They reported later that he had confided that he was not feeling well. They described his cheeks as puffy and his color ashen. He had told them that he was fatigued and that in recent days he had felt the presence of his deceased wife, Fern." 20

After arriving late at Helen's Christmas party—attended also by the prophet's two sisters, Stella and Verda, Verda's husband Charles, and Mary Dean, a convert from the prophet's missionary days in Colorado—the group enjoyed a wonderful meal. As they prepared afterward for the program Helen had prepared, Harold looked so tired that his daughter offered to cancel her plans altogether. "He quickly objected, however, and urged her to proceed. President Lee listened and made comments, but much of the time his eyes were closed. Afterwards, he said to Helen: 'Thank you so much, dearie. That was just beautiful and gives us the real Christmas spirit, to reflect upon the land where Jesus lived and taught.'" 21

It was after 6:00 in the evening when Harold and Joan stood to get their coats. Yet, uncharacteristically, Harold seemed in no hurry to leave, but wandered from room to room for almost

One of the last photographs
taken of Harold and Joan Lee

CA. 1973

Courtesy of the Lee Family Collection

an hour, visiting quietly with many who were there. He appeared to be in good spirits, though perhaps he was a bit more quiet and reflective than usual. After thanking Helen once again and kissing her goodbye, he and Joan were gone.

An hour later Helen received a call informing her that one of her father's associates on the original Church welfare committee had just passed away. Helen called her father to tell him of the man's passing, and Harold agreed to call the family, yet hesitated because he felt too weak to speak at the man's funeral. Helen replied:

"I know, Daddy dear, you looked so tired tonight! I felt guilty about keeping you long enough for our little program. Perhaps we should have let you go home sooner."

"Oh no, no, dear," answered President Lee, "that was lovely! We needed that spiritual touch to our day. It was wonderful to hear Mother's beautiful words about the Savior once more and to listen to the girls sing and play. I enjoyed the spirit in your home all through the afternoon and evening."

Then, responding like a true patriarch to his family, never content until each and every child was accounted for, he expressed his concerns for those who had not been there, and spoke of his desire to keep all his family close together. The last wishes of Helen's mother on the same subject were then recalled, and resolves were renewed as Helen urged her weary father to put his mind at ease about all the family and try to get some rest. Unknown to either of them, this was to be their final conversation. It is significant that though he had the burdens of the world on his mind, he never lost his deep love and concern for each one of his precious family. 22

The next afternoon Joan called Helen to say that her father had been admitted to the hospital two hours earlier. As Brent, the former administrator for LDS Hospital, rushed off to make certain his father-in-law was being properly cared for, Joan explained that Harold had gone to bed early and had slept a full ten hours. Yet upon awakening he still felt fatigued. Sometime later in the day Dr. Orme had recommended hospitalization, and so Harold had called Arthur Haycock, his secretary, asking him to come to the home to conclude some business.

For a time the two men worked together; then Brother Haycock drove Harold to the hospital, where he was admitted and began undergoing a series of tests. Though no one was very concerned, Harold was in a great deal of discomfort, and so Brother Haycock called President Romney to come and help in giving the prophet a blessing. With Brent anointing and President Romney sealing the anointing and pronouncing the blessing while Arthur Haycock assisted, Harold declared: "'I feel much better now. There are not three men of greater faith in the world than you three and I am grateful for that blessing.'" 23

Various doctors and nurses were now working with Harold, yet in a moment of quiet he and Joan prayed together "and enjoyed an 'intimate conversation' in which [he] told his wife, 'God is very near.'" 24

Other doctors began to assemble, including Dr. Alan H. Morris, a brilliant lung specialist. After giving the prophet a thorough examination, Dr. Morris told Brent "that President Lee was anemic, probably due in part to the blood loss from coughing that morning; his lungs were in poor condition, which was not surprising, since he was known to be suffering from chronic bronchitis; and he was in heart failure.

"This latter conclusion came as a great surprise and Brent reminded Dr. Morris that never before had that diagnosis been made.... Doctor Morris firmly, but quietly replied: 'That may be true, but I am certain he is in heart distress now. The blood gas studies confirm this. Perhaps if we get him oxygenated properly these symptoms will disappear.' Immediate steps were taken to introduce more...oxygen through an oxygen mask." 25

After Harold had eaten a bit of supper and everything appeared stable, Brent took Joan to her home and then stopped at his own to give Helen an update. Brother Haycock, meanwhile, was keeping vigil at the bedside. A little later, while he was reading the paper, Harold suddenly "sat up in the bed, took off the oxygen mask, [and] cleared his throat.'" Arthur reported: "'He acted as though he wanted to get out of bed. His face was ashen, covered with perspiration, and his eyes were glazed and bulging. He was staring at me. He didn't respond to my comments. I think he may at that moment have suffered a fatal attack. I laid him back down in his bed.'" 26

Stepping out of the room Brother Haycock told the nurse that Harold had tried to get out of bed. But she, not grasping the gravity of the situation, took that to mean he was doing better and was ready for X-rays. As she wheeled the wheelchair toward his room, she said to someone at the nurse's desk, "'Have someone from Inhalation Therapy come up and accompany us to X-ray.' The comment even surprised herself. She mused:

I had never made such a request before. Why did I say it then? I took the wheelchair into the room. At that brief moment I was alone with President Lee. With super effort and strength I saw him raise himself up in bed so he was resting on both elbows. His eyes were open wide, and he was looking straight up. He appeared to be in a trance, and I took hold of his right arm and said—

"President Lee, can you hear me?" There was no response that he did. His eyes closed slowly and he slipped back onto the bed pillow. I knew his spirit was gone from

his body. I knew, too, what my training had taught me.
I needed to sound the cardiac arrest alarm. 27

As the medical team galvanized into action at the shout of
"Cardiac arrest!" Brent and Arthur Haycock were stunned.
Then each went into action, Brent calling Helen and Brother
Haycock calling President Romney and President Spencer W.
Kimball. "Shortly afterward President Kimball came through the
door. He was stunned, almost in shock. The family asked him
to lead them in a pleading prayer to Heavenly Father, but he was
hardly able to speak. Next, President Romney arrived. The family
could only ask him to help them pray again, to add his faith to the
urgent, broken-hearted petitions. There was nothing else to be
done." 28

As the dozen medical experts in Harold's room labored with
their equipment and expertise to restore his life, Brent, President
Romney, and President Kimball kept their agonizing vigil in the
waiting room. Of that endless few moments, Brent has written:

> Still, despite the obvious bleak medical reports, as
> President Romney and I paced the floor neither of us
> felt that the end could come to our prophet-loved one.
> I still waited for the miracle. He had been saved through
> three other hospitalizations. He was at the pinnacle of his
> performance in Church leadership. The kingdom needed
> him. No one could take his place. We knew the Lord knew
> that, and we had exercised our faith and priesthood.
> Now when was the Lord going to come to our rescue?
> He could send angels to help. I knew it must come soon,
> but I waited, expectantly. It could come any moment now.
> But...it never came.
>
> I was back in the room with Helen and the family
> when Doctor Orme came down the hall and announced
> that they had ceased treatment and that at 8:58 P.M., he

had passed away. No one can describe the emptiness and awfulness of that announcement. It just couldn't be! Yes, he was sick, but certainly in possession of his faculties. Our greatest concern at that time [had been] how we were going to forestall his giving a talk the next Sunday night to the Special Interest members in the Salt Lake Tabernacle. That was then the extent of our worries. Now, he was gone and we were lost in grief, and soon the entire Church membership would be devastated. How could it be? How could the Lord allow this tragedy to happen?

Such were the human, very mortal, protestations of loved ones. But the protests changed nothing. The Lord's will had been announced, and from this verdict there was no appeal. 29

Nurse Hunt was the last to leave Harold's room. She remembered: "Before I left, I stood at his bedside and felt within me that this was according to God's plan. I saw him changed in the twinkling of an eye. All the knowledge and wisdom of medicine or the most skilled physicians could not bring him back. It was simply not to be. Peace and tranquillity filled his room. I quietly closed the door." 30

"Within an hour, the news had been announced over local television and radio. Everywhere it was met with a sense of incredulity. How could it be? The longevity of Mormon church presidents had become legendary. They were expected to live a very long time, at least until they were eighty years old, or older. And the public was accustomed to hearing reports of a prophet's infirmities long in advance of his death, or because of advanced age, as in the case of President Joseph Fielding Smith, the public was conditioned to the idea that he might go at any time. Neither circumstance existed here. Harold B. Lee, age seventy-four, who, as far as the public knew, was in robust health, was gone after having served less than eighteen months. No other Church president had [had] a shorter tenure. No other Church president died so young, except the Prophet Joseph Smith, who was martyred at age thirty-eight. This would take some getting used to." 31

Again, taking advantage of Brother Brent Goates' wonderful memory and records, while still at the hospital, a familiar transition was taking place:

> The three of us, President Romney, President Kimball, and I, stood with our arms about one another, bowed in grief and sick beyond words. After the longest time my administrative training finally overcame the blanket of grief enough for me to realize that some action had to be taken.
>
> Courageously I ventured into the sacred, grief-laden silence and whispered to the new leader of the Church: "Do you want me to phone Wendell Ashton with the news of the President's passing?" Two heads nodded mute approval as the others, too, broke momentarily back into reality. Then President Kimball, senior Apostle and President of the Quorum of the Twelve, in his first executive order as the leader of the Church, said: "I think you'd better tell him to prepare a news release." 32

The change in mortal authority and responsibility was instantaneous, as President Lee himself had seen it time and time before. With the last breath of President Lee, "President Kimball assumed the mantle of leadership over the kingdom of God on earth." 33 Harold B. Lee now belonged to the ages, and a grief-stricken Church, most of whom were only just starting to know and love their dynamic prophet, would now have to go forward without him.

ℰPILOGUE

On Friday, December 29, 1973, in the inner foyer of the Church Administration Building, more than twelve thousand mourners filed past the casket where Harold B. Lee's body lay in state. The viewing lasted from 8:00 A.M. to 8:00 P.M., and some of President Lee's grandsons were present the entire time, standing at each end of the casket. Most of the day it was either raining or snowing, though this in no way diminished the grieving throng.

On Saturday, December 30, it was still raining with intermittent snow. President Spencer W. Kimball conducted the memorial service in the filled-to-capacity Tabernacle, with overflow seating in the Assembly Hall. President Kimball also delivered the main address. In it he traced the major achievements of President Lee's life and his dynamic characteristics. The other speakers, Elders N. Eldon Tanner, Marion G. Romney, and Gordon B. Hinckley, elaborated on these, focusing on their personal relationship with the prophet. The prayers were offered by Elder Marvin J. Ashton and D. Arthur Haycock, and the music was provided by the Tabernacle Choir.

In a heavy downpour, President Lee's body was laid to rest in the Salt Lake Cemetery at the side of his first wife, Fern Lucinda Tanner Lee. Son-in-law L. Brent Goates, at that time a Regional

Representative of the Twelve, began the dedicatory prayer by observing the propriety of the heavens weeping, because the entire Church was also weeping in sorrow and loneliness.

And so closes the story of Harold B. Lee.

And then—too soon—President Harold B. Lee was taken from this earth

CA. 1973

As I completed this manuscript I could not refrain from adding my own tears to theirs. Though it has been more than a quarter of a century since President Lee's passing, and though I knew how the book would end, I found myself desperately wanting it not to happen! I had come to know President Lee—to honor and respect him, to adore him—and yes, to love him, and I did not want him to be gone! I was broken hearted, and I felt cheated, for who knows what more I might have learned from him, what spiritual heights I might have scaled under his inspired direction, had he only been allowed to stay?

Like his family and millions of others back in 1973, I also found myself wondering why. Why was he taken so soon? Why, when it seemed he was only getting started. In his powerful biography, L. Brent Goates writes: "One can only speculate on this, of course. But there could be a clue offered in the prophetic patriarchal blessing given...by Patriarch James Reid McNiel in Clifton, Idaho, on March 18, 1917, when Harold B. Lee was a lad of just eighteen years of age. A portion of the blessing reads:

> Thou shalt assist in the rearing of temples and labor therein for thy kindred dead, until thou art fully satisfied. Thou shalt read the words and works of the Savior, that he performed among the Ten Tribes of Israel after his resurrection and ascension, even in the congregations of the Saints, and labor with that people in bestowing upon them their blessings that they shall receive under the hands of Ephraim.

"This seems to be a calling to a work beyond this earthly sphere. The thought of him laboring amongst the Ten Lost Tribes as an assigned commission brings comfort and consolation to those who felt keenly the loss of President Lee when he was taken in death in 1973. We share him reluctantly in this extra-terrestrial setting." [1]

I found this both intriguing and plausible, yet still I have struggled, trying my best to understand. Yesterday, as I was attending a wedding in one of the temples, I took some time to give thanks to God for the marvelous things President Lee has both taught and shown me during the past few months. If I can hold on to them, I know I will be a better man.

I also asked, almost as an afterthought, and with a great deal of hopefully understandable trepidation, that still-nagging question—Why? As I sat pondering, into my mind came two passages of scripture (Knowing President Lee, why should this have surprised me?), and for myself, they finally brought a measure of peace.

Interestingly, at home I opened Brother Goates' book again and discovered a passage I had somehow missed or forgotten, wherein seemed to be confirmed the message of my two scriptures. Brother Goates writes:

> It seemed as if by the close of his life President Lee had overcome all enemies and weaknesses; that at the end, he was simply too good, too great for this world; that he had run out of challenges worthy of his amazing talents. It was not by any means an easy triumph, however. Consider these tests, among many, which he faced:
>
> He had critics who were jealous of his "beyond his years" abilities.
>
> He was forced to learn patience, to wait behind leaders with more seniority than himself before his ideas could gain acceptance.
>
> He learned how to control his fiery temper and quick, action-oriented disposition which earlier in his life had offended people.
>
> He learned tolerance and unselfishness by subduing all personal desires and placing those of others ahead of his own. This is most notably illustrated in his determination to make his second marriage a happy one, even though it

required an almost complete reversal of habit patterns for himself.

He practiced control and finally excelled, as he had in all other aspects of his life, to gain a mellowing Sainthood that the heavens couldn't reject. 2

To these I would add that he was required to bury both his wife and his daughter, either of which is sufficient to test an individual to the absolute limits of both his courage and his faith.

Thinking of all President Lee overcame, leads me to my two passages of scripture. The first, I believe, had to do with his powerful spirituality, though the passage is actually describing the Brother of Jared:

> Wherefore, having this perfect knowledge of God, he could not be kept from within the veil.... (Ether 3:20)

The second passage, as I suppose, had to do with the way President Lee drove himself, thinking always of the Saints and never of himself—of his own desires and ambitions, his own exhaustion, pain, and discomfort. Surely, I had thought while I wrote, he literally drove himself into the grave. In a way I had felt critical of this—or at least I had until yesterday, when a passage I had always thought might be a mistake or mistranslation suddenly took on clarity—and I could see that President Lee had been heeding the Lord's will all along. In an inspired letter written by Joseph Smith from an attic in Nauvoo where he was hiding from Missouri mobbers, we read:

> Therefore, that we should waste and wear out our lives....
> These should then be attended to with great earnestness.
> (Doctrine & Covenants 123:13–14)

If any man has ever attended to the Lord's work with greater earnestness than did President Lee, I have not heard of him. And certainly no one could have done more to overcome himself while wasting and wearing out his life in God's service. Perhaps that, combined with his painstakingly developed and highly attuned spiritual knowledge, were what finally brought the loving finger of the Lord to touch him so gently that December eve in 1973, drawing him peacefully through the veil and into the loving arms of his Savior and Master.

For myself, it not only makes sense, but gives me greater hope.

Blaine M. Yorgason
June 2001

ENDNOTES

CHAPTER 1

1 The incidents upon which this vignette is based are reported in L. Brent Goates, editor, *He Changed My Life: Personal Experiences with Harold B. Lee*, Glen L. Rudd, essayist, (Salt Lake City, Bookcraft, 1988), pp. 15–22. See also L. Brent Goates, *Harold B. Lee, Prophet & Seer* (Salt Lake City, Bookcraft, 1985), pp. 386–387; Emerson Roy West, *Latter-day Prophets, Their Lives, Teachings, and Testimonies, with Profiles of Their Wives*, (American Fork, Utah: Covenant Communications, 1997), p. 75; *Ensign*, July, 1973, p. 123; and 143RD General Conference Report, Sunday, 8 April 1973, p. 179.

2 Goates, *Prophet & Seer*, pp. 386–387.

3 Ibid., p. 388.

4 Ibid., p. 614.

5 Francis M. Gibbons, *Harold B. Lee: Man of Vision, Prophet of God* (Salt Lake City: Deseret Book Co., 1993), pp. 1–2.

6 Goates, *Prophet & Seer*, pp. 614–615.

7 Goates, *He Changed My Life*, Neal A. Maxwell, essayist, p. 239.

8 Goates, *Prophet & Seer*, pp. 614, 615.

CHAPTER 2

1 The incident on which this vignette is based is taken from L. Brent Goates, *Harold B. Lee, Prophet & Seer* (Salt Lake City: Bookcraft, 1985), p. 40. See also Francis M. Gibbons, *Harold B. Lee, Man of Vision, Prophet of God* (Salt Lake City: Deseret Book, 1993), p. 23.

2   Gibbons, *Man of Vision*, pp. 7–8.

3   Ibid., p. 8.

4   Goates, *Prophet & Seer*, p. 7.

5   Ibid., p. 11.

6   Ibid., p. 23–24.

7   Gibbons, *Man of Vision*, p. 11.

8   Goates, *Prophet & Seer*, pp. 20, 21–22.

9   Ibid., p. 22.

10   Ibid., p. 18–19.

11   Ibid., p. 7.

12   Gibbons, *Man of Vision*, p. 12.

13   Ibid., pp. 12–14.

14   Ibid., pp. 15–16.

15   Harold B. Lee, *Oral History*, 1969. This original tape is in the possession of L. Brent Goates of Salt Lake City, Utah. See also Goates, *Prophet & Seer*, pp. 41, 39, 40.

16   Goates, *Prophet & Seer*, pp. 38.

17   Gibbons, *Man of Vision*, p. 18.

18   Lee, *Oral History*. See also Goates, *Prophet & Seer*, p. 31.

19   Gibbons, *Man of Vision*, p. 18.

20   Goates, *Prophet & Seer*, pp. 32–33.

21   Lee, *Oral History*. See also, Gibbons, *Man of Vision*, p. 20.

22   Goates, *Prophet & Seer*, p. 34.

23   Ibid., p. 26.

24   Ibid., p. 24.

25   Ibid., p. 26.

26   Ibid., p. 25.

CHAPTER 3

1   Francis M. Gibbons, *Harold B. Lee, Man of Vision, Prophet of God* (Salt Lake City: Deseret Book, 1993), pp. 21–22.

2   Brent L. Goates, *Harold B. Lee, Prophet & Seer* (Salt Lake City: Bookcraft, 1985), p. 46.

3   Gibbons, *Man of Vision*, pp. 29–30.

4   Goates, *Prophet & Seer*, pp. 46–48.

5   Ibid., p. 47.

6   Ibid., p. 27. See also Conference Report, April 6, 1941, p. 120.

7   Ibid., p. 27. See also Conference Report, April 6, 1941, p. 120.

8   Gibbons, *Man of Vision*, pp. 33–34.

9   Goates, *Prophet & Seer*, p. 48.

10   Ibid., pp. 48, 51, 53.

11   Gibbons, *Man of Vision*, p. 41.

12   Goates, *Prophet & Seer*, p. 53.

13   Gibbons, *Man of Vision*, p. 42.

14   Goates, *Prophet & Seer*, pp. 26–27.

15   Gibbons, *Man of Vision*, pp. 43–44.

16   Ibid., p. 44–45.

17   Goates, *Prophet & Seer*, p. 38–39.

18   Ibid., p. 17.

19   Harold B. Lee, *Oral History*, 1969.
     See also Goates, *Prophet & Seer*, p. 53.

CHAPTER 4

1   The incidents on which this vignette is based are taken from L.
     Brent Goates, *Harold B. Lee, Prophet & Seer* (Salt Lake City:
     Bookcraft, 1985), pp. 70–71; and Francis M. Gibbons, *Harold B. Lee,
     Man of Vision, Prophet of God* (Salt Lake City: Deseret Book, 1993),
     pp. 61, 67–68. While on several occasions during Harold B. Lee's life
     individuals informed him that they had seen an aura of light
     surrounding his head or face, and Sister Jensen did indeed prophesy
     that he would one day become President of the Church, there is no
     record that such a sighting of sacred light occurred during the
     conference at Sheridan, Wyoming.

2   Gibbons, *Man of Vision*, pp. 46–47.

3   Doctrine and Covenants, 38:32.

4   Gibbons, *Man of Vision*, pp. 48–49.

5   Goates, *Prophet & Seer*, p. 60.

6   Gibbons, *Man of Vision*, p. 51.

7   Harold B. Lee, *Oral History*, 1969.

8   Goates, *Prophet & Seer*, p. 61.

9   Ibid., p. 61.

10   Ibid., pp. 61–62.

11   Ibid., p. 62.

12   Ibid., p. 75. See also Lee, *Oral History*.

13   Lee, *Oral History*.

14   Goates, *Prophet & Seer*, p. 62.

15 Ibid., p. 62.
16 Gibbons, *Man of Vision*, p. 55.
17 Lee, *Oral History*.
18 Goates, *Prophet & Seer*, p. 63.
19 Gibbons, *Man of Vision*, p. 57.
20 Ibid., p. 54.
21 Ibid., pp. 57–58.
22 Ibid., p. 60.
23 Ibid., pp. 60–61.
24 Ibid., p. 61.
25 Goates, *Prophet & Seer*, p. 64.
26 Ibid., p. 66.
27 Ibid., p. 67.
28 Ibid., p. 68.
29 Ibid., p. 68.
30 Gibbons, *Man of Vision*, p. 63.
31 Ibid., pp. 63–64.
32 Goates, *Prophet & Seer*, p. 67.
33 Gibbons, *Man of Vision*, p. 64.
34 Ibid., pp. 64–65.
35 Ibid., pp. 66–67.
36 Goates, *Prophet & Seer*, pp. 70–71.
37 Ibid., p. 70.
38 Ibid., p. 71.
39 Ibid., p. 72.
40 Ibid., p. 72.
41 Ibid., pp. 72–73.
42 Gibbons, *Man of Vision*, p. 62.
43 Ibid., p. 62.
44 Ibid., p. 75.
45 Goates, *Prophet & Seer*, p. 74.
46 See Lee, *Oral History*.
47 Leonard J. Arrington, editor and essayist, *The Presidents of the Church* (Salt Lake City: Deseret Book, 1986), p. 352.

CHAPTER 5
1 The incidents on which this vignette is based are taken from L. Brent Goates, *Harold B. Lee, Prophet & Seer* (Salt Lake City:

Bookcraft, 1985), p. 88; and Francis M. Gibbons, *Harold B. Lee, Man of Vision, Prophet of God* (Salt Lake City: Deseret Book, 1993), p. 88.

2   Gibbons, *Man of Vision*, p. 77.

3   Goates, *Prophet & Seer*, p. 81.

4   Gibbons, *Man of Vision*, pp. 77–78.

5   Ibid., p. 78.

6   Ibid., p. 78.

7   Ibid., p. 80.

8   Goates, *Prophet & Seer*, p. 83.

9   Ibid., p. 84.

10 Arrington, Leonard J., editor and essayist, *The Presidents of the Church* (Salt Lake City: Deseret Book, 1986), p. 353.

11 Goates, *Prophet & Seer*, p. 87.

12 Ibid., pp. 85–86.

13 Gibbons, *Man of Vision*, p. 82.

14 Ibid., p. 83.

15 Ibid., p. 83.

16 Goates, *Prophet & Seer*, pp. 87–88.

17 Ibid., pp. 86–87.

18 Arrington, *Presidents of the Church*, p. 354. A modified version of this essay was published in Preston Nibley, *The Presidents of the Church* (Salt Lake City: Deseret Book, 1974), pp. 427–457. In this vignette, I have used portions from both accounts.

19 Goates, *Prophet & Seer*, p. 86.

20 Ibid., pp. 88–89.

CHAPTER 6

1   The incident on which this vignette is based is taken from L. Brent Goates, *Harold B. Lee, Prophet & Seer* (Salt Lake City: Bookcraft, 1985), pp. 132–133.

2   Francis M. Gibbons, *Harold B. Lee, Man of Vision, Prophet of God* (Salt Lake City: Deseret Book, 1993), pp. 92–93.

3   Goates, *Prophet & Seer*, pp. 89–90.

4   Gibbons, *Man of Vision*, p. 94.

5   Goates, *Prophet & Seer*, pp. 89–90.

6   Ibid., p. 90.

7   Ibid., pp. 92–93.

8   Leonard J. Arrington, editor and essayist, *The Presidents of the Church* (Salt Lake City: Deseret Book, 1986), p. 355. A modified version of this essay was published in Preston Nibley, *The Presidents of the Church* (Salt Lake City: Deseret Book, 1974), pp. 427-457. In the passage above as well as those that follow, I have used portions from both accounts.

9   Ibid., p. 358.

10   Ibid., p. 358.

11   Gibbons, *Man of Vision*, pp. 110–112.

12   Goates, *Prophet & Seer*, pp. 94–96.

13   Ibid., pp. 96–97.

14   Gibbons, *Man of Vision*, p. 113.

15   Goates, *Prophet & Seer*, p. 98.

16   Gibbons, *Man of Vision*, pp. 96–97.

17   Ibid., pp. 99–100.

18   Ibid., pp. 100–101.

19   Goates, *Prophet & Seer*, pp. 110-111.

20   Gibbons, *Man of Vision*, p. 101.

21   Ibid., p. 101.

22   Goates, *Prophet & Seer*, p. 116-117.

23   Ibid., p. 117.

24   Ibid., p. 117.

25   Ibid., p. 119.

26   Ibid., p. 120.

27   Ibid., p. 121.

28   Ibid., p. 118.

29   Ibid., p. 118.

30   Ibid., p. 122.

31   Ibid., p. 133.

32   Ibid., pp. 133–134.

33   Ibid., pp. 132–133.

34   Ibid., p. 137.

35   Ibid., pp. 137–138.

36   Arrington, *Presidents of the Church*, p. 355.

37   Ibid., pp. 355–356.

38   Goates, *Prophet & Seer*, p. 98-99.

39   Gibbons, *Man of Vision*, pp. 115–116.

40   Goates, *Prophet & Seer*, pp. 100-101.

41 Ibid., pp. 111–112.

42 Ibid., p. 112.

43 Ibid., p. 115.

44 Gibbons, *Man of Vision*, p. 108.

CHAPTER 7

1 The incident on which this vignette is based is taken from L. Brent Goates, *Harold B. Lee, Prophet & Seer* (Salt Lake City: Bookcraft, 1985), p. 154.

2 Francis M. Gibbons, *Harold B. Lee, Man of Vision, Prophet of God* (Salt Lake City: Deseret Book, 1993), p. 122.

3 Goates, *Prophet & Seer*, pp. 141–142.

4 Ibid., p. 142.

5 Gibbons, *Man of Vision*, pp. 123-124.

6 Goates, *Prophet & Seer*, pp. 142–143.

7 Leonard J. Arrington, editor and essayist, *The Presidents of the Church* (Salt Lake City: Deseret Book, 1986), pp. 359–360. A modified version of this essay was published in Preston Nibley, *The Presidents of the Church* (Salt Lake City: Deseret Book, 1974), pp. 427–457. In the passage above as well as those that follow, I have used portions from both accounts.

8 Gibbons, *Man of Vision*, pp. 126–127.

9 Goates, *Prophet & Seer*, pp. 144–145.

10 Gibbons, *Man of Vision*, pp. 129–130.

11 Arrington, *Presidents of the Church*, p. 360.

12 Ibid., p. 361.

13 Goates, *Prophet & Seer*, p. 148.

14 Ibid., pp. 148–149.

15 Gibbons, *Man of Vision*, pp. 131–132.

16 Arrington, *Presidents of the Church*, p. 360.

17 Goates, *Prophet & Seer*, p. 147. See also, Marion G. Romney, Conference Report, October 1945, p. 156.

18 Gibbons, *Man of Vision*, p. 132.

19 Goates, *Prophet & Seer*, p. 154.

20 Arrington, *Presidents of the Church*, pp. 361–362.

21 Gibbons, *Man of Vision*, pp. 140–141

22 Ibid., pp. 141–142.

CHAPTER 8

1   The incidents on which this vignette is based are taken from L. Brent Goates, *Harold B. Lee, Prophet & Seer* (Salt Lake City: Bookcraft, 1985), pp. 157–159; and Francis M. Gibbons, *Harold B. Lee, Man of Vision, Prophet of God* (Salt Lake City: Deseret Book, 1993), pp. 146–149.

2   Goates, *Prophet & Seer*, p. 155.

3   Ibid., p. 157.

4   Ibid., p. 170.

5   Ibid., p. 157.

6   Ibid., p. 158.

7   Ibid., pp. 170–171.

8   Gibbons, *Man of Vision*, p. 146.

9   Goates, *Prophet & Seer*, pp. 158–159.

10   Ibid., p. 160.

11   Ibid., p. 160.

12   Gibbons, *Man of Vision*, p. 148.

13   Leonard J. Arrington, editor and essayist, *The Presidents of the Church* (Salt Lake City: Deseret Book, 1986), p. 362.

14   Ibid., pp. 362–363.

15   Goates, *Prophet & Seer*, pp. 162–163.

16   Ibid., p. 163.

17   Gibbons, *Man of Vision*, pp. 153–155.

18   Ibid., p. 155.

19   Goates, *Prophet & Seer*, p. 171.

20   Ibid., pp. 163–164.

21   Gibbons, *Man of Vision*, p. 155.

CHAPTER 9

1.   The incident on which this vignette is based is taken from Francis M. Gibbons, *Harold B. Lee, Man of Vision, Prophet of God* (Salt Lake City: Deseret Book, 1993), pp. 187–190.

2   Ibid., p. 167.

3   Ibid., pp. 165–166.

4   Ibid., pp. 166.

5   Emmerson Roy West, *Latter-day Prophets, Their Lives, Teachings, and Testimonies, with Profiles of Their Wives* (American Fork, Utah: Covenant Communications, 1997, 1999), p. 76.

6   Gibbons, *Man of Vision*, p. 168.

7   L. Brent Goates, *Harold B. Lee, Prophet & Seer* (Salt Lake City: Bookcraft, 1985), pp. 171-172.

8   Gibbons, *Man of Vision*, p. 169.

9   Leonard J. Arrington, editor and essayist, *The Presidents of the Church* (Salt Lake City: Deseret Book, 1986), p. 363.

10   Gibbons, *Man of Vision*, p. 170, 178.

11   Ibid., p. 171.

12   Ibid., p. 189.

13   Ibid., pp. 188—190.

14   L. Brent Goates, editor, *Modern-day Miracles from the Files of President Harold B. Lee* (American Fork, Utah: Covenant Communications, 1996), pp. 15-16.

15   L. Brent Goates, editor, and Paul C. Reimann, essayist, *He Changed My Life: Personal Experiences with Harold B. Lee* (Salt Lake City: Bookcraft, 1988), pp. 162–163.

16   Gibbons, *Man of Vision*, pp. 172–174.

17   Goates, *Prophet & Seer*, p. 172.

18   Ibid., p. 173.

19   Ibid., p. 173.

20   Ibid., p. 173.

21   Arrington, *Presidents of the Church*, pp. 363–364.

22   Goates, *Prophet & Seer*, p. 172.

23   Gibbons, *Man of Vision*, p. 180.

24   Goates, *Prophet & Seer*, p. 176.

25   "Church News," August 19, 1972, p. 3.

26   Clyde J. Williams, editor, *The Teachings of Harold B. Lee* (Salt Lake City: Bookcraft, 1996), p. 574.

27   Goates, *Prophet & Seer*, p. 183.

28   Ibid., pp. 179–180.

29   Ibid., p. 180.

30   Ibid., p. 181.

CHAPTER 10

1   The incidents upon which this vignette is based are reported in L. Brent Goates, *Harold B. Lee, Prophet & Seer* (Salt Lake City: Bookcraft, 1985), pp. 184–186.

2   Ibid., p. 179.

3   Francis M. Gibbons, *Harold B. Lee, Man of Vision, Prophet of God* (Salt Lake City: Deseret Book, 1993), pp. 196–197.

4   Goates, *Prophet & Seer*, pp. 191, 193.

5   Ibid., p. 193.

6   Ibid., pp. 194–195.

7   Gibbons, *Man of Vision*, p. 196.

8   Goates, *Prophet & Seer*, p. 185.

9   Ibid., p. 186.

10   See Brigham Young's speech on June 28, 1857, *Journal of Discourses*, Vol. 4, pp. 371–372.

11   Gibbons, *Man of Vision*, pp. 206–207.

12   Ibid., p. 216.

13   Goates, *Prophet & Seer*, p. 189.

14   Ibid., p. 190.

15   Ibid., p. 190.

16   Ibid., pp. 190–191.

17   Gibbons, *Man of Vision*, p. 217.

18   Goates, *Prophet & Seer*, pp. 197, 199.

19   Gibbons, *Man of Vision*, p. 218.

20   Ibid., p. 223.

21   Ibid., pp. 228–229.

22   Ibid., p. 229.

23   Goates, *Prophet & Seer*, pp. 200–201.

24   Ibid., p. 203.

25   Gibbons, *Man of Vision*, pp. 260–262.

CHAPTER 11

1   This vignette is based on incidents described in Francis M. Gibbons, *Harold B. Lee, Man of Vision, Prophet of God* (Salt Lake City: Deseret Book, 1993), pp. 266–269; and in L. Brent Goates, editor, and Oscar W. McConkie, Jr., essayist, *He Changed My Life: Personal Experiences with Harold B. Lee* (Salt Lake City: Bookcraft, 1988), pp. 30–31. It should be noted that the dialogue between Elder Lee and President McConkie, while based on the records both men left of the experience, is the author's creation.

2   Gibbons, *Man of Vision*, p. 230.

3   Ibid., p. 232.

4   L. Brent Goates, *Harold B. Lee, Prophet & Seer*
    (Salt Lake City: Bookcraft, 1985), p. 205.

5   Ibid., p. 207–208.

6   Gibbons, *Man of Vision*, p. 239.

7   Ibid., p. 208.

8   Goates, *Prophet & Seer*, pp. 214, 216.

9   Ibid., p. 216.

10 Ibid., pp. 217–218.

11 Ibid., p. 218.

12 Ibid., p. 213.

13 Ibid., p. 213.

14 Gibbons, *Man of Vision*, pp. 203–204.

15 Ibid., p. 279.

16 Ibid., p. 257.

17 Ibid., p. 265.

18 Ibid., p. 266.

19 Ibid., pp. 266–267.

20 Ibid., pp. 269–270.

21 Ibid., pp. 275–276.

22 Ibid., p. 276.

23 Ibid., p. 276.

24 Ibid., pp. 277–278.

25 Ibid., p. 278.

26 Ibid., p. 278.

27 Goates, *Prophet & Seer*, p. 230.

28 Leonard J. Arrington, editor and essayist, *The Presidents of the Church*
    (Salt Lake City: Deseret Book, 1986), p. 364.

29 Goates, *Prophet & Seer*, pp. 219–220.

30 Ibid., p. 230.

31 Ibid., p. 231.

32 Arrington, *Presidents of the Church*, p. 364.

33 Gibbons, *Man of Vision*, p. 205.

CHAPTER 12

1   The incident on which this vignette is based is reported in L. Brent
    Goates, editor, and Richard R. Tolman, essayist, *Modern-day Miracles
    from the Files of President Harold B. Lee* (American Fork, Utah:
    Covenant Communications, 1996), pp. 28–31.

2   Francis M. Gibbons, *Harold B. Lee, Man of Vision, Prophet of God*
     (Salt Lake City: Deseret Book, 1993), p. 286.

3   Ibid., p. 286.

4   L. Brent Goates, *Harold B. Lee, Prophet & Seer*
     (Salt Lake City: Bookcraft, 1985), p. 239.

5   Gibbons, *Man of Vision*, p. 288.

6   Goates, *Prophet & Seer*, pp. 240–241.

7   See *Deseret News 1975, Church Almanac*
     (Salt Lake City: Deseret News), Section E.

8   Goates, *Prophet & Seer*, p. 242.

9   Gibbons, *Man of Vision*, p. 296.

10   Ibid., p. 294.

11   Ibid., pp. 294–295.

12   Ibid., p. 297.

13   Ibid., p. 304.

14   Ibid., pp. 304–305.

15   Ibid., pp. 305–306.

16   Ibid., p. 306.

17   Ibid., p. 308.

18   Ibid., pp. 310, 312.

19   Goates, *Prophet & Seer*, p. 317.

20   Gibbons, *Man of Vision*, p. 314.

21   Ibid., p. 314.

22   Goates, *Prophet & Seer*, p. 244.

23   Ibid., pp. 319–320.

24   Ibid., p. 244.

25   Ibid., p. 245.

26   Gibbons, *Man of Vision*, p. 318.

27   Ibid., p. 320.

28   Conference Report, October 1954, pp. 125–131.

29   Ibid., pp. 125–131.

30   Conference Report, October 1954, pp. 125–131. In the above account
     I have used a slight variation to what was recorded in the Conference
     Report. This variation appears in Goates, *Prophet & Seer*, p. 256.

31   Conference Report, October 1954, pp. 125–131. In the above account
     I have used a slight variation to what was recorded in the Conference
     Report. This variation appears in Goates, *Prophet & Seer*, p. 256.

32   Goates, *Prophet & Seer*, pp. 266–267.

33   Ibid., p. 270.

34   Ibid., p. 270.

35   Ibid., pp. 271–272.

36   Ibid., pp. 272, 273

37   Ibid., p. 273.

38   Ibid., p. 29.

39   Ibid., p. 279.

40   Ibid., p. 281.

41   Goates, *Modern-day Miracles*, pp. 30–31.

42   L. Brent Goates, editor, and Asael T. Sorensen, essayist, *He Changed My Life: Personal Experiences with Harold B. Lee* (Salt Lake City: Bookcraft, 1988), pp. 180, 181.

43   Goates, *Prophet & Seer*, p. 282.

44   Ibid., pp. 283–284.

45   Ibid., p. 307.

CHAPTER 13

1   The incident upon which this vignette is based is reported in L. Brent Goates, *Harold B. Lee, Prophet & Seer* (Salt Lake City: Bookcraft, Inc, 1985), pp. 376–377. Information was also taken from L. Brent Goates, editor, and James B. Allen, essayist, *He Changed My Life: Personal Experiences with Harold B. Lee* (Salt Lake City: Bookcraft, 1988), pp. 78–79; Clyde J. Williams, editor, *The Teachings of Harold B. Lee, Eleventh President of The Church of Jesus Christ of Latter-day Saints* (Salt Lake City: Bookcraft, 1996), pp. 261–263; and Arch L. Madsen, Blaine M. Yorgason, and Richard Peterson, *The Infinite Journey: A Brief Overview of the Earthly Life of Arch L. Madsen* (Private Publication), p. 258.

2   "A Study of the Denver and Phoenix Markets" (May, 1980, Message Dissemination Phase II Study, Frank N. Magid Associates, Inc.).

3   Goates, *Prophet & Seer*, p. 377.

4   Francis M. Gibbons, *Harold B. Lee, Man of Vision, Prophet of God* (Salt Lake City: Deseret Book, 1993), p. 387.

5   Ibid., p. 388.

6   Goates, *Prophet & Seer*, p. 341.

7   Ibid., p. 342.

8   Gibbons, *Man of Vision*, pp. 388–389.

9   Ibid., p. 390.

10   Ibid., p. 390.

11   Goates, *Prophet & Seer*, p. 373.

12   Ibid., p. 373.

13   Ibid., p. 373.

14   Gibbons, *Man of Vision*, p. 413.

15   Ibid., p. 414.

16   Goates, *Prophet & Seer*, p. 375.

17   Ibid., p. 375.

18   Ibid., pp. 375–376.

19   Ibid., p. 342.

20   Ibid., p. 343.

21   Ibid., p. 344.

22   Ibid., p. 345.

23   Ibid., pp. 345–346.

24   Ibid., p. 347.

25   Gibbons, *Man of Vision*, p. 396.

26   Ibid., pp. 397–98.

27   Ibid., pp. 398–399.

28   Goates, *Prophet & Seer*, p. 357.

29   Ibid., p. 360.

30   Ibid., p. 360.

31   Ibid., p. 360.

32   Gibbons, *Man of Vision*, p. 400.

33   Ibid., pp. 400–401.

34   Goates, *Prophet & Seer*, p. 362.

35   Gibbons, *Man of Vision*, p. 404.

36   Goates, *Prophet & Seer*, pp. 353–354.

37   Ibid, p. 354.

38   Leonard J. Arrington, editor and essayist, *The Presidents of the Church* (Salt Lake City: Deseret Book, 1986), pp. 364–365.

39   Ibid., p. 365.

40   Gibbons, *Man of Vision*, p. 406.

41   Ibid., pp. 405–406.

42   Goates, *Prophet & Seer*, p. 388.

CHAPTER 14

1   This vignette is based upon an account taken from L. Brent Goates, editor, and Gene R. Cook, essayist, *He Changed My Life: Personal*

Experiences with Harold B. Lee (Salt Lake City: Bookcraft, 1988), pp. 32–37. It should be noted that the circumstances of the incident, including the profession of Elder Lee's questioner, are the creation of the author. Except for minor changes, however, particularly in the last few sentences, the dialogue itself is as it was originally reported.

2   L. Brent Goates, *Harold B. Lee, Prophet & Seer* (Salt Lake City: Bookcraft, 1985), p. 403.

3   Francis M. Gibbons, *Harold B. Lee, Man of Vision, Prophet of God* (Salt Lake City: Deseret Book, 1993), p. 420.

4   Goates, *Prophet & Seer*, p. 404.

5   Ibid., p. 404.

6   Gibbons, *Man of Vision*, p. 421.

7   Goates, *Prophet & Seer*, p. 406.

8   Gibbons, *Man of Vision*, p. 422.

9   Ibid., pp. 423–424.

10   Goates, *Prophet & Seer*, pp. 413–414.

11   Gibbons, *Man of Vision*, p. 425.

12   Ibid., p. 426.

13   Ibid., p. 426.

14   Goates, *Prophet & Seer*, pp. 435–436.

15   Ibid., p. 436.

16   Ibid., pp. 436–437.

17   Ibid., p. 437.

18   Ibid., p. 438.

19   Gibbons, *Man of Vision*, p. 434.

20   Goates, *Prophet & Seer*, pp. 408–409.

21   Ibid., p. 409.

22   Ibid., pp. 421.

23   Gibbons, *Man of Vision*, p. 444.

24   Ibid., p. 445.

25   British Area General Conference Report, Aug. 1971, p. 5.

26   Gibbons, *Man of Vision*, p. 448.

27   British Area General Conference Report, Aug. 1971, pp. 141–42.

28   Gibbons, *Man of Vision*, p. 451.

29   Goates, *Prophet & Seer*, p. 442.

30   Ibid., p. 442.

31   Gibbons, *Man of Vision*, p. 441.

32   Ibid., pp. 441–442.

33   Goates, *Prophet & Seer*, pp. 417–418.

34   Ibid., p. 419.

35   Ibid., p. 447.

36   Ibid., p. 416.

37   Ibid., pp. 449–450.

38   Ibid., p. 450. This tape, now in the possession of President Lee's son–in–law L. Brent Goates, and kindly lent to the author, is one source of the stories in the first few chapters of this volume. The title "Oral History," also used in this volume, was given by the author.

CHAPTER 15

1   The material for this vignette was taken from L. Brent Goates, *Harold B. Lee, Prophet & Seer* (Salt Lake City: Bookcraft, 1985), pp. 453–455.

2   Francis M. Gibbons, *Harold B. Lee, Man of Vision, Prophet of God* (Salt Lake City: Deseret Book, 1993), pp. 455–456.

3   Goates, *Prophet & Seer*, pp. 456–457.

4   Gibbons, *Man of Vision*, p. 456.

5   Goates, *Prophet & Seer*, p. 460.

6   Ibid., pp. 460–461.

7   Gibbons, *Man of Vision*, p. 457.

8   Goates, *Prophet & Seer*, p.461.

9   Ibid., pp. 461–462.

10   Ibid., p. 464.

CHAPTER 16

1   This vignette is based upon accounts taken from L. Brent Goates, editor, and Steven J. Pogue, essayist, *He Changed My Life: Personal Experiences with Harold B. Lee* (Salt Lake City: Bookcraft, 1988), pp. 151–154; Francis M. Gibbons, *Harold B. Lee, Man of Vision, Prophet of God* (Salt Lake City: Deseret Book, 1993), p. 494; and Paul T. Gardner, letter sent to the author, dated 24 June 2001. It should be noted that Steven Pogue's and Paul Gardner's accounts refer to meetings with President Lee that were at least a year apart. Both, however, were impressed with President Lee's use of the scriptures to answer questions. Both were also written in first person and so have been modified by the author for use here.

2   L. Brent Goates, *Harold B. Lee, Prophet & Seer* (Salt Lake City: Bookcraft, 1985), p. 465.

3   Ibid., p. 465.

4   Ibid., p. 465.

5   Ibid., pp. 465–466.

6   Ibid., p. 467.

7   Ibid., p. 466.

8   Gibbons, *Man of Vision*, p. 462.

9   Ibid., p. 459.

10 Goates, *Prophet & Seer*, p. 469.

11 L. Brent Goates, editor, and E. LaMar Buckner, essayist, *Modern–day Miracles from the Files of President Harold B. Lee* (American Fork, Utah: Covenant Communications, 1996), pp. 45–48.

12 Gibbons, *Man of Vision*, p. 463.

13 Goates, *Prophet & Seer*, p. 472.

14 Ibid., pp. 472–473.

15 Gibbons, *Man of Vision*, pp. 461–462.

16 Ibid., pp. 462–463.

17 Goates, *Prophet & Seer*, p. 480.

18 Ibid., pp. 483–484.

19 Ibid., p. 483.

20 Ibid., pp. 485–486.

21 Ibid., p. 486.

22 Ibid., pp. 497–498.

23 Gibbons, *Man of Vision*, pp. 469–471. See also Conference Report, Oct. 1972, pp. 19, 20.

24 Goates, *Prophet & Seer*, pp. 500–501.

25 Ibid., p. 501.

26 Ibid., p. 502.

27 Ibid., pp. 502, 503.

28 Gibbons, *Man of Vision*, pp. 474–475.

29 Ibid., p. 475.

30 Ibid., pp. 476–477.

31 Goates, editor, and Wendell J. Ashton, essayist, *He Changed My Life*, p.86.

32 Goates, editor, and Victor L. Brown, essayist, *He Changed My Life*, p. 65.

33 Goates, editor, and A.M.L., essayist, *Modern–day Miracles*, pp. 56–58.

34 Goates, *Prophet & Seer*, p. 515.

35   Ibid., p. 518.

36   Ibid., p. 519.

37   Ibid., pp. 519–520.

38   Conference Report, October 1973, p. 6–7.

39   Goates, *Prophet & Seer*, p. 544.

40   Conference Report, October, 1973, p. 170–171.

CHAPTER 17

1   The material for this vignette was taken from L. Brent Goates,
     editor, and Marion G. Romney, essayist, *He Changed My Life: Personal
     Experiences with Harold B. Lee* (Salt Lake City: Bookcraft, 1988), pp.
     23–25; and L. Brent Goates, *Harold B. Lee, Prophet and Seer* (Salt Lake
     City, Bookcraft, Inc., 1985), pp. 598–599. This last reference is to
     President Romney's address at Harold B. Lee's funeral. The setting
     of President Romney's information being given in an interview, as
     well as the interviewer, are products of the author's imagination.
     President Romney's quote about Joseph Smith, Oliver Cowdery, and
     W. W. Phelps comes from Joseph Smith, *History of The Church of Jesus
     Christ of Latter-day Saints* (Salt Lake City: Deseret Book, 1974),
     2: 286.

2   Goates, *Prophet & Seer*, p. 549.

3   Francis M. Gibbons, *Harold B. Lee, Man of Vision, Prophet of God*
     (Salt Lake City: Deseret Book, 1993), p. 491.

4   Goates, *Prophet & Seer*, pp. 550–551.

5   Ibid., p. 551.

6   Ibid., p. 551.

7   Ibid., pp. 551–553.

8   Ibid., pp. 558–559.

9   Ibid., pp. 563–564.

10   Gibbons, *Man of Vision*, p. 493.

11   Ibid., p. 494.

12   Goates, editor, and Steven R. Pogue, essayist,
     He Changed My Life, pp. 153–154.

13   Goates, *Prophet & Seer*, p. 565.

14   Gibbons, *Man of Vision*, p. 495.

15   Goates, *Prophet & Seer*, p. 568.

16   Ibid., p. 570.

17   Ibid., p. 570; Gibbons, *Man of Vision*, p. 495.

18 Gibbons, *Man of Vision*, p. 496.

19 Goates, *Prophet & Seer*, p. 572.

20 Ibid., p. 572.

21 Ibid., p. 573.

22 Ibid., p. 575.

23 Ibid., p. 576.

24 Ibid., p. 577.

25 Ibid., p. 577.

26 Ibid., pp. 578–579.

27 Ibid., p. 579.

28 Ibid., p. 580.

29 Ibid., pp. 580–581.

30 Ibid., p. 581.

31 Gibbons, *Man of Vision*, p. 499.

32 Goates, *Prophet & Seer*, p. 582.

33 Ibid., p. 583.

EPILOGUE

1   L. Brent Goates, *Harold B. Lee, Prophet & Seer*
    (Salt Lake City: Bookcraft, 1985), p. 619.

2   Ibid., p. 618.

BIBLIOGRAPHY

Arrington, Leonard J., editor and essayist,
  The Presidents of the Church (Salt Lake City: Deseret Book, 1986).
British Area Conference Report, August 1971.
Deseret News 1975 Church Almanac (Salt Lake City: Deseret News, 1975),
  section E.
Conference Report, April 1941 (Salt Lake City: The Church of Jesus
  Christ of Latter–day Saints), 119–122.
Conference Report, October 1945 (Salt Lake City: The Church of Jesus
  Christ of Latter–day Saints), 155–159.
Conference Report, October 1954 (Salt Lake City: The Church of Jesus
  Christ of Latter–day Saints), 125–131.
Conference Report, October 1972 (Salt Lake City: The Church of Jesus
  Christ of Latter–day Saints), 17–20.
Conference Report, April 1973 (Salt Lake City: The Church of Jesus
  Christ of Latter–day Saints), 176–181.
Conference Report, October 1973 (Salt Lake City: The Church of Jesus
  Christ of Latter–day Saints), 3–10, 166–171.
Gardner, Paul T., letter sent to the author, dated 24 June 2001.
Gibbons, Francis M., *Harold B. Lee: Man of Vision, Prophet of God*
  (Salt Lake City: Deseret Book, 1993).
Goates, L. Brent, *Harold B. Lee, Prophet & Seer*
  (Salt Lake City: Bookcraft, 1985).
Goates, L. Brent, editor, *He Changed My Life: Personal Experiences with
  Harold B. Lee* (Salt Lake City: Bookcraft, 1988).

Goates, L. Brent, editor, *Modern–day Miracles from the Files of President Harold B. Lee* (American Fork, Utah: Covenant Communications, 1996).

Lee, Harold B., Oral History, 1969 (recording). This original tape is in the possession of L. Brent Goates of Salt Lake City, Utah.

Lee, Harold B., "Stand Ye in Holy Places," *Ensign* (July, 1974): 121–124.

Madsen, Arch L., Blaine M. Yorgason, and Richard Peterson, *The Infinite Journey: A Brief Overview of the Earthly Life of Arch L. Madsen* (Private Publication).

Nibley, Preston, *The Presidents of the Church* (Salt Lake City: Deseret Book, 1974).

Smith, Joseph, *History of The Church of Jesus Christ of Latter-day Saints* Vol. 2 (Salt Lake City: Deseret Book, 1974).

"A Study of the Denver and Phoenix Markets" (May, 1980, Message Dissemination Phase II Study, Frank N. Magid Associates, Inc.).

West, Emerson Roy, *Latter–day Prophets, Their Lives, Teachings, and Testimonies, with Profiles of Their Wives* (American Fork, Utah: Covenant Communications, 1997).

Williams, Clyde J., editor, *The Teachings of Harold B. Lee, Eleventh President of The Church of Jesus Christ of Latter–day Saints* Vol. 11 (Salt Lake City: Bookcraft, 1996).

Young, Brigham, *Journal of Discourses,* Vol. 4 (Liverpool: S. W. Richards, 1854–1886).

TOPICAL INDEX